S0-AVS-067

HOMER AND HIS AGE

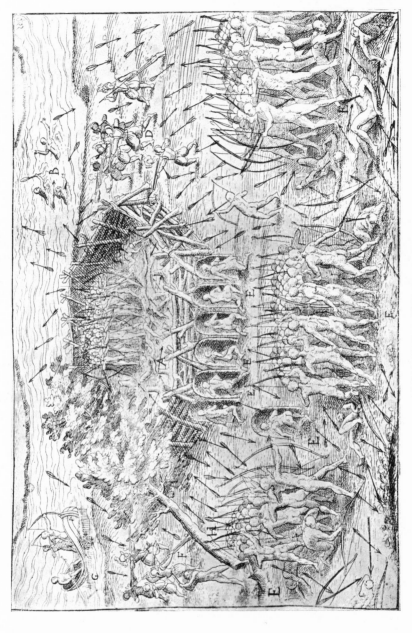

ALGONQUINS UNDER SHIELD

See pp. 135-136

Frontispiece.

HOMER
AND HIS AGE

BY

ANDREW LANG

AMS PRESS
NEW YORK

Reprinted from the edition of 1906, London
First AMS EDITION published 1968
Manufactured in the United States of America

Library of Congress Catalogue Card Number: 68-59285

AMS PRESS, INC.
New York, N.Y. 10003

TO

R. W. RAPER

IN ALL GRATITUDE

PREFACE

IN *Homer and the Epic*, ten or twelve years ago, I examined the literary objections to Homeric unity. These objections are chiefly based on alleged discrepancies in the narrative, of which no one poet, it is supposed, could have been guilty. The critics repose, I venture to think, mainly on a fallacy. We may style it the fallacy of "the analytical reader." The poet is expected to satisfy a minutely critical reader, a personage whom he could not foresee, and whom he did not address. Nor are "contradictory instances" examined —that is, as Blass has recently reminded his countrymen, Homer is put to a test which Goethe could not endure. No long fictitious narrative can satisfy "the analytical reader."

The fallacy is that of disregarding the Homeric poet's audience. He did not sing for Aristotle or for Aristarchus, or for modern minute and reflective inquirers, but for warriors and ladies. He certainly satisfied them ; but if he does not satisfy microscopic professors, he is described as a syndicate of many minstrels, living in many ages.

In the present volume little is said in defence of the poet's consistency. Several chapters on that point have been excised. The way of living which Homer describes is examined, and an effort is made to prove that he depicts the life of a single brief age of culture. The investigation is compelled to a tedious minuteness, because the points of attack—the alleged discrepancies in descriptions of the various details of existence—are so minute as to be all but invisible.

The unity of the Epics is not so important a topic as the methods of criticism. They ought to be sober, logical, and self-consistent. When these qualities are absent, Homeric criticism may be described, in the recent words of Blass, as "a swamp haunted by wandering fires, will o' the wisps."

In our country many of the most eminent scholars are no believers in separatist criticism. Justly admiring the industry and erudition of the separatists, they are unmoved by their arguments, to which they do not reply, being convinced in their own minds. But the number and perseverance of the separatists make on "the general reader" the impression that Homeric unity is *chose jugée*, that *scientia locuta est*, and has condemned Homer. This is far from being the case : the question is still open ; "science" herself is subject to criticism ; and new materials, accruing yearly, forbid a tame acquiescence in hasty theories.

May I say a word to the lovers of poetry who, in reading Homer, feel no more doubt than in reading Milton that, on the whole, they are studying a work of one age, by one author ? Do not let them be driven from their natural impression by the statement that Science has decided against them. The certainties of the exact sciences are one thing: the opinions of Homeric commentators are other and very different things.

Among all the branches of knowledge which the Homeric critic should have at his command, only philology, archæology, and anthropology can be called "sciences"; and they are not exact sciences: they are but skirmishing advances towards the true solution of problems prehistoric and "proto-historic."

Our knowledge shifts from day to day; on every hand, in regard to almost every topic discussed, we find conflict of opinions. There is no certain scientific decision, but there is the possibility of working in the scientific spirit, with breadth of comparison; consistency of logic; economy of conjecture; abstinence from the piling of hypothesis on hypothesis.

Nothing can be more hurtful to science than the dogmatic assumption that the hypothesis most in fashion is scientific.

Twenty years ago, the philological theory of the Solar Myth was preached as "scientific" in the books, primers, and lectures of popular science. To-day its place knows it no more. The separatist theories of the Homeric poems are not more secure than the Solar Myth, "like a wave shall they pass and be passed."

When writing on "The Homeric House" (Chapter X.) I was unacquainted with Mr. Percy Gardner's essay, "The Palaces of Homer" (*Journal of Hellenic Studies*, vol. iii. pp. 264–282). Mr. Gardner says that Dasent's plan of the Scandinavian Hall "offers in most respects not likeness, but a striking contrast to the early Greek hall." Mr. Monro, who was not aware of the parallel which I had drawn between the

Homeric and Icelandic houses, accepted it on evidence more recent than that of Sir George Dasent. *Cf.* his *Odyssey*, vol. ii. pp. 490–494.

Mr. R. W. Raper, of Trinity College, Oxford, has read the proof sheets of this work with his habitual kindness, but is in no way responsible for the arguments. Mr. Walter Leaf has also obliged me by mentioning some points as to which I had not completely understood his position, and I have tried as far as possible to represent his ideas correctly. I have also received assistance from the wide and minute Homeric lore of Mr. A. Shewan, of St. Andrews, and have been allowed to consult other scholars on various points.

The first portion of the chapter on "Bronze and Iron" appeared in the *Revue Archéologique* for April 1905, and the editor, Monsieur Salomon Reinach, obliged me with a note on the bad iron swords of the Celts as described by Polybius.

The design of men in three shields of different shapes, from a Dipylon vase, is reproduced, with permission, from the British Museum *Guide to the Antiquities of the Iron Age;* and the shielded chessmen from Catalogue of Scottish Society of Antiquaries. Thanks for the two ships with men under shield are offered to the Rev. Mr. Browne, S.J., author of *Handbook of Homeric Studies* (Longmans). For the Mycenæan gold corslet I thank Mr. John Murray (Schliemann's *Mycenæ and Tiryns*), and for all the other Mycenæan illustrations Messrs. Macmillan and Mr. Leaf, publishers and author of Mr. Leaf's edition of the *Iliad*.

CONTENTS

CHAPTER VIII

LIST OF ILLUSTRATIONS

HOMER AND HIS AGE

CHAPTER I

THE HOMERIC AGE

THE aim of this book is to prove that the Homeric Epics, as wholes, and apart from passages gravely suspected in antiquity, present a perfectly harmonious picture of the entire life and civilisation of one single age. The faint variations in the design are not greater than such as mark every moment of culture, for in all there is some movement ; in all, cases are modified by circumstances. If our contention be true, it will follow that the poems themselves, as wholes, are the product of a single age, not a mosaic of the work of several changeful centuries.

This must be the case—if the life drawn is harmonious, the picture must be the work of a single epoch—for it is not in the nature of early uncritical times that later poets should adhere, or even try to adhere, to the minute details of law, custom, opinion, dress, weapons, houses, and so on, as presented in earlier lays or sagas on the same set of subjects. Even less are poets in uncritical times inclined to " archaise," either by attempting to draw fancy pictures of the manners of the past, or by making researches in graves, or among old votive offerings in temples, for the purpose of " preserving local colour." The idea of such

A

archaising is peculiar to modern times. To take an instance much to the point, Virgil was a learned poet, famous for his antiquarian erudition, and professedly imitating and borrowing from Homer. Now, had Virgil worked as a man of to-day would work on a poem of Trojan times, he would have represented his heroes as using weapons of bronze.[1] No such idea of archaising occurred to the learned Virgil. It is "the iron" that pierces the head of Remulus (*Æneid*, IX. 633); it is "the iron" that waxes warm in the breast of Antiphates (IX. 701). Virgil's men, again, do not wear the great Homeric shield, suspended by a baldric: Æneas holds up his buckler (*clipeus*), borne "on his left arm" (X. 261). Homer, familiar with no buckler worn on the left arm, has no such description. When the hostile ranks are to be broken, in the *Æneid* it is "with the iron" (X. 372), and so throughout.

The most erudite ancient poet, in a critical age of iron, does not archaise in our modern fashion. He does not follow his model, Homer, in his descriptions of shields, swords, and spears. But, according to most Homeric critics, the later continuators of the Greek Epics, about 800–540 B.C., are men living in an age of iron weapons, and of round bucklers worn on the left arm. Yet, unlike Virgil, they always give their heroes arms of bronze, and, unlike Virgil (as we shall see), they do not introduce the buckler worn on the left arm. They adhere conscientiously to the use of the vast Mycenæan shield, in their time obsolete. Yet, by the theory, in many other respects they innovate at will, introducing corslets and greaves, said to be

---

[1] Looking back at my own poem, *Helen of Troy* (1883), I find that when the metal of a weapon is mentioned the metal is bronze.

unknown to the beginners of the Greek Epics, just as Virgil innovates in bucklers and iron weapons. All this theory seems inconsistent, and no ancient poet, not even Virgil, is an archaiser of the modern sort.

All attempts to prove that the Homeric poems are the work of several centuries appear to rest on a double hypothesis : first, that the later contributors to the *Iliad* kept a steady eye on the traditions of the remote Achæan age of bronze ; next, that they innovated as much as they pleased.

Poets of an uncritical age do not archaise. This rule is overlooked by the critics who represent the Homeric poems as a complex of the work of many singers in many ages. For example, Professor Percy Gardner, in his very interesting *New Chapters in Greek History* (1892), carries neglect of the rule so far as to suppose that the late Homeric poets, being aware that the ancient heroes could not ride, or write, or eat boiled meat, consciously and purposefully represented them as doing none of these things. This they did "on the same principle on which a writer of pastoral idylls in our own day would avoid the mention of the telegraph or telephone." [1] "A writer of our own day,"—there is the pervading fallacy ! It is only writers of the last century who practise this archæological refinement. The authors of *Beowulf* and the *Nibelungenlied*, of the *Chansons de Geste* and of the Arthurian romances, always describe their antique heroes and the details of their life in conformity with the customs, costume, and armour of their own much later ages.

But Mr. Leaf, to take another instance, remarks as to the lack of the metal lead in the Epics, that it is men-

[1] *Op. cit.*, p. 142.

tioned in similes only, as though the poet were aware the
metal was unknown in the heroic age.[1] Here the poet is
assumed to be a careful but ill-informed archæologist,
who wishes to give an accurate representation of the
past. Lead, in fact, was perfectly familiar to the
Mycenæan prime.[2] The critical usage of supposing
that the ancients were like the most recent moderns—
in their archæological preoccupations—is a survival of
the uncritical habit which invariably beset old poets
and artists. Ancient poets, of the uncritical ages, never
worked " on the same principle as a writer in our day,"
as regards archæological precision ; at least we are
acquainted with no example of such accuracy.

Let us take another instance of the critical fallacy.
The age of the Achæan warriors, who dwelt in the
glorious halls of Mycenæ, was followed, at an interval,
by the age represented in the relics found in the older
tombs outside the Dipylon gate of Athens, an age
beginning, probably, about 900–850 B.C. The culture
of this " Dipylon age," a time of geometrical ornaments on vases, and of human figures drawn in geometrical forms, lines, and triangles, was quite unlike that
of the Achæan age in many ways, for example, in mode
of burial and in the use of iron for weapons. Mr.
H. R. Hall, in his learned book, *The Oldest Civilisation of
Greece* (1901), supposes the culture described in the
Homeric poems to be contemporary in Asia with that
of this Dipylon period in Greece.[3] He says, " The
Homeric culture is evidently the culture of the poet's
own days ; there is no attempt to archaise here . . . ."
They do not archaise as to the details of life, but " the

----

[1] *Iliad*, Note on, xi. 237.   [2] Tsountas and Manatt, p. 73.
[3] *Op. cit.*, pp. 49, 222.

Homeric poets consciously and consistently archaised, in regard to the political conditions of continental Greece," in the Achæan times. They give "in all probability a pretty accurate description" of the loose feudalism of Mycenæan Greece.[1]

We shall later show that this Homeric picture of a past political and social condition of Greece is of vivid and delicate accuracy, that it is drawn from the life, not constructed out of historical materials. Mr. Hall explains the fact by "the conscious and consistent" archæological precision of the Asiatic poets of the ninth century. Now to any one who knows early national poetry, early uncritical art of any kind, this theory seems not easily tenable. The difficulty of the theory is increased, if we suppose that the Achæans were the recent conquerors of the Mycenæans. Whether we regard the Achæans as "Celts," with Mr. Ridgeway, victors over an Aryan people, the Pelasgic Mycenæans ; or whether, with Mr. Hall, we think that the Achæans were the Aryan conquerors of a non-Aryan people, the makers of the Mycenæan civilisation ; in the stress of a conquest, followed at no long interval by an expulsion at the hands of Dorian invaders, there would be little thought of archaising among Achæan poets.[2]

A distinction has been made, it is true, between the poet and other artists in this respect. Monsieur Perrot says, " The vase-painter reproduces what he sees ; while the epic poets endeavoured to represent a distant past. If Homer gives swords of bronze to his heroes of times gone by, it is because he knows that such

---

[1] *Op. cit.*, pp. 223, 225.

[2] Mr. Hall informs me that he no longer holds the opinion that the poets archaised.

were the weapons of these heroes of long ago. In arming them with bronze he makes use, in his way, of what we call "local colour . . . ." Thus the Homeric poet is a more conscientious historian than Virgil ![1]

Now we contend that old uncritical poets no more sought for antique "local colour" than any other artists did. M. Perrot himself says with truth, "the *Chanson de Roland*, and all the *Gestes* of the same cycle explain for us the *Iliad* and the *Odyssey*."[2] But the poet of the *Chanson de Roland* accoutres his heroes of old time in the costume and armour of his own age, and the later poets of the same cycle introduce the innovations of their time; they do not hunt for "local colour" in the *Chanson de Roland*. The very words "local colour" are a modern phrase for an idea that never occurred to the artists of ancient uncritical ages. The Homeric poets, like the painters of the Dipylon period, describe the details of life as they see them with their own eyes. Such poets and artists never have the fear of "anachronisms" before them. This, indeed, is plain to the critics themselves, for they detect anachronisms as to land tenure, burial, the construction of houses, marriage customs, weapons, and armour in the *Iliad* and *Odyssey*. These supposed anachronisms we examine later : if they really exist they show that the poets were indifferent to local colour and archæological precision, or were incapable of attaining to archæological accuracy. In fact, such artistic revival of the past in its habit as it lived is a purely modern ideal.

[1] *La Grèce de l'Epopée*, Perrot et Chipiez, p. 230.
[2] *Op. cit.*, p. 5.

We are to show, then, that the Epics, being, as wholes, free from such inevitable modifications in the picture of changing details of life as uncritical authors always introduce, are the work of the one age which they represent. This is the reverse of what has long been, and still is, the current theory of Homeric criticism, according to which the Homeric poems are, and bear manifest marks of being, a mosaic of the poetry of several ages of change.

Till Wolf published his *Prolegomena to the Iliad* (1795) there was little opposition to the old belief that the *Iliad* and *Odyssey* were, allowing for interpolations, the work of one, or at most of two, poets. After the appearance of Wolf's celebrated book, Homeric critics have maintained, generally speaking, that the *Iliad* is either a collection of short lays disposed in sequence in a late age, or that it contains an ancient original " kernel " round which " expansions," made throughout some centuries of changeful life, have accrued, and have been at last arranged by a literary redactor or editor.

The latter theory is now dominant. It is maintained that the *Iliad* is a work of at least four centuries. Some of the objections to this theory were obvious to Wolf himself — more obvious to him than to his followers. He was aware, and some of them are not, of the distinction between reading the *Iliad* as all poetic literature is naturally read, and by all authors is meant to be read, for human pleasure, and studying it in the spirit of " the analytical reader." As often as he read for pleasure, he says, disregarding the purely fanciful " historical conditions " which he invented for Homer ; as often as he yielded himself to that running stream of action and narration ; as often as he considered the *harmony of colour* and of characters in the Epic, no man could be more angry with his own destructive criticism than himself.[1] Wolf ceased to be a Wolfian whenever he placed himself at the point of view of the reader or the listener, to whom alone every poet makes his appeal.

But he deemed it his duty to place himself at another point of view, that of the scientific literary historian, the historian of a period concerning whose history he could know nothing. " How could the thing be possible ? " he asked himself. " How could a long poem like the *Iliad* come into existence in the historical circumstances ? " Wolf was unaware that he did not know what the historical circumstances were. We know how little we know, but we do know more than Wolf. He invented the historical circumstances of the supposed poet. They were, he said, like those of a man who should build a large ship in an inland place, with no sea to launch it upon. The *Iliad* was the large ship ; the sea was the public. Homer could have no *readers*, Wolf said, in an age that, like the old hermit of Prague, " never saw pen and ink," had no knowledge of letters ; or, if letters were dimly known, had never applied them to literature. In such circumstances no man could have a motive for composing a long poem.[2]

Yet if the original poet, " Homer," could make " the greater part of the songs," as Wolf admitted, what physical impossibility stood in the way of his making the whole ? Meanwhile, the historical cir-

[1] Preface to *Homer*, p. xxii., 1794.
[2] *Prolegomena to the Iliad*, p. xxvi.

cumstances, as conceived of by Wolf, were imaginary. He did not take the circumstances of the poet as described in the *Odyssey*. Here a king or prince has a minstrel, honoured as were the minstrels described in the ancient Irish books of law. His duty is to entertain the prince and his family and guests by singing epic chants after supper, and there is no reason why his poetic narratives should be brief, but rather he has an opportunity that never occurred again till the literary age of Greece for producing a long poem, continued from night to night. In the later age, in the Asiatic colonies and in Greece, the rhapsodists, competing for prizes at feasts, or reciting to a civic crowd, were limited in time and gave but snatches of poetry. It is in this later civic age that a poet without readers would have little motive for building Wolf's great ship of song, and scant chance of launching it to any profitable purpose. To this point we return ; but when once critics, following Wolf, had convinced themselves that a long early poem was impossible, they soon found abundant evidence that it had never existed.

They have discovered discrepancies of which, they say, no one sane poet could have been guilty. They have also discovered that the poems had not, as Wolf declared, " one harmony of colour " (*unus color*). Each age, they say, during which the poems were continued, lent its own colour. The poets, by their theory, now preserved the genuine tradition of things old ; cremation, cairn and urn burial ; the use of the chariot in war ; the use of bronze for weapons ; a peculiar stage of customary law ; a peculiar form of semi-feudal society ; a peculiar kind of house. But again, by a

change in the theory, the poets introduced later
novelties; later forms of defensive armour; later
modes of burial; later religious and speculative beliefs; a later style of house; an advanced stage of
law; modernisms in grammar and language.

The usual position of critics in this matter is
stated by Helbig; and we are to contend that the
theory is contradicted by all experience of ancient
literatures, and is in itself the reverse of consistent.
"The *artists* of antiquity," says Helbig, with perfect
truth, "had no idea of archæological studies. . . .
They represented legendary scenes in conformity with
the spirit of their own age, and reproduced the arms and
implements and costume that they saw around them."[1]

Now a poet is an *artist*, like another, and he, too—
no less than the vase painter or engraver of gems—in
dealing with legends of times past, represents (in an
uncritical age) the arms, utensils, costume, and the
religious, geographical, legal, social, and political ideas
of his own period. We shall later prove that this is
true by examples from the early mediæval epic poetry
of Europe.

It follows that if the *Iliad* is absolutely consistent
and harmonious in its picture of life, and of all the
accessories of life, the *Iliad* is the work of a single
age, of a single stage of culture, the poet describing
his own environment. But Helbig, on the other hand,
citing Wilamowitz Moellendorff, declares that the *Iliad*
—the work of four centuries, he says—maintains its
unity of colour by virtue of an uninterrupted poetical
tradition.[2] If so, the poets must have archæologised,

---

[1] *L'Épopée Homerique*, p. 5; *Homerische Epos*, p. 4.
[2] *Homerische Untersuchungen*, p. 292; *Homerische Epos*, p. 1.

must have kept asking themselves, " Is this or that detail true to the past ? " which artists in uncritical ages never do, as we have been told by Helbig. They must have carefully pondered the surviving old Achæan lays, which " were born when the heroes could not read, or boil flesh, or back a steed." By carefully observing the earliest lays the late poets, in times of changed manners, " could avoid anachronisms by the aid of tradition, which gave them a very exact idea of the epic heroes." Such is the opinion of Wilamo-witz Moellendorff. He appears to regard the tradition as keeping the later poets in the old way automatically, not consciously, but this, we also learn from Helbig, did not occur. The poets often wandered from the way.[1] Thus old Mycenæan lays, if any existed, would describe the old Mycenæan mode of burial. The Homeric poet describes something radically different. We vainly ask for proof that in any early national literature known to us poets have been true to the colour and manners of the remote times in which their heroes moved, and of which old minstrels sang. The thing is without example : of this proofs shall be offered in abundance.

Meanwhile, the whole theory which regards the *Iliad* as the work of four or five centuries rests on the postulate that poets throughout these centuries did what such poets never do, kept true to the details of a life remote from their own, and also—did not.

For Helbig does not, after all, cleave to his opinion. On the other hand, he says that the later poets of the *Iliad* did *not* cling to tradition. " They allowed them-selves to be influenced by their own environment : *this*

[1] Helbig, *Homerische Epos*, pp. 2, 3.

influence bewrays itself in the descriptions of details. . . .
The rhapsodists," (reciters, supposed to have altered
the poems at will), " did not fail to interpolate relatively recent elements into the oldest parts of the
Epic." [1]

At this point comes in a complex inconsistency.
The Tenth Book of the *Iliad*, thinks Helbig—in common
with almost all critics—" is one of the most recent lays
of the *Iliad*." But in this recent lay (say of the eighth
or seventh century) the poet describes the Thracians as
on a level of civilisation with the Achæans, and, indeed,
as even more luxurious, wealthy, and refined in the
matter of good horses, glorious armour, and splendid
chariots. But, by the time of the Persian wars, says
Helbig, the Thracians were regarded by the Greeks
as rude barbarians, and their military equipment was
totally un-Greek. They did not wear helmets, but
caps of fox-skin. They had no body armour ; their
shields were small round bucklers ; their weapons
were bows and daggers. These customs could not,
at the time of the Persian wars, be recent innovations
in Thrace.[2]

Had the poet of *Iliad*, Book X., known the Thracians
in *this* condition, says Helbig, as he was fond of details
of costume and arms, he would have certainly described
their fox-skin caps, bows, bucklers, and so forth. He
would not here have followed the Epic tradition, which
represented the Thracians as makers of great swords
and as splendidly armed charioteers. His audience
had met the Thracians in peace and war, and would
contradict the poet's description of them as heavily
armed charioteers. It follows, therefore, that the latest

[1] *Homerische Epos*, p. 2.   [2] Herodotus, vii. 75.

poets, such as the author of Book X., did not introduce recent details, those of their own time, but we have just previously been told that to do so was their custom in the description of details.

Now Studniczka[1] explains the picture of the Thracians in *Iliad*, Book X., on Helbig's *other* principle, namely, that the very late author of the Tenth Book merely conforms to the conventional tradition of the Epic, adheres to the model set in ancient Achæan, or rather ancient Ionian times, and scrupulously preserved by the latest poets—that is, when the latest poets do not bring in the new details of their own age. But Helbig will not accept his own theory in this case, whence does it follow that the author of the Tenth Book must, in his opinion, have lived in Achæan times, and described the Thracians as they then were, charioteers, heavily armed, not light-clad archers ? If this is so, we ask how Helbig can aver that the Tenth Book is one of the latest parts of the *Iliad* ?

In studying the critics who hold that the *Iliad* is the growth of four centuries—say from the eleventh to the seventh century B.C.—no consistency is to be discovered; the earth is never solid beneath our feet. We find now that the poets are true to tradition in the details of ancient life—now that the poets introduce whatever modern details they please. The late poets have now a very exact knowledge of the past ; now, the late poets know nothing about the past, or, again, some of the poets are fond of actual and very minute archæological research ! The theory shifts its position as may suit the point to be made at the moment by the critic. All

[1] *Homerische Epos*, pp. 7–11, *cf.* Note 1 ; *Zeitschrift für die Oesterr. Gymnasien*, 1886, p. 195.

is arbitrary, and it is certain that logic demands a very different method of inquiry. If Helbig and other critics of his way of thinking mean that in the *Iliad* (1) there are parts of genuine antiquity ; other parts (2) by poets who, with stern accuracy, copied the old modes ; other parts (3) by poets who tried to copy but failed ; with passages (4) by poets who deliberately innovated ; and passages (5) by poets who drew fanciful pictures of the past "from their inner consciousness," while, finally (6), some poets made minute antiquarian researches ; and if the argument be that the critics can detect these six elements, then we are asked to repose unlimited confidence in critical powers of discrimination. The critical standard becomes arbitrary and subjective.

It is our effort, then, in the following pages to show that the *unus color* of Wolf does pervade the Epics, that recent details are not often, if ever, interpolated, that the poems harmoniously represent one age, and that a brief age, of culture ; that this effect cannot, in a thoroughly uncritical period, have been deliberately aimed at and produced by archæological learning, or by sedulous copying of poetic tradition, or by the scientific labours of an editor of the sixth century B.C. We shall endeavour to prove, what we have already indicated, that the hypotheses of expansion are not self-consistent, or in accordance with what is known of the evolution of early national poetry. The strongest part, perhaps, of our argument is to rest on our interpretation of archæological evidence, though we shall not neglect the more disputable or less convincing contentions of literary criticism.

CHAPTER II

HYPOTHESES AS TO THE GROWTH OF THE EPICS

ANY theorist who believes that the Homeric poems are the growth of four changeful centuries, must present a definite working hypothesis as to how they escaped from certain influences of the late age in which much of them is said to have been composed. We must first ask to what manner of audiences did the poets sing, in the alleged four centuries of the evolution of the Epics. Mr. Leaf, as a champion of the theory of ages of "expansion," answers that "the *Iliad* and *Odyssey* are essentially, and above all, Court poems. They were composed to be sung in the palaces of a ruling aristocracy . . . the poems are aristocratic and courtly, not popular."[1] They are not *Volkspoesie;* they are not ballads. "It is now generally recognised that this conception is radically false."

These opinions, in which we heartily agree—there never was such a thing as a "popular" Epic—were published fourteen years ago. Mr. Leaf, however, would not express them with regard to "our" *Iliad* and *Odyssey*, because, in his view, a considerable part of the *Iliad*, as it stands, was made, not by Court bards in the Achæan courts of Europe, not for an audience of noble warriors and dames, but by wandering minstrels in the later Ionian colonies of Asia. They did not chant for a

[1] *Companion to the Iliad*, pp. 2, 3. 1892.

military aristocracy, but for the enjoyment of town
and country folk at popular festivals.[1]   The poems
were *begun*, indeed, he thinks, for "a wealthy aristocracy living on the product of their lands," in European
Greece ; were begun by contemporary court minstrels,
but were continued, vastly expanded, and altered to
taste by wandering singers and reciting rhapsodists,
who amused the holidays of a commercial, expansive,
and bustling Ionian democracy.[2]

We must suppose that, on this theory, the later poets
pleased a commercial democracy by keeping up the
tone that had delighted an old land-owning military
aristocracy.   It is not difficult, however, to admit this
as possible, for the poems continued to be admired in
all ages of Greece and under every form of society.
The real question is, would the modern poets be the
men to keep up a tone some four or five centuries old,
and to be true, if they were true, to the details of the
heroic age ?   "It is not beyond the bounds of possibility that some part of the most primitive *Iliad* may
have been actually sung by the court minstrel in the
palace whose ruins can still be seen in Mycenæ."[3]   But,
by the expansionist theory, even the oldest parts of our
Iliad are now full of what we may call quite recent
Ionian additions, full of late retouches, and full, so to
speak, of omissions of old parts.

Through four or five centuries, by the hypothesis,
every singer who could find an audience was treating
as much as he knew of a vast body of ancient lays
exactly as he pleased, adding here, lopping there, alter-
ing everywhere.   Moreover, these were centuries full

---

[1] *Iliad*, vol. i. p. xvi. 1900.   [2] *Companion to the Iliad*, p. 11.
[3] Leaf, *Iliad*, vol. i. p. xv.

of change. The ancient Achæan palaces were becoming the ruins which we still behold. The old art had faded, and then fallen under the disaster of the Dorian conquest. A new art, or a recrudescence of earlier art, very crude and barbaric, had succeeded, and was beginning to acquire form and vitality. The very scene of life was altered : the new singers and listeners dwelt on the Eastern side of the Ægean. Knights no longer, as in Europe, fought from chariots : war was conducted by infantry, for the most part, with mounted auxiliaries. With the disappearance of the war chariot the huge Mycenæan shields had vanished or were very rarely used. The early vase painters do not, to my knowledge, represent heroes as fighting from war chariots. They had lost touch with that method. Fighting men now carried relatively small round bucklers, and iron was the metal chiefly employed for swords, spears, and arrow points. Would the new poets, in deference to tradition, abstain from mentioning cavalry, or small bucklers, or iron swords and spears ? or would they avoid puzzling their hearers by speaking of obsolete and unfamiliar forms of tactics and of military equipment ? Would they therefore sing of things familiar— of iron weapons, small round shields, hoplites, and cavalry ? We shall see that confused and self-contradictory answers are given by criticism to all these questions by scholars who hold that the Epics are not the product of one, but of many ages.

There were other changes between the ages of the original minstrel and of the late successors who are said to have busied themselves in adding to, mutilating, and altering his old poem. Kings and courts had passed away ; old Ionian myths and religious usages, unknown

B

to the Homeric poets, had come out into the light ;
commerce and pleasure and early philosophies were the
chief concerns of life.   Yet the poems continued to be
aristocratic in manners ; and, in religion and ritual, to be
pure from recrudescences of savage poetry and super-
stition, though the Ionians " did not drop the more
primitive phases of belief which had clung to them;
these rose to the surface with the rest of the marvellous
Ionic genius, and many an ancient survival was enshrined
in the literature or mythology of Athens which had long
passed out of all remembrance at Mycenæ." [1]

Amazing to say, none of these " more primitive
phases of belief," none of the recrudescent savage
magic, was intruded by the late Ionian poets into
the *Iliad* which they continued, by the theory.   Such
phases of belief were, indeed, by their time popular,
and frequently appeared in the Cyclic poems on the
Trojan war ; continuations of the *Iliad*, which were
composed by Ionian authors at the same time as much
of the *Iliad* itself (by the theory) was composed.   The
authors of these Cyclic poems—authors contemporary
with the makers of much of the *Iliad*—were eminently
" un-Homeric " in many respects.[2]   They had ideas
very different from those of the authors of the *Iliad*
and *Odyssey*, as these ideas have reached us.

Helbig states this curious fact, that the Homeric
poems are free from many recent or recrudescent ideas
common in other Epics composed during the later
centuries of the supposed four hundred years of Epic
growth.[3]   Thus a signet ring was mentioned in the

---

[1] *Companion to the Iliad*, p. 7.
[2] *Cf.* Monro, *The Cyclic Poets ; Odyssey*, vol. ii. pp. 342–384.
[3] *Homerische Epos*, p. 3.

Ilias Parva, and there are no rings in *Iliad* or *Odyssey.* But Helbig does not perceive the insuperable difficulty which here encounters his hypothesis. He remarks : " In certain poems which were grouping themselves around the *Iliad* and *Odyssey,* we meet data absolutely opposed to the conventional style of the Epic." He gives three or four examples of perfectly un-Homeric ideas occurring in Epics of the eighth to seventh centuries, B.C., and a large supply of such cases can be adduced. But Helbig does not ask how it happened that, if poets of these centuries had lost touch with the Epic tradition, and had wandered into a new region of thought, as they had, examples of their notions do not occur in the *Iliad* and *Odyssey.* By his theory these poems were being added to and altered, even in their oldest portions, at the very period when strange fresh, or old and newly revived fancies were flourishing. If so, how were the *Iliad* and *Odyssey,* unlike the Cyclic poems, kept uncontaminated, as they confessedly were, by the new romantic ideas ?

Here is the real difficulty. Cyclic poets of the eighth and seventh centuries had certainly lost touch with the Epic tradition ; their poems make that an admitted fact. Yet poets of the eighth to seventh centuries were, by the theory, busily adding to and altering the ancient lays of the *Iliad.* How did *they* abstain from the new or revived ideas, and from the new *genre* of romance ? Are we to believe that one set of late Ionian poets—they who added to and altered the *Iliad*—were true to tradition, while another contemporary set of Ionian poets, the Cyclics—authors of new Epics on Homeric themes—are known to have quite lost touch with the Homeric taste, religion, and ritual ?

The reply will perhaps be—a Cyclic poet said, "Here I am going to compose quite a new poem about the old heroes. I shall make them do and think and believe as I please, without reference to the evidence of the old poems." But, it will have to be added, the rhapsodists of 800–540 B.C., and the general editor of the latter date, thought, "*we* are continuing an *old* set of lays, and we must be very careful in adhering to manners, customs, and beliefs as described by our predecessors. For instance, the old heroes had only bronze, no iron,"—and then the rhapsodists forgot, and made iron a common commodity in the *Iliad*. Again, the rhapsodists knew that the ancient heroes had no corslets—the old lays, we learn, never spoke of corslets —but they made them wear corslets of much splendour.[1] This theory does not help us. In an uncritical age poets could not discern that their *genre* of romance and religion was alien from that of Homer.

To return to the puzzle about the careful and precise continuators of the *Iliad*, as contrasted with their heedless contemporaries, the authors of the Cyclic poems. How "non-Homeric" the authors of these Cyclic poems were, before and after 660 B.C., we illustrate from examples of their left hand backslidings and right hand fallings off. They introduced (1) The Apotheosis of the Dioscuri, who in Homer (*Iliad*, III. 243) are merely dead men (*Cypria*). (2) Story of Iphigenia (*Cypria*). (3) Story of Palamedes, who is killed when angling by Odysseus and Diomede (*Cypria*).

---

[1] The reader must remember that the view of the late poets as careful adherents of tradition in usages and ideas only obtains *sometimes ;* at others the critics declare that archæological precision is *not* preserved, and that the Ionic continuators introduced, for example, the military gear of their own period into a poem which represents much older weapons and equipments.

Homer's heroes never fish, except in stress of dire necessity, in the *Odyssey*, and Homer's own Diomede and Odysseus would never stoop to assassinate a companion when engagèd in the contemplative man's recreation. We here see the heroes in late degraded form as on the Attic stage. (4) The Cyclics introduce Helen as daughter of Nemesis, and describe the flight of Nemesis from Zeus in various animal forms, a *Märchen* of a sort not popular with Homer ; an Ionic *Märchen*, Mr. Leaf would say. There is nothing like this in the *Iliad* and *Odyssey*. (5) They call the son of Achilles, not Neoptolemus, as Homer does, but Pyrrhus. (6) They represent the Achæan army as obtaining supplies through three magically gifted maidens, who produce corn, wine, and oil at will, as in fairy tales. Another Ionic non-Achæan *Märchen !* They bring in ghosts of heroes dead and buried. Such ghosts, in Homer's opinion, were impossible if the dead had been cremated.

All these non-Homeric absurdities, save the last, are from the *Cypria*, dated by Sir Richard Jebb about 776 B.C., long before the *Odyssey* was put into shape, namely, after 660 B.C. in his opinion. Yet the alleged late compiler of the *Odyssey*, in the seventh century, never wanders thus from the Homeric standard in taste. What a skilled archæologist he must have been ! The author of the *Cypria* knew the *Iliad*,[1] but his know-ledge could not keep him true to tradition. (7) In the *Æthiopis* (about 776 B.C.) men are made immortal after death, and are worshipped as heroes, an idea foreign to *Iliad* and *Odyssey*. (8) There is a savage ritual of purification from blood shed by a homicide (compare *Eumenides*, line 273). This is unheard of in *Iliad* and

---

[1] Monro, *Odyssey*, vol. ii. p. 354.

Odyssey, though familiar to Æschylus.   (9) Achilles, after death, is carried to the isle of Leukê.   (10) The fate of Ilium, in the Cyclic *Little Iliad*, hangs on the Palladium, of which nothing is known in *Iliad* or *Odyssey*.   The *Little Iliad* is dated about   700 B.C. (11) The *Nostoi* mentions Molossians, not named by Homer (which is a trifle) ; it also mentions the Asiatic city of Colophon, an Ionian colony, which is not a trivial self-betrayal on the part of the poet.   He is dated about 750 B.C.

Thus, more than a century before the *Odyssey* received its final form, after 660 B.C., from the hands of one man (according to the theory), the other Ionian poets who attempted Epic were betraying themselves as non-Homeric on every hand.[1]

Our examples are but a few derived from the brief notices of the Cyclic poets' works, as mentioned in ancient literature ; these poets probably, in fact, betrayed themselves constantly.   But their contemporaries, the makers of late additions to the *Odyssey*, and the later mosaic worker who put it together, never betrayed themselves to anything like the fatal extent of anachronism exhibited by the Cyclic poets.   How, if the true ancient tone, taste, manners, and religion were lost, as the Cyclic poets show that they were, did the contemporary Ionian poets or rhapsodists know and preserve the old manner ?

The best face we can put on the matter is to say that all the Cyclic poets were recklessly independent of tradition, while all men who botched at the *Iliad* were very learned, and very careful to maintain harmony in their pictures of life and manners, except

---

[1] Monro, *Odyssey*, vol. ii. pp. 347-383.

when they introduced changes in burial, bride-price, houses, iron, greaves, and corslets, all of them things, by the theory, modern, and when they sang in modern grammar.

Yet despite this conscientiousness of theirs, most of the many authors of our *Iliad* and *Odyssey* were, by the theory, strolling irresponsible rhapsodists, like the later *jongleurs* of the thirteenth and fourteenth centuries in mediæval France. How could these strollers keep their modern Ionian ideas, or their primitive, recrudescent phases of belief, out of their lays, as far as they *did* keep them out, while the contemporary authors of the *Cypria*, *The Sack of Ilios*, and other Cyclic poets were full of new ideas, legends, and beliefs, or primitive notions revived, and, save when revived, quite obviously late and quite un-Homeric in any case?

The difficulty is the greater if the Cyclic poems were long poems, with one author to each Epic. Such authors were obviously men of ambition ; they produced serious works *de longue haleine*. It is from them that we should naturally expect conservative and studious adhesion to the traditional models. From casual strollers like the rhapsodists and chanters at festivals, we look for nothing of the sort. *They* might be expected to introduce great feats done by sergeants and privates, so to speak—men of the nameless λαός, the host, the foot men—who in Homer are occasionally said to perish of disease or to fall under the rain of arrows, but are never distinguished by name. The strollers, it might be thought, would also be the very men to introduce fairy tales, freaks of primitive Ionian myth, discreditable anecdotes of the princely heroes, and references to the Ionian colonies.

But it is not so ; the serious, laborious authors of the long Cyclic poems do such un-Homeric things as these ; the gay, irresponsible strolling singers of a lay here and a lay there—lays now incorporated in the *Iliad* and *Odyssey*—scrupulously avoid such faults. They never even introduce a signet ring. These are difficulties in the theory of the *Iliad* as a patchwork by many hands, in many ages, which nobody explains ; which, indeed, nobody seems to find difficult. Yet the difficulty is insuperable. Even if we take refuge with Wilamowitz in the idea that the Cyclic and Homeric poems were at first mere protoplasm of lays of many ages, and that they were all compiled, say in the sixth century, into so many narratives, we come no nearer to explaining why the tone, taste, and ideas of two such narratives—*Iliad* and *Odyssey*—are confessedly distinct from the tone, taste, and ideas of all the others. The Cyclic poems are certainly the production of a late and changed age.[1] The *Iliad* is not in any degree—save perhaps in a few interpolated passages—touched by the influences of that late age. It is not a complex of the work of four incompatible centuries, as far as this point is concerned—the point of legend, religion, ritual, and conception of heroic character.

---

[1] For what manner of audience, if not for readers, the Cyclic poems were composed is a mysterious question.

CHAPTER III

HYPOTHESES OF EPIC COMPOSITION

WHOSOEVER holds that the Homeric poems were evolved out of the lays of many men, in many places, during many periods of culture, must present a consistent and logical hypothesis as to how they attained their present plots and forms. These could not come by accident, even if the plots are not good—as all the world held that they were, till after Wolf's day—but very bad, as some critics now assert. Still plot and form, beyond the power of chance to produce, the poems do possess. Nobody goes so far as to deny that ; and critics make hypotheses explanatory of the fact that a single ancient " kernel " of some 2500 lines, a " kernel " altered at will by any one who pleased during four centuries, became a constructive whole. If the hypotheses fail to account for the fact, we have the more reason to believe that the poems are the work of one age, and, mainly, of one man.

In criticising Homeric criticism as it is to-day, we cannot do better than begin by examining the theories of Mr. Leaf which are offered by him merely as " a working hypothesis." His most erudite work is based on a wide knowledge of German Homeric specu-lation, of the exact science of Grammar, of archæo-logical discoveries, and of manuscripts.[1] His volumes are, I doubt not, as they certainly deserve to be, on the

---

[1] *The Iliad.* Macmillan & Co. 1900, 1902.

shelves of every Homeric student, old or young, and
doubtless their contents reach the higher forms in
schools, though there is reason to suppose that, about
the unity of Homer, schoolboys remain conservative.

In this book of more than 1200 pages Mr. Leaf's
space is mainly devoted to textual criticism, philology,
and pure scholarship, but his Introductions, Notes, and
Appendices also set forth his mature ideas about the
Homeric problem in general.　He has altered some of
his opinions since the publication of his *Companion to the
Iliad* (1892), but the main lines of his old system are,
except on one crucial point, unchanged.　His theory
we shall try to state and criticise ; in general outline it
is the current theory of separatist critics, and it may
fairly be treated as a good example of such theories.

The system is to the following effect : Greek tradition, in the classical period, regarded the *Iliad* and
Odyssey as the work of one man, Homer, a native of
one or other of the Ionian colonies of Asia Minor.
But the poems show few obvious signs of origin in
Asia.　They deal with dwellers, before the Dorian
invasion (which the poet never alludes to), on the
continent of Europe and in Crete.[1]　The lays are concerned with "good old times" ; presumably between
1500 and 1100 B.C.　Their pictures of the details of
life harmonise more with what we know of the society
of that period from the evidence of buildings and

---

[1] If the poet sang after the tempest of war that came down with the
Dorians from the north, he would probably have sought a topic in the Achæan
exploits and sorrows of that period.　The Dorians, not the Trojans, would
have been the foes.　The epics of France of the eleventh and twelfth
centuries dwell, not on the real victories of the remote Charlemagne so much
as on the disasters of Aliscans and Roncesvaux—defeats at Saracen hands,
Saracens being the enemies of the twelfth-century poets.　No Saracens, in
fact, fought at Roncesvaux.

recent excavations, than with what we know of the life and the much more rude and barbaric art of the so-called "Dipylon" period of "geometrical" ornament considerably later. In the Dipylon age though the use of iron, even for swords (made on the lines of the old bronze sword), was familiar, art was on a most barbaric level, not much above the Red Indian type, as far, at least, as painted vases bear witness. The human figure is de-signed as in Tommy Traddles's skeletons ; there is, how-ever, some crude but promising idea of composition.

The picture of life in the Homeric poems, then, is more like that of, say, 1500–1100 B.C. than of, say, 1000–850 B.C. in Mr. Leaf's opinion. Certainly Homer describes a wealthy aristocracy, subject to an Over-Lord, who rules, by right divine, from "golden Mycenæ." We hear of no such potentate in Ionia. Homer's accounts of contemporary art seem to be inspired by the rich art generally dated about 1500–1200. Yet there are "many traces of apparent anachronism," of divergence from the more antique picture of life. In these divergences are we to recognise the picture of a later development of the ancient existence of 1500–1200 B.C.? Or have elements of the life of a much later age of Greece (say, 800–550 B.C.) been consciously or unconsciously introduced by the late poets ? Here Mr. Leaf recognises a point on which we have insisted, and must keep insisting, for it is of the first importance. "It is à priori the most probable" supposition that, "in an uncritical age," poets do not "reproduce the circumstances of the old time," but "only clothe the old tale in the garb of their own days." Poets in an uncritical age always, in our experience, "clothe old tales with the garb of their own time," but Mr. Leaf

thinks that, in the case of the Homeric poems, this idea
" is not wholly borne out by the facts."

In fact, Mr. Leaf's hypothesis, like Helbig's, exhibits
a come-and-go between the theory that his late poets
clung close to tradition and so kept true to ancient details
of life, and the theory that they did quite the reverse
in many cases. Of this frequent examples will occur.
He writes, "The Homeric period is certainly later than
the shaft tombs " (discovered at Mycenæ by Dr. Schliemann), " but it does not necessarily follow that it is
post-Mycenæan. It is quite possible that certain notable differences between the poems and the monuments " (of Mycenæ) " in burial, for instance, and in
women's dress may be due to changes which arose
within the Mycenæan age itself, in that later part of it
of which our knowledge is defective—almost as defective as it is of the subsequent ' Dipylon ' period. On
the whole, the resemblance to the typical Mycenæan
culture is more striking than the difference." [1]

So far Mr. Leaf states precisely the opinion for
which we argue. The Homeric poems describe an age
later than that of the famous tombs—so rich in relics—
of the Mycenæan acropolis, and earlier than the tombs
of the Dipylon of Athens. The poems thus spring out
of an age of which, except from the poems themselves,
we know little or nothing, because, as is shown later,
no cairn burials answering to the frequent Homeric
descriptions have ever been discovered—so relics cor-
roborating Homeric descriptions are to seek. But the
age attaches itself in many ways to the age of the
Mycenæan tombs, while, in our opinion, it stands quite
apart from the post-Dorian culture.

[1] Leaf, *Iliad*, vol. i. pp. xiii.-xv. 1900.

Where we differ from Mr. Leaf is in believing that the poems, as wholes, were composed in that late Mycenæan period of which, from material remains, we know very little ; that "much new" was *not* added, as he thinks, in "the Ionian development" which lasted perhaps "from the ninth century B.C. to the seventh." We cannot agree with Mr. Leaf, when he, like Helbig, thinks that much of the detail of the ancient life in the poems had early become so "stereotyped" that no continuator, however late, dared "intentionally to sap" the type, "though he slipped from time to time into involuntary anachronism." Some poets are also asserted to indulge in *voluntary* anachronism when, as Mr. Leaf supposes, they equip the ancient warriors with corslets and greaves and other body armour of bronze such as, in his opinion, the old heroes never knew, such as never were mentioned in the oldest parts or "kernel" of the poems. Thus the traditional details of Mycenæan life sometimes are regarded as "stereotyped" in poetic tradition ; sometimes as subject to modern alterations of a sweeping and revolutionary kind.

As to deliberate adherence to tradition by the poets, we have proved that the Cyclic epic poets of 800–660 B.C. wandered widely from the ancient models. If, then, every minstrel or rhapsodist who, anywhere, added at will to the old "kernel" of the *Wrath of Achilles* was, so far as he was able, as conscientiously precise in his stereotyped archæological details as Mr. Leaf sometimes supposes, the fact is contrary to general custom in such cases. When later poets in an uncritical age take up and rehandle the poetic themes of their predecessors, they always give to the stories "a new costume," as M. Gaston Paris remarks in reference to

thirteenth century dealings with French epics of the
eleventh century. But, in the critics' opinion, the late
rehandlers of old Achæan lays preserved the archaic
modes of life, war, costume, weapons, and so forth,
with conscientious care, except in certain matters to
be considered later, when they deliberately did the
very reverse. Sometimes the late poets devoutly
follow tradition. Sometimes they deliberately innovate.
Sometimes they pedantically "archaise," bringing in
genuine, but by their time forgotten, Mycenæan things,
and criticism can detect their doings in each case.

Though the late continuators of the *Iliad* were able,
despite certain inadvertencies, to keep up for some four
centuries in Asia the harmonious picture of ancient
Achæan life and society in Europe, critics can distinguish four separate strata, the work of many different
ages, in the *Iliad*. Of the first stratum composed in
Europe, say about 1300–1150 B.C. (I give a conjectural
date under all reserves), the topic was *The Wrath of
Achilles*. Of this poem, in Mr. Leaf's opinion, (*a*) the
First Book and fifty lines of the Second Book remain
intact or, perhaps, are a blend of two versions. (*b*) The
Valour of Agamemnon and *Defeat of the Achæans*. Of
this there are portions in Book XI., but they were
meddled with, altered, and generally doctored, "down
to the latest period," namely, the age of Pisistratus in
Athens, the middle of the sixth century B.C. (*c*) The
fight in which, after their defeat, the Achæans try to
save the ships from the torch of Hector, and the *Valour
of Patroclus* (but some critics do not accept this), with
his death (XV., XVI. in parts). (*d*) Some eighty lines
on the *Arming of Achilles* (XIX.). (*e*) Perhaps an incident or two in Books XX., XXI. (*f*) The *Slaying of*

Hector by Achilles, in Books XXI., XXII. (but some of the learned will not admit this, and we shall, unhappily, have to prove that, if Mr. Leaf's principles be correct, we really know nothing about the *Slaying of Hector* in its original form).

Of these six elements only did the original poem consist, Mr. Leaf thinks ; a rigid critic will reject as original even the *Valour of Patroclus* and the *Death of Hector*, but Mr. Leaf refuses to go so far as that. The original poem, as detected by him, is really "the work of a single poet, perhaps the greatest in all the world's history." If the original poet did no more than is here allotted to him, especially if he left out the purpose of Zeus and the person of Thetis in Book I., we do not quite understand his unapproachable greatness. He must certainly have drawn a rather commonplace Achilles, as we shall see, and we confess to preferring the *Iliad* as it stands.

The brief narrative cut out of the mass by Mr. Leaf, then, was the genuine old original poem or "kernel." What we commonly call the *Iliad*, on the other hand, is, by his theory, a thing of shreds and patches, combined in a manner to be later described. The blend, we learn, has none of the masterly unity of the old original poem. Meanwhile, as criticism of literary composition is a purely literary question, critics who differ from Mr. Leaf have a right to hold that the *Iliad* as it stands contains, and always did contain, a plot of masterly perfection. We need not attend here so closely to Mr. Leaf's theory in the matter of the First Expansions, (2) and the Second Expansions, (3) but the latest Expansions (4) give the account of *The Embassy to Achilles* with his refusal of *Agamemnon's Apology*

(Book IX.), the *Ransoming of Hector* (Book XXIV.), the *Reconciliation of Achilles and Agamemnon,* and the *Funeral Games of Patroclus* (XXIII.).   In all these parts of the poem there are, we learn, countless alterations, additions, and expansions, with, last of all, many transitional passages, "the work of the editor inspired by the statesman," that is, of an hypothetical editor who really by the theory made *our Iliad,* being employed to that end by Pisistratus about 540 B.C.[1]

Mr. Leaf and critics who take his general view are enabled to detect the patches and tatters of many ages by various tests, for example, by discovering discrepancies in the narrative, such as in their opinion no one sane poet could make.   Other proofs of multiplex authorship are discovered by the critic's private sense of what the poem ought to be, by his instinctive knowledge of style, by detection of the poet's supposed errors in geography, by modernisms and false archaisms in words and grammar, and by the presence of many objects, especially weapons and armour, which the critic believes to have been unknown to the original minstrel.

Thus criticism can pick out the things old, fairly old, late, and quite recent, from the mass, evolved through many centuries, which is called the *Iliad.*

If the existing *Iliad* is a mass of "expansions," added at all sorts of dates, in any number of places, during very different stages of culture, to a single short old poem of the Mycenæan age, science needs an hypothesis which will account for the *Iliad* "as it stands." Everybody sees the need of the hypothesis.   How was the medley of new songs by many generations of irresponsible hands codified into a plot which used to

[1] Leaf, *Iliad,* vol. ii. pp. x., xiv. 1900.

be reckoned fine ?   How were the manners, customs, and characters, *unus color*, preserved in a fairly coherent and uniform aspect ?   How was the whole Greek world, throughout which all manner of discrepant versions and incongruous lays must, by the theory, have been current, induced to accept the version which has been bequeathed to us ?   Why, and for what audience or what readers, did somebody, in a late age of brief lyrics and of philosophic poems, take the trouble to harmonise the body of discrepant wandering lays, and codify them in the *Iliad* ?

An hypothesis which will answer all these questions is the first thing needful, and hypotheses are produced.

Believers like Mr. Leaf in the development of the *Iliad* through the changing revolutionary centuries, between say 1200 and 600 B.C., consciously stand in need of a working hypothesis which will account, above all, for two facts : first, the relatively correct preservation of .the harmony of the picture of life, of ideas political and religious, of the characters of the heroes, of the customary law (such as the bride-price in marriage), and of the details as to weapons, implements, dress, art, houses, and so forth, when these are not (according to the theory) deliberately altered by late poets.

Next, the hypothesis must explain, in Mr. Leaf's own words, how a single version of the *Iliad* came to be accepted, " where many rival versions must, from the necessity of the case, have once existed side by side." [1]

Three hypotheses have, in fact, been imagined : the first suggests the preservation of the original poems in very early written texts ; not, of course, in " Homer's

[1] *Iliad*, vol. i. p. xviii.   1900.

autograph." This view Mr. Leaf, we shall see, discards. The second presents the notion of *one* old sacred college for the maintenance of poetic uniformity. Mr. Leaf rejects this theory, while supposing that there were schools for professional reciters.

Last, there is the old hypothesis of Wolf : " Pisistratus " (about 540 B.C.) " was the first who had the Homeric poems committed to writing, and brought into that order in which we now possess them."

This hypothesis, now more than a century old, would, if it rested on good evidence, explain how a single version of the various lays came to be accepted and received as authorised. The Greek world, by the theory, had only in various places various sets of incoherent chants *orally* current on the *Wrath of Achilles*. The public was everywhere a public of listeners, who heard the lays sung on rare occasions at feasts and fairs, or whenever a strolling rhapsodist took up his pitch, for a day or two, at a street corner. There was, by the theory, no reading public for the Homeric poetry.   But, by the time of Pisistratus, a reading public was coming into existence. The tyrant had the poems collected, edited, arranged into a continuous narrative, primarily for the purpose of regulating the recitals at the Panathenaic festival. When once they were written, copies were made, and the rest of Hellas adopted these for their public purposes.

On a small scale we have a case analogous. The old songs of Scotland existed, with the airs, partly in human memory, partly in scattered broadsheets. The airs were good, but the words were often silly, more often they were Fescennine—"more dirt than wit." Burns rewrote the words, which were published in handsome volumes, with the old airs, or with these airs altered, and his became the authorised versions, while the ancient anonymous chants were almost entirely forgotten.

The parallel is fairly close, but there are points of difference. Burns was a great lyric poet, whereas we hear of no great epic poet in the age of Pisistratus. The old words which Burns's songs superseded were wretched doggerel ; not such were the ancient Greek heroic lays. The old Scottish songs had no sacred historic character ; they did not contain the history of the various towns and districts of Scotland. The heroic lays of Greece were believed, on the other hand, to be a kind of Domesday book of ancient principalities, and cities, and worshipped heroes. Thus it was much easier for a great poet like Burns to supersede with his songs a mass of unconsidered "sculdudery" old lays, in which no man or set of men had any interest, than for a mere editor, in the age of Pisistratus, to supersede a set of lays cherished, in one shape or another, by every State in Greece. This holds good, even if, prior to Pisistratus, there existed in Greece no written texts of Homer, and no reading public, a point which we shall show reasons for declining to concede.

The theory of the edition of Pisistratus, if it rested on valid evidence, would explain " how a single version of the poems came to be accepted," namely, because the poem was now *written* for the first time, and oral versions fell out of memory. But it would not, of course, explain how, before Pisistratus, during four or five centuries of change, the new poets and reciters, throughout the Greek world, each adding such fresh verses as he pleased, and often introducing such modern details of life as he pleased, kept up the harmony of the Homeric picture of life, and character, and law, as far as it confessedly exists.

To take a single instance : the poems never allude to the personal armorial bearings of the heroes. They are unknown to or unnamed by Homer, but are very familiar on the shields in seventh century and sixth century vases, and Æschylus introduces them with great poetic effect in *The Seven against Thebes*. How did late continuators, familiar with the serpents, lions, bulls' heads, crabs, doves, and so forth, on the contemporary shields, keep such picturesque and attractive details out of their new rhapsodies ? In mediæval France, we shall show, the epics (eleventh to thirteenth centuries) deal with Charlemagne and his peers of the eighth century A.D. But they provide these heroes with the armorial bearings which came in during the eleventh to twelfth century A.D. The late Homeric rhapsodists avoided such tempting anachronisms.

Wolf's theory, then, explains "how a single version came to be accepted." It was the first *written* version ; the others died out, like the old Scots orally repeated songs, when Burns published new words to the airs. But Wolf's theory does not explain the harmony of the picture of life, the absence of post-Homeric ideas and ways of living, in the first written version, which, practically, is our own version.

In 1892 (*Companion to the Iliad*) Mr. Leaf adopted a different theory, the hypothesis of a Homeric "school" "which busied itself with the tradition of the Homeric poetry," for there must have been some central authority to preserve the text intact when it could not be preserved in writing. Were there no such body to maintain a fixed standard, the poems must have ended by varying indefinitely, according to the caprice of their various reciters. This is perfectly obvious.

Such a school could keep an eye on anachronisms and excise them ; in fact, the Maori priests, in an infinitely more barbarous state of society, had such schools for the preservation of their ancient hymns in purity. The older priests "insisted on a critical and verbatim rehearsal of all the ancient lore." Proceedings were sanctioned by human sacrifices and many mystic rites. We are not told that new poems were produced and criticised ; it does not appear that this was the case. Pupils attended from three to five years, and then qualified as priests or *tohunga*.[1] Suppose that the Asiatic Greeks, like the Maoris and Zuñis, had Poetic Colleges of a sacred kind, admitting new poets, and keeping them up to the antique standard in all respects. If this were so, the relative rarity of "anachronisms" and of modernisms in language in the Homeric poems is explained. But Mr. Leaf has now entirely and with a light heart abandoned his theory of a school, which is unsupported by evidence, he says.[2]

"The great problem," he writes, "for those who maintain the gradual growth of the poems by a process of crystallisation has been to understand how a single version came to be accepted, where many rival versions must, from the necessity of the case, have once existed side by side. The assumption of a school or guild of singers has been made," and Mr. Leaf, in 1892, made

---

[1] White, *The Ancient History of the Maori*, vol. i. pp. 8–13.

[2] *Cf. Companion to the Iliad*, pp. 20, 21 ; *Iliad*, vol. i. pp. xviii., xix. 1900.

the assumption himself ; " as some such hypothesis we are bound to make in order to explain the possibility of any theory " (1892).[1]

But now (1900) he says, after mentioning "the assumption of a school or guild of singers," that "the rare mention of Ὁμηρίδαι in Chios gives no support to this hypothesis, which lacks any other confirmation."[2] He therefore now adopts the Wolfian hypothesis that " an official copy of Homer was made in Athens at the time of Solon or Pisistratus," from the rhapsodies existing in the memory of reciters.[3] But Mr. Leaf had previously said[4] that "the legend which connects his" (Pisistratus's) "name with the Homeric poems is itself probably only conjectural, and of late date." Now the evidence for Pisistratus which, in 1892, he thought "conjectural and of late date," seems to him a sufficient basis for an hypothesis of a Pisistratean editor of the *Iliad*, while the evidence for an Homeric school which appeared to him good enough for an hypothesis in 1892 is rejected as worthless, though, in each case, the evidence itself remains just what it used to be.

This is not very satisfactory, and the Pisistratean hypothesis is much less useful to a theorist than the former hypothesis of an Homeric school, for the Pisistratean hypothesis cannot explain the harmony of the characters and the details in the *Iliad*, nor the absence of such glaring anachronisms as the Cyclic poets made, nor the general " pre-Odyssean " character of the language and grammar. By the Pisistratean hypothesis there was not, what Mr. Leaf in 1892 justly deemed essential, a school " to maintain a fixed

---

[1] *Companion to the Iliad*, pp. 20, 21. [2] *Iliad*, vol. i. xviii. p. xix.
[3] *Iliad*, vol. i. p. xix. [4] *Companion to the Iliad*, p. 190.

standard," throughout the changes of four centuries, and against the caprice of many generations of fresh reciters and irresponsible poets. The hypothesis of a school was really that which, of the two, best explained the facts, and there is no more valid evidence for the first making and writing out of our *Iliad* under Pisistratus than for the existence of a Homeric school.

The evidence for the *Iliad* edited for Pisistratus is examined in a Note at the close of this chapter. Meanwhile Mr. Leaf now revives Wolf's old theory to account for the fact that somehow "a single version" (of the Homeric poems) "came to be accepted." His present theory, if admitted, does account for the acceptation of a single version of the poems, the first standard *written* version, but fails to explain how "the caprice of the different reciters" (as he says) did not wander into every variety of anachronism in detail and in diction, thus producing a chaos which no editor of about 540 A.D. could force into its present uniformity.

Such an editor is now postulated by Mr. Leaf. If his editor's edition, as being *written*, was accepted by Greece, then we " understand how a single version came to be accepted." But we do not understand how the editor could possibly introduce a harmony which could only have characterised his materials, as Mr. Leaf has justly remarked, if there was an Homeric school " to maintain a fixed standard." But now such harmony in the picture of life as exists in the poems is left without any explanation. We have now, by the theory, a crowd of rhapsodists, many generations of uncontrolled wandering men, who, for several centuries,

" Rave, recite, and madden through the land,"

with no written texts, and with no " fixed body to maintain a standard." Such men would certainly not adhere
strictly to a stereotyped early tradition : *that* we cannot
expect from them.

Again, no editor of about 540 B.C. could possibly
bring harmony of manners, customs, and diction into
such of their recitals as he took down in writing.

Let us think out the supposed editor's situation.
During three centuries nine generations of strollers
have worked their will on one ancient short poem, *The
Wrath of Achilles*. This is, in itself, an unexampled
fact. Poets turn to new topics ; they do not, as a
rule, for centuries embroider one single situation out
of the myriads which heroic legend affords. Strolling
reciters are the least careful of men, each would recite
in the language and grammar of his day, and introduce
the newly evolved words and idioms, the new and
fashionable manners, costume, and weapons of his
time. When war chariots became obsolete, he would
bring in cavalry ; when there was no Over-Lord, he
would not trouble himself to maintain correctly the
character and situation of Agamemnon. He would
speak of coined money, in cases of buying and selling ;
his European geography would often be wrong ; he
would not ignore the Ionian cities of Asia ; most
weapons would be of iron, not bronze, in his lays.
Ionian religious ideas could not possibly be excluded,
nor changes in customary law, civil and criminal. Yet,
we think, none of these things occurs in Homer.

The editor of the theory had to correct all these
anachronisms and discrepancies. What a task in an
uncritical age ! The editor's materials would be the
lays known to such strollers as happened to be gathered

in Athens, perhaps at the Panathenaic festival. The *répertoire* of each stroller would vary indefinitely from those of all the others. One man knew this chant, as modified or made by himself ; other men knew others, equally unsatisfactory.

The editor must first have written down from recitation all the passages that he could collect. Then he was obliged to construct a narrative sequence containing a plot, which he fashioned by a process of selection and rejection ; and then he had to combine passages, alter them, add as much as he thought fit, remove anachronisms, remove discrepancies, accidentally bring in fresh discrepancies (as always happens), weave transitional passages, look with an antiquarian eye after the too manifest modernisms in language and manners, and so produce the *Iliad*. That, in the sixth century B.C., any man undertook such a task, and succeeded so well as to impose on Aristotle and all the later Greek critics, appears to be a theory that could only occur to a modern man of letters, who is thinking of the literary conditions of his own time. The editor was doing, and doing infinitely better, what Lönnrot, in the nineteenth century, tried in vain to achieve for the Finnish *Kalewala*.[1]

Centuries later than Pisistratus, in a critical age, Apollonius Rhodius set about writing an epic of the Homeric times. We know how entirely he failed, on all hands, to restore the manner of Homer. The editor of 540 B.C. was a more scientific man. Can any one who sets before himself the nature of the editor's task believe in him and it ? To the masterless floating jellyfish of old poems and new, Mr. Leaf supposes that

[1] See Comparetti, *The Kalewala*.

" but small and unimportant additions were made after
the end of the eighth century or thereabouts," especially
as " the creative and imaginative forces of the Ionian
race turned to other forms of expression," to lyrics
and to philosophic poems. But the able Pisistratean
editor, after all, we find, introduced quantities of new
matter into the poems—in the middle of the sixth
century ; that kind of industry, then, did *not* cease
towards the end of the eighth century, as we have
been told. On the other hand, as we shall learn, the
editor contributed to the *Iliad*, among other things,
Nestor's descriptions of his youthful adventures, for
the purpose of flattering Nestor's descendant, the tyrant
Pisistratus of Athens.

One hypothesis, the theory of an Homeric school
—which would answer our question, " How was the
harmony of the picture of life in remote ages preserved
in poems composed in several succeeding ages, and in
totally altered conditions of life ? "—Mr. Leaf, as we
know, rejects. We might suggest, again, that there
were written texts handed down from an early period,
and preserved in new copies from generation to generation. Mr. Leaf states his doubt that there were any
such texts. "The poems were all this time handed
down orally only by tradition among the singers (*sic*),
who used to wander over Greece reciting them at
popular festivals. Writing was indeed known through
the whole period of epic development" (some four
centuries at least), " but it is in the highest degree
unlikely that it was ever employed to form a standard
text of the Epic or any part of it. There can hardly
have been any standard text ; at best there was a continuous tradition of those parts of the poems which

were especially popular, and the knowledge of which was a valuable asset to the professional reciter."

Now we would not contend for the existence of any *standard* text much before 600 B.C., and I understand Mr. Leaf not to deny, now, that there may have been texts of the *Odyssey* and *Iliad* before, say, 600–540 B.C. If cities and reciters had any ancient texts, then texts existed, though not "standard" texts ; and by this means the harmony of thought, character, and detail in the poems might be preserved. We do not think that it is "in the highest degree unlikely" that there were no texts. Is this one of the many points on which every savant must rely on his own sense of what is "likely"? To this essential point, the almost certain existence of written texts, we return in our conclusion.

What we have to account for is not only the relative lack of anachronisms in poems supposed to have been made through a period of at least four hundred years, but also the harmony of the *characters* in subtle details. Some of the characters will be dealt with later ; meanwhile it is plain that Mr. Leaf, when he rejects both the idea of written texts prior to 600–540 B.C., and also the idea of a school charged with the duty of "maintaining a fixed standard," leaves a terrible task to his supposed editor of orally transmitted poems which, he says—if unpreserved by text or school—"must have ended by varying infinitely according to the caprice of their various reciters."[1]

On that head there can be no doubt ; in the supposed circumstances no harmony, no *unus color*, could have survived in the poems till the days of the sixth century editor.

[1] *Companion to the Iliad*, p. 21.

Here, then, is another difficulty in the path of the theory that the *Iliad* is the work of four centuries. If it was, we are not enabled to understand how it came to be what it is. No editor could possibly tinker it into the whole which we possess ; none could steer clear of many absurd anachronisms. These are found by critics, but it is our hope to prove that they do not exist.

NOTE

THE LEGEND OF THE MAKING OF THE "ILIAD" UNDER PISISTRATUS

It has been shown in the text that in 1892 Mr. Leaf thought the story about the making of the *Iliad* under Pisistratus, a legend without authority, while he regarded the traditions concerning an Homeric school as sufficient basis for an hypothesis, " which we are bound to make in order to explain the possibility of any theory." In 1900 he entirely reversed his position, the school was abandoned, and the story of Pisistratus was accepted. One objection to accepting any of the various legends about the composing and writing out, for the first time, of the *Iliad*, in the sixth century, the age of Pisistratus, was the silence of Aristarchus on the subject. He discussed the authenticity of lines in the *Iliad* which, according to the legend, were interpolated for a political purpose by Solon or Pisistratus, but, as far as his comments have reached us in the scholia, he never said a word about the tradition of Athenian interpolation. Now Aristarchus must, at least, have known the tradition of the political use of a disputed line, for Aristotle writes (*Rhetoric*, i. 15) that the Athenians, early in the sixth century, quoted *Iliad*, II. 558, to prove their right to Salamis. Aristarchus also discussed *Iliad*, II. 553, 555, to which the

Spartans appealed on the question of supreme command against Persia (Herodotus, vii. 159). Again Aristarchus said nothing, or nothing that has reached us, about Athenian interpolation. Once more, *Odyssey*, II. 631, was said by Hereas, a Megarian writer, to have been interpolated by Pisistratus (Plutarch.) But "the scholia that represent the teaching of Aristarchus" never make any reference to the alleged dealings of Pisistratus with the *Iliad*. The silence of Aristarchus, however, affords no safe ground of argument to believers or disbelievers in the original edition written out by order of Pisistratus.

It can never be proved that the scholiasts did not omit what Aristarchus said, though we do not know why they should have done so ; and it can never be proved that Aristarchus was ignorant of the traditions about Pisistratus, or that he thought them unworthy of notice. All is matter of conjecture on these points. Mr. Leaf's conversion to belief in the story that our *Iliad* was practically edited and first committed to writing under Pisistratus appears to be due to the probability that Aristarchus must have known the tradition. But if he did, there is no proof that he accepted it as historically authentic. There is not, in fact, any proof even that Aristarchus must have known the tradition. He had probably read Dieuchidas of Megara, for "Wilamowitz has shown that Dieuchidas wrote in the fourth century."[1] But, unluckily, we do not know that Dieuchidas stated that the *Iliad* was made and first committed to writing in the sixth century B.C. No mortal knows what Dieuchidas said ; and, again, what Dieuchidas said is not evidence. He wrote as a partisan in a historical dispute.

The story about Pisistratus and his editor, the practical maker of the *Iliad*, is interwoven with a legend about an early appeal, in the beginning of the sixth century B.C., to Homer as an historical authority. The Athenians and Megarians, contending for the possession of the island of Salamis, the home of the hero Aias, are said to have laid their differences before the Spartans (*cir.* 600–580 B.C.). Each party quoted Homer as evidence. Aristotle, who, as we saw, mentions the tale (*Rhetoric*, i. 15), merely says that the Athenians cited *Iliad*, II. 558 : "Aias led and stationed his men where the phalanxes of the Athenians

---

[1] *Iliad*, vol. i. p. xix.

were posted." Aristarchus condemned this line, not (as far as evidence goes) because there was a tradition that the Athenians had interpolated it to prove their point, but because he thought it inconsistent with *Iliad*, III. 230 ; IV. 251, which, if I may differ from so great a critic, it is not ; these two passages deal, not with the position of the camps, but of the men in the field on a certain occasion. But if Aristarchus had thought the tradition of Athenian interpolation of II. 558 worthy of notice, he might have mentioned it in support of his opinion. Perhaps he did. No reference to his notice has reached us. However this may be, Mr. Leaf mainly bases his faith in the Pisistratean editor (apparently, we shall see, an Asiatic Greek, residing in Athens), on a fragmentary passage of Diogenes Laertius (third century A.D.), concerned with the tale of Homer's being cited about 600–580 B.C. as an authority for the early ownership of Salamis. In this text Diogenes quotes Dieuchidas as saying something about Pisistratus in relation to the Homeric poems, but what Dieuchidas really said is unknown, for a part has dropped out of the text.

The text of Diogenes Laertius runs thus (*Solon*, i. 57) : " He (Solon) decreed that the Homeric poems should be recited by rhapsodists ἐξ ὑποβολῆς " (words of disputed sense), so that where the first reciter left off thence should begin his successor. It was rather Solon, then, than Pisistratus who brought Homer to light (ἐφώτισεν), as Diogenes says in the Fifth Book of his *Megarica*. *And the lines were especially these :* " They who held Athens," &c. (*Iliad*, II. 546–558), the passage on which the Athenians rested in their dispute with the Megarians.

And *what* " lines were especially these " ? Mr. Leaf fills up the gap in the sense, after " Pisistratus " thus, " for it was he " (Solon) " who interpolated lines in the *Catalogue*, and not Pisistratus." He says : " The natural sense of the passage as it stands " (in Diogenes Laertius) " is this : It was not Peisistratos, as is generally supposed, but Solon *who collected the scattered Homer of his day,* for he it was who interpolated the lines in the *Catalogue of the Ships.*" . . . But Diogenes neither says for himself nor quotes from Dieuchidas anything about " collecting the scattered Homer of his day." That Pisistratus did so is Mr. Leaf's theory, but there is not a hint about anybody collecting anything in the Greek. Ritschl, indeed, conjecturally supplying the gap in the text of Diogenes, invented the words, " Who *collected* the Homeric poems, and inserted some things to please the Athenians." But Mr. Leaf rejects that conjecture as "clearly wrong." Then why does he adopt, as "the natural sense of the passage," "it was not Peisistratos but Solon who *collected* the scattered Homer of his day?"[1] The testimony of Dieuchidas, as far as we can see in the state of the text, "refers," as Mr. Monro says, "to the *interpolation* that has just been mentioned, and need not extend further back." "Interpolation is a process that postulates a text in which the additional verses can be inserted," whereas, if I understand Mr. Leaf, the very first text, in his opinion, was that compiled by the editor for Pisistratus.[2]

Mr. Leaf himself dismisses the story of the Athenian appeal to Homer for proof of their claim as "a fiction." If so, it does not appear that ancient commentaries on a fiction are of any value as proof that Pisistratus produced the earliest edition of the *Iliad*.[3]

---

[1] *Iliad*, vol. i. p. xviii.

[2] Monro, *Odyssey*, vol. ii. pp. 400–410, especially pp. 408–409.

[3] Mr. Leaf adds that, except in one disputed line (*Iliad*, II. 558), Aias "is not, in the *Iliad*, encamped next the Athenians." His proofs of this odd oversight of the fraudulent interpolator, who should have altered the line, are *Iliad*, IV. 327 *ff*, and XIII. 681 *ff*. In the former passage we find Odysseus stationed next to the Athenians. But Odysseus would have neighbours *on either hand*. In the second passage we find the Athenians stationed next to the Bœotians and Ionians, but the Athenians, too, had neighbours on either side. The arrangement was, on the Achæan extreme left, Protesilaus's command (he was dead), and that of Aias ; then the Bœotians and Ionians, with "the picked men of the Athenians " ; and then Odysseus, on the Bœoto-Iono-Athenian right ; or so the Athenians would read the passage. The texts must have seemed favourable to the fraudulent Athenian interpolator denounced by the Megarians, or he would have altered them. Mr. Leaf, however, argues that line 558 of Book II. "cannot be original, as is patent from the fact that Aias in the rest of the *Iliad* is not encamped next the Athenians" (see IV. 327 ; XIII. 681). The Megarians do not seem to have seen it, or they would have cited these passages. But why argue at all about the Megarian story if it be a fiction? Mr. Leaf takes the brief bald mention of Aias in *Iliad*, II. 558 as "a mocking cry from Athens over the conquest of the island of the Aiakidai." But as, in this same *Catalogue*, Aias is styled " by far the best of warriors" after Achilles (II. 768), while there is no more honourable mention made of Diomede than that he had "a loud war cry " (II. 568), or of Menelaus but that he was also sonorous, and while Nestor, the ancestor of Pisistratus, receives not even that amount of praise (line 601), " the mocking cry from Athens" appears a vain imagination.

The lines disputed by the Megarians occur in the *Catalogue*, and, as to the date and original purpose of the *Catalogue*, the most various opinions prevail. In Mr. Leaf's earlier edition of the *Iliad* (vol. i. p. 37), he says that "nothing convincing has been urged to show" that the *Catalogue* is "of late origin." We know, from the story of Solon and the Megarians, that the *Catalogue* "was considered a classical work—the Domesday Book of Greece, at a very early date "—say 600–580 B.C. "It agrees with the poems in being pre-Dorian" (except in lines 653–670).

"There seems therefore to be no valid reason for doubting that it, like the bulk of the *Iliad* and *Odyssey*, was composed in Achæan times, and carried with the emigrants to the coast of Asia Minor. . . ."

In his new edition (vol. ii. p. 86), Mr. Leaf concludes that the *Catalogue* "originally formed an introduction to the whole Cycle," the compiling of "the whole Cycle" being of uncertain date, but very late indeed, on any theory. The author "studiously preserves an ante-Dorian standpoint. It is admitted that there can be little doubt that some of the material, at least, is old."

These opinions are very different from those expressed by Mr. Leaf in 1886. He cannot now give "even an approximate date for the composition of the *Catalogue*," which, we conceive, must be the latest thing in Homer, if it was composed "for that portion of the whole Cycle which, as worked up in a separate poem, was called the *Kypria*," for the *Kypria* is obviously a very late performance, done as a prelude to the *Iliad*.

I am unable to imagine how this mutilated passage of Diogenes, even if rightly restored, proves that Dieuchidas, a writer of the fourth century B.C., alleged that Pisistratus made a collection of scattered Homeric poems—in fact, made "a standard text."

The Pisistratean hypothesis "was not so long ago unfashionable, but in the last few years a clear reaction has set in," says Mr. Leaf.[1]

The reaction has not affected that celebrated scholar, Dr. Blass, who, with Teutonic frankness, calls the Pisistratean edition "an absurd legend."[2] Meyer says that the Alexandrians rejected the

---

[1] *Iliad*, i. p. xix.
[2] Blass, *Die Interpolationen in der Odyssee*, pp. 1, 2. Halle, 1904.

Pisistratean story "as a worthless fable," differing here from
Mr. Leaf and Wilamowitz ; and he spurns the legend, saying
that it is incredible that the whole Greek world would allow the
tyrants of Athens to palm off a Homer on them.[1]

Mr. T. W. Allen, an eminent textual scholar, treats the Pisistratean editor with no higher respect. In an Egyptian papyrus
containing a fragment of Julius Africanus, a Christian chrono-
loger, Mr. Allen finds him talking confidently of the Pisistratidæ.
They "stitched together the rest of the epic," but excised some
magical formulæ which Julius Africanus preserves. Mr. Allen
remarks : "The statements about Pisistratus belong to a well-
established category, that of Homeric mythology. . . . The anecdotes about Pisistratus and the poet himself are on a par with
Dares, who ' wrote the *Iliad* before Homer.' "[2]

The editor of Pisistratus is hardly in fashion, though that is
of no importance. Of importance is the want of evidence for the
editor, and, as we have shown, the impossible character of the
task allotted to him by the theory.

As I suppose Mr. Leaf to insinuate, "fashion" has really
nothing to do with the question. People who disbelieve in written
texts must, and do, oscillate between the theory of an Homeric
"school" and the Wolfian theory that Pisistratus, or Solon, or
somebody procured the making of the first written text at Athens
in the sixth century—a theory which fails to account for the harmony of the picture of life in the poems, and, as Mr. Monro,
Grote, Nutzhorn, and many others argue, lacks evidence.

As Mr. Monro reasons, and as Blass states the case bluntly,
" Solon, or Pisistratus, or whoever it was, put a stop, at least as
far as Athens was concerned, to the mangling of Homer " by the
rhapsodists or reciters, each anxious to choose a pet passage, and
not going through the whole *Iliad* in due sequence. " But the
unity existed before the mangling. That this has been so long
and so stubbornly misunderstood is no credit to German scholarship : blind uncritical credulity on one side, limitless and arbitrary
theorising on the other ! " We are not solitary sceptics when we
decline to accept the theory of Mr. Leaf. It is neither bottomed
on evidence nor does it account for the facts in the case. That

[1] Meyer, *Geschichte des Alterthums*, ii. 390, 391. 1893.
[2] *Classical Review*, xviii. 148.

D

is to say, the evidence appeals to Mr. Leaf as valid, but is thought worse than inadequate by other great scholars, such as Monro and Blass ; while the fact of the harmony of the picture of life, preserved through four or five centuries, appears to be left without explanation.

Mr. Leaf holds that, in order to organise recitations in due sequence, the making of a text, presenting, for the first time, a due sequence, was necessary. His opponents hold that the sequence already existed, but was endangered by the desultory habits of the rhapsodists. We must here judge each for himself; there is no court of final appeal.

I confess to feeling some uncertainty about the correctness of my statement of Mr. Leaf's opinions. He and I both think an early Attic " recension " probable, or almost certain. But (see " Conclusion ") I regard such recension as distinct from the traditional " edition " of Pisistratus. Mr. Leaf, I learn, does not regard the " edition " as having " made " the *Iliad;* yet his descriptions of the processes and methods of his Pisistratean editor correspond to my idea of the " making " of our *Iliad* as it stands. See, for example, Mr. Leaf's Introduction to *Iliad,* Book II. He will not even insist on the early Attic as the first *written* text ; if it was not, its general acceptance seems to remain a puzzle. He discards the idea of one Homeric " school " of paramount authority, but presumes that, as recitation was a profession, there must have been schools. We do not hear of them or know the nature of their teaching. The Beauvais " school " of *jongleurs* in Lent (fourteenth century A.D.) seems to have been a holiday conference of strollers.

CHAPTER IV

LOOSE FEUDALISM : THE OVER-LORD IN "ILIAD," BOOKS I. AND II.

WE now try to show that the Epics present an historical unity, a complete and harmonious picture of an age, in its political, social, legal, and religious aspects ; in its customs, and in its military equipment. A long epic can only present an unity of historical ideas if it be the work of one age. Wandering minstrels, living through a succession of incompatible ages, civic, commercial, democratic, could not preserve, without flaw or failure, the attitude, in the first place, of the poet of feudal princes towards an Over-Lord who rules them by undisputed right divine, but rules weakly, violently, unjustly, being subject to gusts of arrogance, and avarice, and repentance. Late poets not living in feudal society, and unfamiliar alike with its customary law, its jealousy of the Over-Lord, its conservative respect for his consecrated function, would inevitably miss the proper tone, and fail in some of the many *nuances* of the feudal situation. This is all the more certain, if we accept Mr. Leaf's theory that each poet-rhapsodist's *répertoire* varied from the *répertoires* of the rest. There could be no unity of treatment in their handling of the character and position of the Over-Lord and of the customary law that regulates his relations with his peers. Again, no editor of 540 B.C. could construct an harmonious picture of the Over-Lord in relation to the princes out of the fragmentary *répertoires* of strolling rhapsodists, which now lay before him in written versions. If the editor could do this, he was a man of Shakespearian genius, and had minute knowledge of a dead society. This becomes evident when, in place of examining the *Iliad* through microscopes, looking out for discrepancies, we study it in its large lines as a literary whole. The question being, Is the *Iliad* a literary whole or a mere literary mosaic? we must ask "What, taking it provisionally as a literary whole, are the qualities of the poet as a painter of what we may call feudal society?"

Choosing the part of the Over-Lord Agamemnon, we must not forget that he is one of several analogous figures in the national poetry and romance of other feudal ages. Of that great analogous figure, Charlemagne, and of his relations with his peers in the earlier and later French mediæval epics we shall later speak. Another example is Arthur, in some romances "the blameless king," in others *un roi fainéant.*

The parallel Irish case is found in the Irish saga of Diarmaid and Grainne. We read Mr. O'Grady's introduction on the position of Fionn Mac Cumhail, the legendary Over-Lord of Ireland, the Agamemnon of the Celts. "Fionn, like many men in power, is variable; he is at times magnanimous, at other times tyrannical and petty. Diarmaid, Oisin, Oscar, and Caoilte Mac Rohain are everywhere the καλοὶ καγαθοὶ of the Fenians ; of them we never hear anything bad." [1]

Human nature eternally repeats itself in similar conditions of society, French, Norse, Celtic, and Achæan. "We never hear anything bad" of Diomede, Odysseus, or Aias, and the evil in Achilles's resentment up to a

---

[1] *Transactions of the Ossianic Society*, vol. iii. p. 39.

certain point is legal, and not beyond what the poet thinks natural and pardonable in his circumstances.

The poet's view of Agamemnon is expressed in the speeches and conduct of the peers. In Book I. we see the bullying truculence of Agamemnon, wreaked first on the priest of Apollo, Chryses, then in threats against the prophet Chalcas, then in menaces against any prince on whom he chooses to avenge his loss of fair Chryseis, and, finally, in the Seizure of Briseis from Achilles.

This part of the First Book of the *Iliad* is confessedly original, and there is no varying, throughout the Epic, from the strong and delicate drawing of an historical situation, and of a complex character. Agamemnon is truculent, and eager to assert his authority, but he is also possessed of a heavy sense of his responsibilities, which often unmans him. He has a legal right to a separate "prize of honour" (γέρας) after each capture of spoil. Considering the wrath of Apollo for the wrong done in refusing his priest's offered ransom for his daughter, Agamemnon will give her back, " if that is better ; rather would I see my folks whole than perishing." [1]

Here we note points of feudal law and of kingly character. The giving and taking of ransom exists as it did in the Middle Ages ; ransom is refused, death is dealt, as the war becomes more fierce towards its close. Agamemnon has sense enough to waive his right to the girlish prize, for the sake of his people, but is not so generous as to demand no compensation. But there are no fresh spoils to apportion, and the Over-Lord threatens to take the prize of one of his peers, even of Achilles.

[1] *Iliad*, I. 115–117.

Thereon Achilles does what was frequently done in
the feudal age of western Europe, he "renounces his
fealty," and will return to Phthia. He adds insult,
"thou dog-face!" The whole situation, we shall show,
recurs again and again in the epics of feudal France,
the later epics of feudal discontent. Agamemnon replies that Achilles may do as he pleases. "I have
others by my side that shall do me honour, and, above
all, Zeus, Lord of Counsel" (I. 175). He rules,
literally, by divine right, and we shall see that, in the
French feudal epics, as in Homer, this claim of divine
right is granted, even in the case of an insolent and
cowardly Over-Lord. Achilles half draws "his great
sword," one of the long, ponderous cut-and-thrust
bronze swords of which we have actual examples from
Mycenæ and elsewhere. He is restrained by Athene,
visible only to him. "With words, indeed," she says,
"revile him . . . . hereafter shall goodly gifts come to
thee, yea, in threefold measure . . . ."

Gifts of atonement for "surquedry," like that of
Agamemnon, are given and received in the French
epics, for example, in the *Chanson de Roland*. The *Iliad*
throughout exhibits much interest in such gifts, and in
the customary law as to their acceptance, and other
ritual or etiquette of reconciliation. This fact, it will
be shown, accounts for a passage which critics reject,
and which is tedious to our taste, as it probably was
tedious to the age of the supposed late poets themselves.
(Book XIX.). But the taste of a feudal audience, as of
the audience of the Saga men, delighted in "realistic"
descriptions of their own customs and customary law,
as in descriptions of costume and armour. This is
fortunate for students of customary law and costume,

but wearies hearers and readers who desire the action to advance. Passages of this kind would never be inserted by late poets, who had neither the knowledge of, nor any interest in, the subjects.

To return to Achilles, he is now within his right ; the moral goddess assures him of that, and he is allowed to give the reins to his tongue, as he does in passages to which the mediæval epics offer many parallels. In the mediæval epics, as in Homer, there is no idea of recourse to a duel between the Over-Lord and his peer. Achilles accuses Agamemnon of drunkenness, greed, and poltroonery. He does not return home, but swears by the sceptre that Agamemnon shall rue his *outrecuidance* when Hector slays the host. By the law of the age Achilles remains within his right. His violent words are not resented by the other peers. They tacitly admit, as Athene admits, that Achilles has the right, being so grievously injured, to " renounce his fealty," till Agamemnon makes apology and gives gifts of atonement. Such, plainly, is the unwritten feudal law, which gives to the Over-Lord the lion's share of booty, the initiative in war and council, and the right to command ; but limits him by the privilege of the peers to renounce their fealty under insufferable provocation. In no Book is Agamemnon so direfully insulted as in the First, which is admitted to be of the original " kernel." Elsewhere the sympathy of the poet occasionally enables him to feel the elements of pathos in the position of the over-tasked King of Men.

As concerns the apology and the gifts of atonement, the poet has feudal customary law and usage clearly before his eyes. He knows exactly what is due, and

the limits of the rights of Over-Lord and prince, matters
about which the late Ionian poets could only pick up
information by a course of study in constitutional
history—the last thing they were likely to attempt—
unless we suppose that they all kept their eyes on the
"kernel," and that steadily, through centuries, generations of strollers worked on the lines laid down in that
brief poem.

Thus the poet of Book IX.—one of "the latest
expansions,"—thoroughly understands the legal and
constitutional situation, as between Agamemnon and
Achilles.   Or rather *all* the poets who collaborated
in Book IX., which "had grown by a process of
accretion," [1] understood the legal situation.

Returning to the poet's conception of Agamemnon,
we find in the character of Agamemnon himself the
key to the difficulties which critics discover in the
Second Book.   The difficulty is that when Zeus, won
over to the cause of Achilles by Thetis, sends a false
Dream to Agamemnon, the Dream tells the prince that
he shall at once take Troy, and bids him summon the
host to arms.   But Agamemnon, far from doing that,
summons the host to a *peaceful* assembly, with the
well-known results of demoralisation.

Mr. Leaf explains the circumstances on his own
theory of expansions compiled into a confused whole
by a late editor.   He thinks that probably there were
two varying versions even of this earliest Book of the
poem.   In one (A), the story went on from the quarrel
between Agamemnon and Achilles, to the holding of
a general assembly "to consider the altered state of
affairs."   This is the Assembly of Book II., but debate,

---

[1] Leaf, *Iliad*, vol. i. p. 371.

in version A, was opened by Thersites, not by Agamemnon, and Thersites proposed instant flight! That was probably the earlier version.

In the other early version (B), after the quarrel between the chiefs, the story did not, as in A, go on straight to the Assembly, but Achilles appealed to his mother, the fair sea-goddess, as in our *Iliad*, and she obtained from Zeus, as in the actual *Iliad*, his promise to honour Achilles by giving victory, in his absence, to the Trojans. The poet of version B, in fact, created the beautiful figure of Thetis, so essential to the development of the tenderness that underlies the ferocity of Achilles. The other and earliest poet, who treated of the *Wrath of Achilles*, the author of version A, neglected that opportunity with all that it involved, and omitted the purpose of Zeus, which is mentioned in the fifth line of the Epic. The editor of 540 B.C., seeing good in both versions, A and B, "combined his information," and produced Books I. and II. of the *Iliad* as they stand.[1]

Mr. Leaf suggests that "there is some ground for supposing that the oldest version of the *Wrath of Achilles* did not contain the promise of Zeus to Thetis ; it was a tale played exclusively on the earthly stage."[2] In that case the author of the oldest form (A) must have been a poet very inferior indeed to the later author of B who took up and altered his work. In *his* version, Book I. does not end with the quarrel of the princes, but Achilles receives, with all the courtesy of his character, the unwelcome heralds of Agamemnon, and sends Briseis with them to the Over-Lord. He then with tears appeals to his goddess-mother, Thetis of the

[1] Leaf, *Iliad*, vol. i. p. 47.   [2] *Ibid.*, vol. i. p. xxiii.   Note.

Sea, who " rose from the grey mere like a mist, leaving
the sea deeps where she dwelt beside her father, the
ancient one of the waters.   Then sat she face to face
with her son as he let the tears down fall, and caressed
him, saying, 'Child, wherefore weepest thou, for what
sorrow of heart ?   Hide it not, tell it to me ; that I
may know it as well as thou.' "   Here the poet strikes
the keynote of the character of Achilles, the deadly in
war, the fierce in council, who weeps for his lost lady
and his wounded honour, and cries for help to his
mother, as little children cry.

Such is the Achilles of the *Iliad* throughout and
consistently, but such he was not to the mind of Mr.
Leaf's probably elder poet, the author of version A.
Thetis, in version B, promises to persuade Zeus to
honour Achilles by making Agamemnon rue his absence,
and, twelve days after the quarrel, wins the god's
consent.

In Book II. Zeus reflects on his promise, and sends
a false Dream to beguile Agamemnon, promising that
now he shall take Troy.   Agamemnon, while asleep, is
full of hope ; but when he wakens he dresses in mufti,
in a soft doublet, a cloak, and sandals ; takes his sword
(swords were then worn as part of civil costume), and
the ancestral sceptre, which he wields in peaceful
assemblies.   Day dawns, and " he bids the heralds. . . ."
A break here occurs, according to the theory.

Here (*Iliad*, Book II., line 50) the kernel ceases,
Mr. Leaf says, and the editor of 540 B.C. plays his
pranks for a while.

The kernel (or one of the *two* kernels), we are to
take up again at Book II., 443–483, and thence "skip"
to XI. 56, and now "we have a narrative masterly in

conception and smooth in execution,"[1] says Mr. Leaf. This kernel is kernel B, probably the later kernel of the pair, that in which Achilles appeals to his lady mother, who wins from Zeus the promise to cause Achæan defeat, till Achilles is duly honoured. The whole Epic turns on this promise of Zeus, as announced in the fifth, sixth, and seventh lines of the very first Book. If kernel A is the first kernel, the poet left out the essence of the plot he had announced. However, let us first examine probable kernel B, reading, as advised, Book II. 1–50, 443–483 ; XI. 56 ff.

We left Agamemnon (though the Dream bade him summon the host to arms) *dressed in civil costume.* His ancestral sceptre in his hand, he is going to hold a deliberative assembly of the unarmed host. His attire proves that fact (πρεπώδης δὲ ἡ στολὴ τῷ ἐπὶ βουλὴν ἐξίοντι, says the scholiast). Then if we skip, as advised, to II. 443–483 he bids the heralds call the host not to peaceful council, for which his costume is appropriate, but to *war!* The host gathers, "and in their midst the lord Agamemnon,"—still in civil costume, with his sceptre (he has not changed his attire as far as we are told)— "in face and eyes like Zeus ; in waist like Ares" (god of war) ; "in breast like Poseidon,"—yet, for all that we are told, entirely unarmed ! The host, however, were dressed "in innumerable bronze," "war was sweeter to them than to depart in their ships to their dear native land,"—so much did Athene encourage them.

But nobody had been speaking of flight, *in the kernel B : that* proposal was originally made by Thersites, in kernel A, and was attributed to Agamemnon in the part of Book II. where the editor blends A and B.

[1] *Iliad*, vol. i. p. 47.

This part, at present, Mr. Leaf throws aside as a very late piece of compilation. Turning next, as directed, to XI. 56, we find the Trojans deploying in arms, and the hosts encounter with fury—Agamemnon still, for all that appears, in the raiment of peace, and with the sceptre of constitutional monarchy. " In he rushed, first of all, and slew Bienor," and many other gentlemen of Troy, not with his sceptre !

Clearly all this is the reverse of " a narrative masterly in conception and smooth in execution :" it is an impossible narrative.

Mr. Leaf has attempted to disengage one of two forms of the old original poem from the parasitic later growths ; he has promised to show us a smooth and masterly narrative, and the result is a narrative on which no Achæan poet could have ventured. In II. 50 the heralds are bidden κηρύσσειν, that is to summon the host—*to what?* To a peaceful assembly, as Agamemnon's costume proves, says the next line (II. 51), but that is excised by Mr. Leaf, and we go on to II. 443, and the reunited passage now reads, "Agamemnon bade the loud heralds " (II. 50) " call the Achæans to battle " (II. 443), and they came, in harness, but their leader— when did *he* exchange chiton, cloak, and sceptre for helmet, shield, and spear ? A host appears in arms ; a king who set out with sceptre and doublet is found with a spear, in bronze armour·: and not another word is said about the Dream of Agamemnon.

It is perfectly obvious and certain that the two pieces of the broken kernel B do not fit together at all. Nor is this strange, if the kernel was really broken and endured the insertion of matter enough to fill nine Books (II.–XI.). If kernel B really contained Book II.,

line 50, as Mr. Leaf avers, if Agamemnon, as in that
line (50) "bade the clear-voiced heralds do. . . . ."
something—what he bade them do was, necessarily, as
his peaceful costume proves, to summon the peaceful
assembly which he was to moderate with his sceptre.
At such an assembly, or at a preliminary council of
Chiefs, he would assuredly speak of his Dream, as he
does in the part excised.   Mr. Leaf, if he will not have
a peaceful assembly as part of kernel B, must begin his
excision at the middle of line 42, in *Iliad*, II., where
Agamemnon wakens ; and must make him dress not in
mufti but in armour, and call the host of the Achæans
to arm, as the Dream bade him do, and as he does in
II. 443.   Perhaps we should then excise II. 452, 453,
with the reference to the plan of retreat, for *that* is part
of kernel A where there was no promise of Zeus, and no
Dream sent to Agamemnon.   Then from II. 483, the
description of the glorious armed aspect of Agamemnon,
Mr. Leaf may pass to XI. 56, the account of the
Trojans under Hector, of the battle, of the prowess of
Agamemnon, inspired by the Dream which he, contrary
to Homeric and French epic custom, has very wisely
mentioned to nobody—that is, in the part not excised.

This appears to be the only method by which Mr.
Leaf can restore the continuity of his kernel B.

Though Mr. Leaf has failed to fit Book XI. to any
point in Book II., of course it does not follow that
Book XI. cannot be a continuation of the original
Wrath of Achilles (version B).   If so, we understand
why Agamemnon plucks up heart, in Book XI., and is
the chief cause of a temporary Trojan reverse.   He relies
on the Dream sent from Zeus in the opening lines of
Book II., the Dream which was not in kernel A ; the

Dream which he communicated to nobody ; the Dream
conveying the promise that he should at once take
Troy. This is perhaps a tenable theory, though
Agamemnon had much reason to doubt whether the
host would obey his command to arm, but an alternative theory of why and wherefore Agamemnon does
great feats of valour, in Book XI., will later be pro-
pounded. Note that the events of Books XI.–XVIII.,
by Mr. Leaf's theory, all occur on the very day after
Thetis (according to kernel B) obtains from Zeus his
promise to honour Achilles by the discomfiture of the
Achæans; they have suffered nothing till that moment,
as far as we learn, from the absence of Achilles and
his 2500 men : allowing for casualties, say 2000.

So far we have traced—from Books I. and II. to
Book XI.—the fortunes of kernel B, of the supposed
later of two versions of the opening of the *Iliad*. But
there may have been a version (A) probably earlier,
we have been told, in which Achilles did not appeal to
his mother, nor she to Zeus, and Zeus did not promise
victory to the Trojans, and sent no false Dream of
success to Agamemnon. What were the fortunes of
that oldest of all old kernels ? In this version (A)
Agamemnon, having had no Dream, summoned a
peaceful assembly to discuss the awkwardness caused
by the mutiny of Achilles. The host met (*Iliad*, II. 87–
99). Here we pass from line 99 to 212–242 : Thersites
it is who opens the debate, (in version A) insults
Agamemnon, and advises flight. The army rushed off
to launch the ships, as in II. 142–210, and were
brought back by Odysseus, who made a stirring speech,
and was well backed by Agamemnon, urging to battle.

Version A appears to us to have been a version

that no heroic audience would endure. A low person like Thersites opens a debate in an assembly called by the Over-Lord ; this could not possibly pass unchallenged among listeners living in the feudal age. When a prince called an assembly, he himself opened the debate, as Achilles does in Book I. 54–67. That a lewd fellow, the buffoon and grumbler of the host, of " the people," nameless and silent throughout the Epic, should rush in and open debate in an assembly convoked by the Over-Lord, would have been regarded by feudal hearers, or by any hearers with feudal traditions, as an intolerable poetical license. Thersites would have been at once pulled down and beaten ; the host would not have rushed to the ships on *his* motion. Any feudal audience would know better than to endure such an impossibility ; they would have asked, " How could Thersites speak—without the sceptre ? "

As the poem stands, and ought to stand, nobody less than the Over-Lord, acting within his right, (ἢ θέμις ἐστί, II. 73), could suggest the flight of the host, and be obeyed.

It is the absolute demoralisation of the host, in consequence of the strange test of their Lord, Agamemnon, making a feigned proposal to fly, and it is their confused, bewildered return to the assembly under the persuasions of Odysseus, urged by Athene, that alone, in the poem, give Thersites his unique opportunity to harangue. When the Over-Lord had called an assembly the first word, of course, was for *him* to speak, as he does in the poem as it stands. That Thersites should rise in the arrogance bred by the recent disorderly and demoralised proceedings is one thing ; that he should open the debate when excitement was eager to hear Agamemnon, and before demoralisation set in, is quite another. We never hear again of Thersites, or of any one of the commonalty, daring to open his mouth in an assembly. Thersites sees his one chance, the chance of a life time, and takes it; because Agamemnon, by means of the test—a proposal to flee homewards—which succeeded, it is said, in the case of Cortès,—has reduced the host, already discontented, to a mob.

Before Agamemnon thus displayed his ineptitude, as he often does later, Thersites had no chance. All this appears sufficiently obvious, if we put ourselves at the point of view of the original listeners. Thersites merely continues, in full assembly, the mutinous babble which he has been pouring out to his neighbours during the confused rush to launch the ships and during the return produced by the influence of Odysseus. The poet says so himself (*Iliad*, II. 212). "The rest sat down . . . only Thersites still chattered on." No original poet could manage the situation in any other way.

We have now examined Mr. Leaf's two supposed earliest versions of the beginning of the *Iliad*. His presumed earlier version (A), with no Thetis, no promise of Zeus, and no Dream, and with Thersites opening debate, is jejune, unpoetical, and omits the gentler and most winning aspect of the character of Achilles, while it could not possibly have been accepted by a feudal audience for the reasons already given. His presumed later version (B), with Thetis, Zeus, and the false Dream, cannot be, or certainly has not been, brought by Mr. Leaf into congruous connection with Book XI., and it results in the fighting of the *unarmed*

Agamemnon, which no poet could have been so careless as to invent. Agamemnon could not go into battle without helmet, shield, and spears (the other armour we need not dwell upon here), and Thersites could not have opened a debate when the Over-Lord had called the Assembly, nor could he have moved the chiefs to prepare for flight, unless, as in the actual *Iliad*, they had already been demoralised by the result of the feigned proposal of flight by Agamemnon, and its effect upon the host. Probably every reader who understands heroic society, temper, and manners will, so far, agree with us.

Our own opinion is that the difficulties in the poem are caused partly by the poet's conception of the violent, wavering, excitable, and unstable character of Agamemnon; partly by some accident, now indiscoverable, save by conjecture, which has happened to the text.

The story in the actual *Iliad* is that Zeus, planning disaster for the Achæans, in accordance with his promise to Thetis, sends a false Dream, to tell Agamemnon that he will take Troy instantly. He is bidden by the Dream to summon the host to arms. Agamemnon, *still asleep*, "has in his mind things not to be fulfilled: Him seemeth that he shall take Priam's town that very day" (II. 36, 37). "Then he awoke" (II. 41), and, obviously, was no longer so sanguine, once awake!

Being a man crushed by his responsibility, and, as commander-in-chief, extremely timid, though personally brave, he disobeys the Dream, dresses in civil costume, and summons the host *to a peaceful assembly, not* to *war*, as the Dream bade him do. Probably he thought that

E

the host was disaffected, and wanted to argue with them, in place of commanding.

Here it is that the difficulty comes in, and our perplexity is increased by our ignorance of the regular procedure in Homeric times. Was the host not in arms and fighting every day, when there was no truce ? There seems to have been no armistice after the mutiny of Achilles, for we are told that, in the period between his mutiny and the day of the Dream of Agamemnon, Achilles " was neither going to the Assembly, nor into battle, but wasted his heart, abiding there, longing for war and the slogan " (I. 489, 492). Thus it seems that war went on, and that assemblies were being held, in the absence of Achilles. It appears, however, that the fighting was mere skirmishing and raiding, no general onslaught was attempted ; and from Book II. 73, 83 it seems to have been a matter of doubt, with Agamemnon and Nestor, whether the army would venture a pitched battle.

It also appears, from the passage cited (I. 489, 492) that assemblies were being regularly held ; we are told that Achilles did not attend them. Yet, when we come to the assembly (II. 86–100) it seems to have been a special and exciting affair, to judge by the brilliant picture of the crowds, the confusion, and the cries. Nothing of the sort is indicated in the meeting of the assembly in I. 54–58. Why is there so much excitement at the assembly of Book II. ? Partly because it was summoned *at dawn*, whereas the usual thing was for the host to meet in arms before fighting on the plain or going on raids ; assemblies were held when the day's work was over. The host, therefore, when summoned to an assembly *at dawn*,

expects to hear of something out of the common—
as the mutiny of Achilles suggests—and is excited.

We must ask, then, why does Agamemnon, after the
Dream has told him merely to summon the host to arm
—a thing of daily routine—call a deliberative *morning*
assembly, a thing clearly not of routine ? If Agamemnon is really full of confidence, inspired by the Dream,
why does he determine, not to do what is customary,
call the men to arms, but as Jeanne d'Arc said to the
Dauphin, to "hold such long and weary councils"?
Mr. Jevons speaks of Agamemnon's "confidence in
the delusive dream" as at variance with his proceedings, and would excise II. 35-41, "the only lines
which represent Agamemnon as confidently believing
in the Dream." [1] But the poet never once says that
Agamemnon, awake, did believe confidently in the
Dream ! Agamemnon dwelt with hope *while asleep ;*
when he wakened—he went and called a peaceful
morning assembly, though the Dream bade him call
to arms. He did not dare to risk his authority. This
was exactly in keeping with his character. The poet
should have said, "When he woke, the Dream appeared to him rather poor security for success" (saying
so in poetic language, of course), and then there would
be no difficulty in the summoning of an assembly at
dawn. But either the poet expected us to understand
the difference between the hopes of Agamemnon sleeping, and the doubts of Agamemnon waking to chill
realities—an experience common to all of us who
dream—or some explanatory lines have been dropped
out—one or two would have cleared up the matter.

If I am right, the poet has not been understood.

---

[1] *Journal of Hellenic Studies*, vol. vii. pp. 306, 307.

People have not observed that Agamemnon hopes while
asleep, and doubts, and acts on his doubt, when awake.
Thus Mr. Leaf writes : " Elated by the dream, as we
are led to suppose, Agamemnon summons the army—
to lead them into battle ? Nothing of the sort ; he
calls them to assembly." [1] But we ought not to have
been led to suppose that the waking Agamemnon was
so elated as the sleeping Agamemnon. He was " dis-
illusioned " on waking ; his conduct proves it ; he did
not know what to think about the Dream ; he did not
know how the host would take the Dream ; he doubted
whether they would fight at his command, so he called
an assembly.

Mr. Jevons very justly cites a parallel case. Grote
has remarked that in Book VII. of Herodotus, " The
dream sent by the Gods to frighten Xerxes when
about to recede from his project," has "a marked
parallel in the *Iliad*." Thus Xerxes, after the defection
of Artabanus, was despondent, like Agamemnon after
the mutiny of Achilles, and was about to recede from
his project. " To both a delusive dream is sent urging
them to proceed. Xerxes calls an assembly, however,
and says that he will *not* proceed. Why ? Because,
says Herodotus, " when day came, he thought nothing
of his dream." Agamemnon, once awake, thought
doubtfully of *his* dream ; he called a Privy Council,
told the princes about his dream—of which Nestor
had a very dubious opinion—and said that he would
try the temper of the army by proposing instant flight :
the chiefs should restrain the men if they were eager to
run away.

Now the epic prose narrative of Herodotus is here

1 *Iliad*, vol. ii. p. 46.

clearly based on *Iliad*, II., which Herodotus must have
understood as I do. But in Homer there is no line to
say—and one line or two would have been enough—
that Agamemnon, when awake, doubted, like Xerxes,
though Agamemnon, when asleep, had been confident.
The necessary line, for all that we know, still existed in
the text used by Herodotus. Homer may lose a line
as well as Dieuchidas of Megara, or rather Diogenes
Laertius. Juvenal lost a whole passage, re-discovered
by Mr. Winstedt in a Bodleian manuscript. If Homer
expected modern critics to note the delicate distinction
between Agamemnon asleep and Agamemnon awake,
or to understand Agamemnon's character, he expected
too much.[1] The poet then treats the situation on these
lines : Agamemnon, awake and free from illusion, does
not obey the dream, does *not* call the army to war ; he
takes a middle course.

In the whole passage the poet's main motive, as
Mr. Monro remarks with obvious truth, is " to let his
audience become acquainted with the temper and spirit
of the army as it was affected by the long siege . . .
and by the events of the First Book." [2] The poet could
not obtain his object if Agamemnon merely gave the
summons to battle ; and he thinks Agamemnon precisely
the kind of waverer who will call, first the Privy Council
of the Chiefs, and then an assembly. Herein the home-
sick host will display its humours, as it does with a
vengeance. Agamemnon next tells his Dream to the
chiefs (if he had a dream of this kind he would most
certainly tell it), and adds (as has been already stated)
that he will first test the spirit of the army by a feigned

[1] *Cf.* Jevons, *Journal of Hellenic Studies*, vol. vii. pp. 306, 307.
[2] Monro, *Iliad*, vol. i. p. 261.

proposal of return to Greece, while the chiefs are to restrain them if they rush to launch the ships. Nestor hints that there is not much good in attending to dreams ; however, this is the dream of the Over-Lord, who is the favoured of Zeus.

Agamemnon next, addressing the assembly, says that posterity will think it a shameful thing that the Achæans raised the siege of a town with a population much smaller than their own army ; but allies from many cities help the Trojans, and are too strong for him, whether posterity understands that or not. " Let us flee with our ships ! "

On this the host break up, in a splendid passage of poetry, and rush to launch the ships, the passion of *nostalgie* carrying away even the chiefs, it appears—a thing most natural in the circumstances. But Athene finds Odysseus in grief : " neither laid *he* any hand upon his ship," as the others did, and she encouraged him to stop the flight. This he does, taking the sceptre of Agamemnon from his unnerved hand.

He goes about reminding the princes "have we not heard Agamemnon's real intention in council ? " (II. 188–197), and rating the common sort. The assembly meets again in great confusion ; Thersites seizes the chance to be insolent, and is beaten by Odysseus. The host then arms for battle.

The poet has thus shown Agamemnon in the colours which he wears consistently all through the *Iliad*. He has, as usual, contrasted with him Odysseus, the type of a wise and resolute man. This contrast the poet maintains without fail throughout. He has shown us the temper of the weary, home-sick army, and he has persuaded us that he knows how subtle, dangerous, and

contagious a thing is military panic. Thus, at least, I
venture to read the passage, which, thus read, is perfectly intelligible. Agamemnon is no personal coward,
but the burden of the safety of the host overcomes him
later, and he keeps suggesting flight in the ships, as we
shall see. Suppose, then, we read on from II. 40 thus :
" The Dream left him thinking of things not to be, even
that on this day he shall take the town of Priam. . . .
But he awoke from sleep with the divine voice ringing
in his ears. (*Then it seemed him that some dreams are true
and some false, for all do not come through the Gate of
Horn.*) So he arose and sat up and did on his soft
tunic, and his great cloak, and grasped his ancestral
sceptre . . . and bade the clear-voiced heralds summon
the Achæans of the long locks to the deliberative assembly." He then, as in II. 53–75, told his Dream to
the preliminary council, and proposed that he should
try the temper of the host by proposing flight—which,
if it began, the chiefs were to restrain—before giving
orders to arm. The test of the temper of the host
acted as it might be expected to act ; all rushed to
launch the ships, and the princes were swept away in
the tide of flight, Agamemnon himself merely looking
on helpless. The panic was contagious ; only Odysseus
escaped its influence, and redeemed the honour of the
Achæans, as he did again on a later day.

The passage certainly has its difficulties. But
Erhardt expresses the proper state of the case, after
giving his analysis. "The hearer's imagination is so
captured, first by the dream, then by the brawling
assembly, by the rush to the ships, by the intervention
of Odysseus, by the punishment of Thersites—all these
living pictures follow each other so fleetly before the

eyes that we have scarcely time to make objections."[1] The poet aimed at no more and no less effect than he has produced, and no more should be required by any one, except by that anachronism—"the analytical reader." *He* has "time to make objections": the poet's audience had none; and he must be criticised from *their* point of view. Homer did not sing for analytical readers, for the modern professor; he could not possibly conceive that Time would bring such a being into existence.

To return to the character of Agamemnon. In moments of encouragement Agamemnon is a valiant fighter, few better spearmen, yet "he attains not to the first Three," Achilles, Aias, Diomede. But Agamemnon is unstable as water; again and again, as in Book II., the lives and honour of the Achæans are saved in the Over-Lord's despite by one or other of the peers. The whole *Iliad*, with consistent uniformity, pursues the scheme of character and conduct laid down in the two first Books. It is guided at once by feudal allegiance and feudal jealousy, like the *Chansons de Geste* and the early sagas or romances of Ireland. A measure of respect for Agamemnon, even of sympathy, is preserved; he is not degraded as the kings and princes are often degraded on the Attic stage, and even in the Cyclic poems. Would wandering Ionian reciters at fairs have maintained this uniformity? Would the tyrant Pisistratus have made his literary man take this view?

[1] *Die Enstehung der Homerische Gedichte*, p. 29.

CHAPTER V

IN the Third Book, Agamemnon receives the compliments due to his supremacy, aspect, and valour from the lips of Helen and Priam. There are other warriors taller by a head, and Odysseus was shorter than he by a head, so Agamemnon was a man of middle stature. He is "beautiful and royal" of aspect ; "a good king and a mighty spearman," says Helen.

The interrupted duel between Menelaus and Paris follows, and then the treacherous wounding of Menelaus by Pandarus. One of Agamemnon's most sympathetic characteristics is his intense love of his brother, for whose sake he has made the war. He shudders on seeing the arrow wound, but consoles Menelaus by the certainty that Troy will fall, for the Trojans have broken the solemn oath of truce. Zeus "doth fulfil at last, and men make dear amends." But with characteristic inconsistency he discourages Menelaus by a picture of many a proud Trojan leaping on his tomb, while the host will return home—an idea constantly present to Agamemnon's mind. He is always the first to propose flight, though he will "return with shame" to Mycenæ. Menelaus is of much better cheer : " Be of good courage, *neither dismay all the host of the Achœans*,"—a thing which Agamemnon does habitually, though he is not a personal poltroon. As Menelaus has only a slight flesh wound

after all, and as the Trojans are doomed men, Agamemnon is now "eager for glorious battle." He encourages the princes, but, of all men, rebukes Odysseus
as "last at a fray and first at a feast": such is his
insolence, for which men detest him.

This is highly characteristic in Agamemnon, who
has just been redeemed from ruin by Odysseus. Re-
buked by Odysseus, he "takes back his word" as
usual, and goes on to chide Diomede as better at
making speeches than at fighting! But Diomede
made no answer, "having respect to the chiding of the
revered King." He even rebukes the son of Capaneus
for answering Agamemnon haughtily. Diomede, however, does not forget ; he bides his time. He now does
the great deeds of his day of valour (Book V.). Agamemnon meanwhile encourages the host.

During Books V., VI. Agamemnon's business is "to
bid the rest keep fighting." When Hector, in Book
VII., challenges any Achæan, nobody volunteers except
Menelaus, who has a strong sense of honour. Agamemnon restrains him, and lots are cast : the host
pray that the lot may fall on Aias, Diomede, or
Agamemnon (VII. 179-180). Thus the Over-Lord
is acknowledged to be a man of his hands, especially good at hurling the spear, as we see again in
Book XXIII.

A truce is proposed for the burial of the dead, and
Paris offers to give up the wealth that he brought to
Troy, and more, if the Achæans will go home, but
Helen he will not give up. We expect Agamemnon
to answer as becomes him. But no ! All are silent,
till Diomede rises. They will not return, he says, even
if Helen be restored, for even a fool knows that Troy

is doomed, because of the broken oath. The rest shout acquiescence, and Agamemnon refuses the compromise. Apparently he would not have disdained it, but for Diomede's reply.

On the following day the Trojans have the better in the battle, and Agamemnon " has no heart to stand," nor have some of his peers. But Diomede has more courage, and finally Agamemnon begins to call to the host to fight, but breaks down, weeps, and prays to Zeus "that we ourselves at least flee and escape ;" he is not an encouraging commander-in-chief ! Zeus, in pity, sends a favourable omen ; Aias fights well ; night falls, and the Trojans camp on the open plain.

Agamemnon, in floods of tears, calls an assembly, and proposes to " return to Argos with dishonour." " Let us flee with our ships to our dear native land, for now shall we never take wide-wayed Troy." All are silent, till Diomede rises and reminds Agamemnon that " thou saidst I was no man of war, but a coward." (In Book V. ; we are now in Book IX.) " Zeus gave thee the honour of the sceptre above all men, but valour he gave thee not. . . . Go thy way ; thy way is before thee, and thy ships stand beside the sea. But all the other flowing-haired Achæans will tarry here until we waste Troy."

Nestor advises Agamemnon to set an advanced guard, which that martialist had never thought of doing, and to discuss matters over supper. A force of 700 men, under Meriones and the son of Nestor, was posted between the foss and the wall round the camp ; the council met, and Nestor advised Agamemnon to approach Achilles with gentle words and gifts of atonement. Agamemnon, full of repentance, acknow-

ledges his folly and offers enormous atonement.
Heralds and three ambassadors are sent ; and how
Achilles received them, with perfect courtesy, but with
absolute distrust of Agamemnon and refusal of his
gifts, sending the message that he will fight only when
fire comes to his own ships, we know.

Achilles is now entirely in the wrong, and the Over-
Lord is once more within his right. He has done all,
or more than all, that customary law demands. In
Book IX. Phœnix states the case plainly. " If Agamemnon brought thee not gifts, and promised thee
more hereafter, . . . then were I not he that should
bid thee cast aside thine anger, and save the Argives
. . ." (IX. 515–517). The case so stands that, if
Achilles later relents and fights, the gifts of atonement
will no longer be due to him, and he " will not be held
in like honour " (IX. 604).

The poet knows intimately, and, like his audience,
is keenly interested in the details of the customary law.
We cannot easily suppose this frame of mind and this
knowledge in a late poet addressing a late Ionian
audience.

The ambassadors return to Agamemnon ; their evil
tidings are received in despairing silence. But Diomede
bids Agamemnon take heart and fight next day, with
his host arrayed " before the ships " (IX. 708). This
appears to counsel defensive war ; but, in fact, and for
reasons, when it comes to fighting they do battle in
the open.

The next Book (X.) is almost universally thought
a late interpolation ; an opinion elsewhere discussed
(see *The Doloneia*). Let us, then, say with Mr. Leaf
that the Book begins with " exaggerated despondency "

and ends with "hasty exultation," in consequence of
a brilliant camisade, wherein Odysseus and Diomede
massacre a Thracian contingent. Our point is that
the poet carefully (see *The Doloneia*) continues the
study of Agamemnon in despondency, and later, by
his "hasty exultation," preludes to the valour which
the Over-Lord displays in Book XI.

The poet knows that something in the way of
personal valour is due to Agamemnon's position ; he
fights brilliantly, receives a flesh wound, retires, and
is soon proposing a general flight in his accustomed
way. When the Trojans, in Book XIV., are attacking
the ships, Agamemnon remarks that he fears the dis-
affection of his whole army (XIV. 49, 51), and, as for
the coming defeat, that he "knew it," even when Zeus
helped the Greeks. They are all to perish far from
Argos. Let them drag the ships to the sea, moor them
with stones, and fly, "For there is no shame in fleeing
from ruin, even in the night. Better doth he fare who
flees from trouble than he that is overtaken." It is
now the turn of Odysseus again to save the honour
of the army. "Be silent, lest some other of the
Achæans hear this word, that no man should so much
as suffer to pass through his mouth. . . . And now
I wholly scorn thy thoughts, such a word hast thou
uttered." On this Agamemnon instantly repents.
"Right sharply hast thou touched my heart with
thy stern reproof :" he has not even the courage of
his nervousness.

The combat is now in the hands of Aias and
Patroclus, who is slain. Agamemnon, who is wounded,
does not reappear till Book XIX., when Achilles, anxious
to fight and avenge Patroclus at once, without for-

malities of reconciliation, professes his desire to let bygones be bygones. Agamemnon excuses his insolence to Achilles as an inspiration of Atê : a predestined fault—"Not I am the cause, but Zeus and Destiny."

Odysseus, to clinch the reunion and fulfil customary law, advises Agamemnon to bring out the gifts of atonement (the gifts prepared in Book IX.), after which the right thing is for him to give a feast of reconciliation, "that Achilles may have nothing lacking of his right." [1] The case is one which has been provided for by customary law in every detail. Mr. Leaf argues that all this part must be late, because of the allusion to the gifts offered in Book IX. But we reply, with Mr. Monro, that the Ninth Book is "almost necessary to any Achilleis." The question is, would a late editor or poet know all the details of customary law in such a case as a quarrel between Over-Lord and peer ? would a feudal audience have been satisfied with a poem which did not wind the quarrel up in accordance with usage ? and would a late poet, in a society no longer feudal, know how to wind it up ? Would he find any demand on the part of his audience for a long series of statements, which to a modern seem to interrupt the story ? To ourselves it appears that a feudal audience desired the customary details ; to such an audience they were most interesting.

This is a taste which, as has been said, we find in all early poetry and in the sagas ; hence the long "runs" of the Celtic sagas, minutely repeated descriptions of customary things. The Icelandic saga-men never weary, though modern readers do, of legal details. For these reasons we reckon the passages

[1] Book XIX. 179, 180.

in Book XIX. about the reconciliation as original, and think they can be nothing else. It is quite natural that, in a feudal society of men who were sticklers for custom, the hearers should insist on having all things done duly and in order—the giving of the gifts and the feast of reconciliation—though the passionate Achilles himself desires to fight at once. Odysseus insists that what we may call the regular routine shall be gone through. It is tedious to the modern reader, but it is surely much more probable that a feudal poet thus gratified his peculiar audience (he looked for no other) than that a late poet, with a different kind of audience, thrust the Reconciliation in as an " after-thought." [1] The right thing must be done, Odysseus assures Achilles, "for I was born first, and know more things." It is *not* the right thing to fight at once, unfed, and before the solemn sacrifice by the Over-Lord, the prayer, the Oath of Agamemnon, and the reception of the gifts by Achilles ; only after these formalities, and after the army has fed, can the host go forth. " I know more than you do ; you are a younger man," says Odysseus, speaking in accordance with feudal character, at the risk of wearing later unforeseen generations.

This is not criticism inspired by mere " literary feeling," for " literary feeling " is on the side of Achilles, and wishes the story to hurry to his revenge. But ours is *historical* criticism ; we must think of the poet in relation to his audience and of their demands, which we can estimate by similar demands, vouched for by the supply, in the early national poetry of other peoples and in the Icelandic sagas.

[1] Leaf, *Iliad*, vol. ii. p. 317.

We hear no more of Agamemnon till, in Book XXIII. 35–38, after the slaying of Hector, Achilles "was brought to noble Agamemnon" (for that, as Odysseus said, was the regular procedure) "by the Achæan chiefs, hardly persuading him thereto, for his heart was wroth for his comrade." Here they feast, Achilles still full of grief and resentment. He merely goes through the set forms, much against his will. It does appear to us that the later the poet the less he would have known or cared about the forms. An early society is always much interested in forms and in funerals and funeral games, so the poet indulges their taste with the last rites of Patroclus. The last view of Agamemnon is given when, at the end of the games, Achilles courteously presents him with the flowered *lebes*, the prize for hurling the spear, without asking him to compete, since his superior skill is notorious. This act of courtesy is the real reconciliation ; previously Achilles had but gone reluctantly through the set forms in such cases provided. Even when Agamemnon offered the gifts of atonement, Achilles said, "Give them, as is customary, or keep them, as you please" (XIX. 146, 148). Achilles, young and passionate, cares nothing for the feudal procedure.

This rapid survey seems to justify the conclusion that the poet presents an uniform and historically correct picture of the Over-Lord and of his relations with his peers, a picture which no late editor could have pieced together out of the widely varying *répertoires* of late strolling reciters. Such reciters would gladly have forgotten, and such an editor would gladly have "cut" the "business" of the reconciliation. They

would also, in a democratic spirit, have degraded the
Over-Lord into the tyrant, but throughout, however
low Agamemnon may fall, the poet is guided by the
knowledge that his right to rule is *jure divino*, that he
has qualities, that his responsibilities are crushing,
" I, whom among all men Zeus hath planted for ever
among labours, while my breath abides within me, and
my limbs move," says the Over-Lord (X. 89, 90). In
short, the poet's conception of the Over-Lord is
throughout harmonious, is a contemporary conception
entertained by a singer who lives among peers that
own, and are jealous of, and obey an Over-Lord. The
character and situation of Agamemnon are a poetic
work of one age, one moment of culture.

CHAPTER VI

ARCHÆOLOGY OF THE "ILIAD"

BURIAL AND CREMATION

IN archæological discoveries we find the most convincing proofs that the *Iliad*, on the whole, is the production of a single age, not the patchwork of several changeful centuries. This may seem an audacious statement, as archæology has been interpreted of late in such a manner as to demand precisely the opposite verdict. But if we can show, as we think we can, that many recent interpretations of the archæological evidence are not valid, because they are not consistent, our contention, though unexpected, will be possible. It is that the combined testimony of archæology and of the Epic proves the *Iliad* to represent, as regards customs, weapons, and armour, a definite moment of evolution ; a period between the age recorded in the art of the Mycenæan shaft graves and the age of early iron swords and the " Dipylon " period.

Before the discoveries of the material remains of the " Mycenæan " times, the evidence of archæology was seldom appropriately invoked in discussions of the Homeric question. But in the thirty years since Schliemann explored the buried relics of the Mycenæan Acropolis, his " Grave of Agamemnon," a series of excavations has laid bare the interments, the works of art, and the weapons and ornaments of years long prior to the revolution commonly associated with the " Dorian Invasion " of about 1100–1000 B.C. The objects of all sorts which have been found in many sites of Greece and the isles, especially of Cyprus and Crete, in some respects tally closely with Homeric descriptions, in others vary from them widely. Nothing can be less surprising, if the heroes whose legendary feats inspired the poet lived centuries before his time, as Charlemagne and his Paladins lived some three centuries before the composition of the earliest extant *Chansons de Geste* on their adventures. There was, in such a case, time for much change in the details of life, art, weapons and implements. Taking the relics in the graves of the Mycenæan Acropolis as a starting-point, some things would endure into the age of the poet, some would be modified, some would disappear.

We cannot tell how long previous to his own date the poet supposes the Achæan heroes to have existed. He frequently ascribes to them feats of strength which "no man of such as now are" could perform. This gives no definite period for the interval ; he might be speaking of the great grandfathers of his own generation. But when he regards the heroes as closely connected by descent of one or two generations with the gods, and as in frequent and familiar intercourse with gods and goddesses, we must suppose that he did not think their period recent. The singers of the *Chansons de Geste* knew that angels' visits were few and far between at the period, say, of the Norman Conquest ; but they allowed angels to appear in epics dealing with the earlier time, almost as freely as gods intervene in Homer.

In short, the Homeric poet undeniably treats the age of his heroes as having already, in the phrase of Thucydides, "won its way to the mythical," and therefore as indefinitely remote.

It is impossible here to discuss in detail the complex problems of Mycenæan chronology. If we place the Mycenæan " bloom-time " from " the seventeenth or sixteenth to the twelfth century B.C.,"[1] it is plain that there is space to spare, between the poet's age and that of his heroes, for the rise of changes in war, weapons, and costume. Indeed, there are traces enough of change even in the objects and art discovered in the bloom-time, as represented by the Mycenæan acropolis itself and by other " Mycenæan " sites. The art of the fragment of a silver vase in a grave, on which a siege is represented, is not the art, the costumes are not the costumes, of the inlaid bronze dagger-blade. The men shown on the vase and the lion-hunters on the dagger both have their hair close cropped, but on the vase they are naked, on the dagger they wear short drawers. On the Vaphio cups, found in a *tholos* chamber-tomb near Amyclae, the men are "long-haired Achæans," with heavy, pendent locks, like the man on a pyxis from Knossos, published by Mr. Evans ; they are of another period than the close-cropped men of the vase and dagger.[2] Two of the men on the silver vase are covered either with shields of a shape and size elsewhere unknown in Mycenæan art, or with cloaks of an unexampled form. The masonry of the city wall, shown on the vase in the Mycenæan grave, is not the ordinary masonry of

[1] Tsountas and Manatt, p. 322.
[2] *Journal of Hellenic Studies*, vol. xvi. p. 102.

Mycenæ itself. On the vase the wall is "isodomic," built of cut stones in regular layers. Most of the Mycenæan walls, on the other hand, are of "Cyclopean" style, in large irregular blocks.

Art, good and very bad, exists in many various stages in Mycenæan relics. The drawing of a god, with a typical Mycenæan shield in the form of a figure 8, on a painted sarcophagus from Milato in Crete, is more crude and savage than many productions of the Australian aboriginals,[1] the thing is on the level of Red Indian work. Meanwhile at Vaphio, Enkomi, Knossos, and elsewhere the art is often excellent.

In one essential point the poet describes a custom without parallel among the discovered relics of the Mycenæan age—namely, the disposal of the bodies of the dead. They are neither buried with their arms, in stately *tholos* tombs nor in shaft graves, as at Mycenæ : whether they be princes or simple oarsmen, they are cremated. A pyre of wood is built ; on this the warrior's body is laid, the pyre is lighted, the body is reduced to ashes, the ashes are placed in a vessel or box of gold, wrapped round with precious cloths (no arms are buried, as a general rule), and a mound, howe, barrow, or tumulus is raised over all. Usually a *stêlê* or pillar crowns the edifice. This method is almost uniform, and, as far as cremation and the cairn go, is universal in the *Iliad* and *Odyssey* whenever a burial is described. Now this mode of interment must be the mode of a single age in Greek civilisation. It is confessedly not the method of the Mycenæans of the shaft grave, or of the latter *tholos* or stone beehive-

[1] *Journal of Hellenic Studies*, vol. xvi. p. 174, fig. 50. Grosse. *Les Débuts de l'Art*, pp. 124-176.

shaped grave ; again, the Mycenæans did not burn the
dead ; they buried. Once more, the Homeric method
is not that of the Dipylon period (say 900–750 B.C.)
represented by the tombs outside the Dipylon gate
of Athens. The people of that age now buried, now
burned, their dead, and did not build cairns over them.
Thus the Homeric custom comes between the shaft
graves and the latter *tholos* graves, on the one hand,
and the Dipylon custom of burning or burying, with
sunk or rock-hewn graves, on the other.

The Homeric poets describe the method of their
own period. They assuredly do not adhere to an
older epic tradition of shaft graves or *tholos* graves,
though these must have been described in lays of the
period when such methods of disposal of the dead
were in vogue. The altar above the shaft-graves in
Mycenæ proves the cult of ancestors in Mycenæ ; of this
cult in the *Iliad* there is no trace, or only a dim trace
of survival in the slaughter of animals at the funeral.
The Homeric way of thinking about the state of the
dead, weak, shadowy things beyond the river Oceanus,
did not permit them to be worshipped as potent
beings. Only in a passage, possibly interpolated, of
the *Odyssey*, do we hear that Castor and Polydeuces,
brothers of Helen, and sons of Tyndareus, through
the favour of Zeus have immortality, and receive
divine honours.[1]

These facts are so familiar that we are apt to over-
look the strangeness of them in the history of religious
evolution. The cult of ancestral spirits begins in the
lowest barbarism, just above the level of the Australian
tribes, who, among the Dieri, show some traces of the

[1] *Odyssey*, XI. 298–304.

practice, at least, of ghost feeding.[1] Sometimes, as in many African tribes, ancestor worship is almost the whole of practical cult. Usually it accompanies polytheism, existing beside it on a lower plane. It was prevalent in the Mycenæ of the shaft graves ; in Attica it was uninterrupted ; it is conspicuous in Greece from the ninth century onwards. But it is unknown to or ignored by the Homeric poets, though it can hardly have died out of folk custom. Consequently, the poems are of one age, an age of cremation and of burial in barrows, with no ghost worship. Apparently some revolution as regards burial occurred between the age of the graves of the Mycenæan acropolis and the age of Homer. That age, coming with its form of burning and its absence of the cult of the dead, between two epochs of inhumation, ancestor worship, and absence of cairns, is as certainly and definitely an age apart, a peculiar period, as any epoch can be.

Cremation, with cairn burial of the ashes, is, then, the only form of burial mentioned by Homer, and, as far as the poet tells us, the period was not one in which iron was used for swords and spears. At Assarlik (Asia Minor) and in Thera early graves prove the use of cremation, but also, unlike Homer, of iron weapons.[2] In these graves the ashes are inurned. There are examples of the same usage in Salamis, without iron. In Crete, in graves of the period of geometrical ornament (" Dipylon "), burning is more common than inhumation. Cremation is attested in a *tholos* or beehive-shaped grave in Argos, where the vases were late

---

[1] Howitt, *Native Tribes of South-Eastern Australia*, p. 448. There are also traces of propitiation in Western Australia (MS. of Mrs. Bates).

[2] Paton, *Journal of Hellenic Studies*, viii. 64 ff. For other references, cf. Poulsen, *Die Dipylongräben*, p. 2. Notes. Leipzig 1905.

Mycenæan. Below this stratum was an older shaft
grave, as is usual in *tholos* interments; it had been
plundered.[1]

The cause of the marked change from Mycenæan
inhumation to Homeric cremation is matter of conjecture. It has been suggested that burning was introduced during the migrations after the Dorian invasion.
Men could carry the ashes of their friends to the place
where they finally settled.[2] The question may, perhaps,
be elucidated by excavation, especially in Asia Minor,
on the sites of the earliest Greek colonies. At Colophon are many cairns unexplored by science. Mr.
Ridgeway, as is well known, attributes the introduction
of cremation to a conquering northern people, the
Achæans, his "Celts." It is certain that cremation
and urn burial of the ashes prevailed in Britain during
the Age of Bronze, and co-existed with inhumation in
the great cemetery of Hallstatt, surviving into the Age
of Iron.[3] Others suppose a change in Achæan ideas
about the soul; it was no longer believed to haunt
the grave and grave goods and be capable of haunt-
ing the living, but to be wholly set free by burning,
and to depart for ever to the House of Hades, power-
less and incapable of hauntings.

It is never easy to decide as to whether a given
mode of burial is the result of a definite opinion about
the condition of the dead, or whether the explanation
offered by those who practise the method is an after-
thought. In Tasmania among the lowest savages,
now extinct, were found monuments over cremated

---

[1] Poulsen, p. 2.   [2] Helbig, *Homerische Epos*, p. 83.
[3] Cf. *Guide to Antiquities of Early Iron Age*, British Museum, 1905, by
Mr. Reginald A. Smith, under direction of Mr. Charles H. Read, for a brief
account of Hallstatt culture.

human remains, accompanied with "characters crudely marked, similar to those which the aborigines tattooed on their forearms." In one such grave was a spear, "for the dead man to fight with when he is asleep," as a native explained. Some Tasmanian tribes burned the dead and carried the ashes about in amulets; others buried in hollow trees ; others simply inhumed. Some placed the dead in a hollow tree, and cremated the body after lapse of time. Some tied the dead up tightly (a common practice with inhumation), and then burned him. Some buried the dead in an erect posture. The common explanation of burning was that it prevented the dead from returning, thus it has always been usual to burn the bodies of vampires. Did a race so backward hit on an idea unknown to the Mycenæan Greeks ?[1] If the usual explanation be correct—burning prevents the return of the dead—how did the Homeric Greeks come to substitute burning for the worship and feeding of the dead, which had certainly prevailed ? How did the ancient method return, overlapping and blent with the method of cremation, as in the early Dipylon interments ? We can only say that the Homeric custom is definite and isolated, and that but slight variations occur in the methods of Homeric burial.

(1) In *Iliad*, VI. 416 *ff*, Andromache says that Achilles slew her father, "yet he despoiled him not, for his soul had shame of that; but he burnt him in his inlaid armour, and raised a barrow over him." We are not told that the armour was interred with the ashes of Eetion. This is a peculiar case. We always hear in the

---

[1] Ling Roth., *The Tasmanians*, pp. 128–134. Reports of Early Discoverers.

Iliad that the dead are burned, and the ashes of princes are placed in a vessel of gold within an artificial hillock; but we do not hear, except in this passage, that they are burned in their armour, or that it is burned, or that it is buried with the ashes of the dead. The invariable practice is for the victor, if he can, to despoil the body of the fallen foe ; but Achilles for some reason spared that indignity in the case of Eetion.[1]

(2) *Iliad*, VII. 85. Hector, in his challenge to a single combat, makes the conditions that the victor shall keep the arms and armour of the vanquished, but shall restore his body to his friends. The Trojans will burn him, if he falls ; if the Achæan falls, the others will do something expressed by the word ταρχύσωσι, probably a word surviving from an age of embalment.[2] It has come to mean, generally, to do the funeral rites. The hero is to have a barrow or artificial howe or hillock built over him, " beside wide Hellespont," a memorial of him, and of Hector's valour.

On the River Helmsdale, near Kildonan, on the left bank, there is such a hillock which has never, it is believed, been excavated. It preserves the memory of its occupant, an early Celtic saint; whether he was cremated or not it is impossible to say. But his memory is not lost, and the howe, cairn, or hillock, in Homer is desired by the heroes as a *memorial*.

On the terms proposed by Hector the arms of the dead could not be either burned or buried with him.

(3) *Iliad*, IX. 546. Phœnix says that the Calydonian

---

[1] German examples of burning the arms of the cremated dead and then burying them are given by Mr. Ridgeway, *Early Age of Greece*, vol. i. pp. 498, 499.

[2] Helbig, *Homerische Epos*, pp. 55, 56.

boar " brought many to the mournful pyre." All were cremated.

(4) *Iliad*, XXII. 510–515. Andromache in her dirge (the *regret* of the French mediæval epics) says that Hector lies unburied by the ships and naked, but she will burn raiment of his, " delicate and fair, the work of women . . . to thee no profit, since thou wilt never lie therein, yet this shall be honour to thee from the men and women of Troy." Her meaning is not very clear, but she seems to imply that if Hector's body were in Troy it would be clad in garments before cremation.

Helbig appears to think that to clothe the dead in *garments* was an Ionian, not an ancient epic custom. But in Homer the dead always wear at least one garment, the φᾶρος, a large mantle, either white or purple, such as Agamemnon wears in peace (*Iliad*, II. 43), except when, like Eetion and Elpenor in the *Odyssey*, they are burned in their armour. In *Iliad*, XXIII. 69 *ff.*, the shadow of the dead unburned Patroclus appears to Achilles in his sleep asking for " his dues of fire." The whole passage, with the account of the funeral of Patroclus, must be read carefully, and compared with the funeral rites of Hector at the end of Book XXIV. Helbig, in an essay of great erudition, though perhaps rather fantastic in its generalisations, has contrasted the burials of the two heroes. Patroclus is buried, he says, in a true portion of the old Æolic epic (Sir Richard Jebb thought the whole passage " Ionic "), though even into this the late Ionian *bearbeiter* (a spectral figure), has introduced his Ionian notions. But the Twenty-fourth Book itself is late and Ionian, Helbig says, not genuine early Æolian epic poetry.[1] The burial of Patroclus, then, save for Ionian late interpolations, easily detected by Helbig, is, he assures us, genuine "kernel," [2] while Hector's burial " is partly Ionian, and describes the destiny of the dead heroes otherwise than as in the old Æolic epos."

Here Helbig uses that one of his two alternate theories according to which the late Ionian poets do *not* cling to old epic tradition, but bring in details of the life of their own date. By Helbig's other alternate theory, the late poets cling to the model set in old epic tradition in their pictures of details of life.

Disintegrationists differ: far from thinking that the late Ionian poet who buried Hector varied from the Æolic minstrel who buried Patroclus (in Book XXIII.), Mr. Leaf says that Hector's burial is "almost an abstract" of that of Patroclus.[3] He adds that Helbig's attempts "to distinguish the older Æolic from the newer and more sceptical 'Ionic' faith seem to me visionary." [4] Visionary, indeed, they do seem, but they are examples of the efforts made to prove that the *Iliad* bears marks of composition continued through several centuries. We must remember that, according to Helbig, the Ionians, colonists in a new country, "had no use for ghosts." A fresh colony does not produce ghosts. "There is hardly an English or Scottish castle without its spook (*spuck*). On the other hand, you look in vain for such a thing in the United States "— spiritualism apart.[5]

This is a hasty generalisation ! Helbig will, if he

---

[1] Helbig, *Zu den Homerischen Bestattungsgebraüchen.* Aus den Sitzungsberichten der philos. philol. und histor. Classe der Kgl. bayer. Academie der Wissenschaften. 1900. Heft. ii. pp. 199–299.

[2] *Op. laud.*, p. 208.　　　[3] Leaf, *Iliad*, XXIII. Note to 791.

[4] *Iliad*, vol. ii. p. 619. Note 2.　　[5] *Op. laud.*, p. 204.

looks, find ghosts enough in the literature of North
America while still colonial, and in Australia, a still
more newly settled country, sixty years ago Fisher's
ghost gave evidence of Fisher's murder, evidence which,
as in another Australian case, served the ends of justice.[1]
More recent Australian ghosts are familiar to psychical
research.

This colonial theory is one of Helbig's too ven-
turous generalisations.   He studies the ghost, or
rather dream-apparition, of Patroclus after examining
the funeral of Hector ; but we shall begin with Patroclus.   Achilles (XXIII. 4–16) first hails his friend
"even in the House of Hades" (so he believes that
spirits are in Hades), and says that he has brought
Hector "raw for dogs to devour," and twelve Trojans
of good family "to slaughter before thy pyre." That
night, when Achilles is asleep (XXIII. 65) the spirit
(ψύχη) of Patroclus appears to him, says that he is
forgotten, and begs to be burned at once, that he may
pass the gates of Hades, for the other spirits drive him
off and will not let him associate with them "beyond
the River," and he wanders vaguely along the wide-
gated dwelling of Hades.   "Give me thy hand, for
never more again shall I come back from Hades, when
ye have given me my due of fire."   Patroclus, being
newly discarnate, does not yet know that a spirit
cannot take a living man's hand, though, in fact, tactile
hallucinations are not uncommon in the presence of
phantasms of the dead.   "Lay not my bones apart
from thine . . . let one coffer" (σορός) "hide our
bones."

Σορός, like *larnax*, is a coffin (*Sarg*), or what the

[1] See, in *The Valet's Tragedy* (A. L.) : "Fisher's Ghost."

Americans call a "casket," in the opinion of Helbig :[1]
it is an oblong receptacle of the bones and dust.
Hector was buried in a *larnax;* so will Achilles and
Patroclus be when Achilles falls, but the dust of
Patroclus is kept, meanwhile, in a golden covered cup
(φιάλη) in the quarters of Achilles ; it is not laid in
howe after his cremation (XXIII. 243).

Achilles tries to embrace Patroclus, but fails, like
Odysseus with the shade of his mother in Hades, in
the *Odyssey.* He exclaims that "there remaineth then
even in the House of Hades a spirit and phantom of
the dead, albeit the life " (or the wits) " be not anywise
therein, for all night hath the spirit of hapless Patroclus
stood over me. . . ."

In this speech Helbig detects the hand of the late
Ionian poet. What goes before is part of the genuine
old Epic, the kernel, done at a time when men believed
that spooks could take part in the affairs of the upper
world. Achilles therefore (in his dream), thought that
he could embrace his friend. It was the sceptical
Ionian, in a fresh and spookless colony, who knew
that he could not ; *he* thinks the ghost a mere dream,
and introduces his scepticism in XXIII. 99–107. He
brought in " the ruling ideas of his own period." The
ghost, says the Ionian *bearbeiter*, is intangible, though
in the genuine old epic the ghost himself thought
otherwise—he being new to the situation and without
experience. This is the first sample of the critical
Ionian spirit, later so remarkable in philosophy and
natural science, says Helbig.[2]

We need not discuss this acute critical theory. The
natural interpretation of the words of Achilles is obvious;

[1] *Op. laud.*, p. 217.   [2] *Op. laud.*, pp. 233, 234.

as Mr. Leaf remarks, the words are "the cry of sudden personal conviction in a matter which has hitherto been lazily accepted as an orthodox dogma." [1] Already, as we have seen, Achilles has made promises to Patroclus in the House of Hades, now he exclaims "there really is something in the doctrine of a feeble future life."

It is vain to try to discriminate between an old epic belief in able-bodied *ghosts* and an Ionian belief in mere futile *shades*, in the Homeric poems. Everywhere the dead are too feeble to be worth worshipping after they are burned; but, as Mr. Leaf says with obvious truth, and with modern instances, "men are never so inconsistent as in their beliefs about the other world." We ourselves hold various beliefs simultaneously. The natives of Australia and of Tasmania practise, or did practise, every conceivable way of disposing of the dead—burying, burning, exposure in trees, carrying about the bodies or parts of them, eating the bodies, and so forth. If each such practice corresponded, as archæologists believe, to a different opinion about the soul, then all beliefs were held together at once, and this, in fact, is the case. There is not now one and now another hard and fast orthodoxy of belief about the dead, though now we find ancestor worship prominent and now in the shade.

After gifts of hair and the setting up of jars full of oil and honey, Achilles has the body laid on the top of the pyre in the centre. Bodies of sheep and oxen, two dogs and four horses, are strewed around; why, we know not, for the dead is not supposed to need food: the rite may be a survival, for there were sacrifices at the burials of the Mycenæan shaft graves. Achilles

[1] *Iliad*, vol. ii. p. 620.

slays also the twelve Trojans, " because of mine anger at thy slaying," he says (XXIII. 23). This was his reason, as far as he consciously had any reason, not that his friend might have twelve thralls in Hades. After the pyre is alit Achilles drenches it all night with wine, and, when the flame dies down, the dead hero's bones are collected and placed in the covered cup of gold. The circle of the barrow is then marked out, stones are set up round it (we see them round Highland tumuli), and earth is heaped up ; no more is done ; the tomb is empty ; the covered cup holding the ashes is in the hut of Achilles.

We must note another trait. After the body of Patroclus was recovered, it was washed, anointed, laid on a bier, and covered from head to foot ἑανῷ λιτὶ, translated by Helbig, " with a linen sheet " (cf. XXIII. 254). The golden cup with the ashes is next wrapped ἑανῷ λιτὶ ; here Mr. Myers renders the words " with a linen veil." Scottish cremation burials of the Bronze Age retain traces of linen wrappings of the urn.[1] Over all a white φᾶρος (mantle) was spread. In Iliad, XXIV. 231, twelve φάρεα with chitons, single cloaks, and other articles of dress, are taken to Achilles by Priam as part of the ransom of Hector's body. Such is the death-garb of Patroclus ; but Helbig, looking for Ionian innovations in Book XXIV., finds that the death-garb of Hector is not the same as that of Patroclus in Book XXIII. One difference is that when the squires of Achilles took the ransom of Hector from the waggon of Priam, they left in it two φάρεα and a well-spun chiton. The women washed and

---

[1] Proceedings of the Scottish Society of Antiquaries, 1905, p. 552. For other cases, cf. Leaf, Iliad, XXIV. 796. Note.

anointed Hector's body ; they clad him in the chiton,
and threw one φᾶρος over it ; we are not told what
they did with the other. Perhaps, as Mr. Leaf says,
it was used as a cover for the bier, perhaps it was
not, but was laid under the body (Helbig). All we
know is that Hector's body was restored to Priam
in a chiton and a φᾶρος, which do not seem to have
been removed before he was burned; while Patroclus
had no chiton in death, but a φᾶρος and, apparently,
a linen sheet.

To the ordinary reader this does not seem, in the
circumstances, a strong mark of different ages and different burial customs. Priam did not bring any linen
sheet—or whatever ἑανὸς λίς may be—in the waggon as
part of Hector's ransom ; and it neither became Achilles
to give nor Priam to receive any of Achilles's stuff as
death-garb for Hector. The squires, therefore, gave
back to Priam, to clothe his dead son, part of what he
had brought ; nothing can be more natural, and there,
we may say, is an end on't. They did what they could
in the circumstances. But Helbig has observed that,
in a Cean inscription of the fifth century B.C., there is
a sumptuary law, forbidding a corpse to wear more
than three white garments, a sheet under him, a chiton,
and a mantle cast over him.[1] He supposes that Hector
wore the chiton, and had one φᾶρος over him and the
other under him, though Homer does not say that.
The Laws of Solon also confined the dead man to three
articles of dress.[2] In doing so Solon sanctioned an
old custom, and that Ionian custom, described by the
author of Book XXIV., bewrays him, says Helbig, for

---

[1] *Op. laud.*, p. 209.
[2] Plutarch, *Solon*, 21.

a late Ionian *bearbeiter*, deserting true epic usages and inserting those of his own day. But in some Attic Dipylon vases, in the pictures of funerals, we see no garments or sheets over the corpses.

Penelope also wove a φᾶρος against the burial of old Laertes, but surely she ought to have woven *two* for him ; on Helbig's showing Hector had *two*, Patroclus had only one ; Patroclus is in the old epic, Hector and Laertes are in the Ionian epics ; therefore, Laertes should have had two φάρεα, but we only hear of one. Penelope had to finish the φᾶρος and show it ;[1] now if she wanted to delay her marriage, she should have begun the second φᾶρος, just as necessary as the first, if Hector, with a pair of φάρεα, represents Ionian usage. But Penelope never thought of what, had she read Helbig, she would have seen to be so obvious. She thought of no funeral garments for the old man but one shroud (σπεῖρον, *Odyssey*, II. 102 ; XIX. 147) ; yet, being, by the theory, a character of late Ionian, not of genuine old Æolic epic, she should have known better. It is manifest that if even the acuteness and vast erudition of Helbig can only find such invisible differences as these between the manners of the genuine old epic and the late Ionian innovations, there is really no difference, beyond such trifles as diversify custom in any age.

Hector, when burned and when his ashes have been placed in the casket, is laid in a κάπετος, a ditch or trench (*Iliad*, XV. 356 ; XVIII. 564) ; but here (XXIV. 797) κάπετος is a chamber covered with great stones, within the howe, the casket being swathed with purple robes, and this was the end. The ghost of Hector would not

[1] *Odyssey*, XXIV. 147.

revisit the sun, as ghosts do freely in the Cyclic poems, a proof that the Cyclics are later than the Homeric poems.[1]

If the burning of the weapons of Eetion and Elpenor are traces of another than the *old* Æolic epic faith,[2] they are also traces of another than the late *Ionic* epic faith, for no weapons are burned with Hector. In the *Odyssey* the weapons of Achilles are not burned ; in the *Iliad* the armour of Patroclus is not burned. No victims of any kind are burned with Hector : possibly the poet was not anxious to repeat what he had just described (his last book is already a very long book) ; possibly the Trojans did not slay victims at the burning.

The howes or barrows built over the Homeric dead were hillocks high enough to be good points of outlook for scouts, as in the case of the barrow of Æsyetes (*Iliad*, II. 793) and "the steep mound," the howe of lithe Myrine (II. 814). We do not know that women were usually buried in howe, but Myrine was a warrior maiden of the Amazons. We know, then, minutely what the Homeric mode of burial was, with such variations as have been noted. We have burning and howe even in the case of an obscure oarsman like Elpenor. It is not probable, however, that every peaceful mechanic had a howe all to himself ; he may have had a small family cairn ; he may not have had an expensive cremation.

The interesting fact is that no barrow burial precisely of the Homeric kind has ever been discovered in Greek sites. The old Mycenæans buried either in shaft graves or in a stately *tholos;* and in rock

---

[1] Helbig, *op. laud.*, pp. 240, 241.   [2] *Ibid.*, p. 253.

chambers, later, in the town cemetery: they did not
burn the bodies. The people of the Dipylon period
sometimes cremated, sometimes inhumed, but they
built no barrow over the dead.[1] The Dipylon was
a period of early iron swords, made on the lines of
not the best type of bronze sword. Now, in Mr. Leaf's
opinion, our Homeric accounts of burial " are all late ;
the oldest parts of the poems tell us nothing." [2] We
shall show, however, that Mr. Leaf's " kernel " alludes to
cremation. What is " late " ? In this case it is not the
Dipylon period, say 900–750 B.C. It is not any later
period ; one or two late barrow burials do not answer
to the Homeric descriptions. The " late " parts of the
poems, therefore, dealing with burials, in Books VI.,
VII., XIX., XXIII., XXIV., and the *Odyssey*, are of an
age not in " the Mycenæan prime," not in the Dipylon
period, not in any later period, say the seventh or sixth
centuries B.C., and, necessarily, not of any subsequent
period. Yet nobody dreams of saying that the poets
describe a purely fanciful form of interment. They
speak of what they know in daily life. If it be argued
that the late poets preserve, by sheer force of epic
tradition, a form of burial unknown in their own age,
we ask, " Why did epic tradition not preserve the burial
methods of the Mycenæan prime, the shaft grave, or
the *tholos*, without cremation ? "

Mr. Leaf's own conclusion is that the people of
Mycenæ were " spirit worshippers, practising inhumation,

[1] *Annal. de l'Inst.*, 1872, pp. 135, 147, 167. Plausen, *ut supra.*
[2] *Iliad*, vol. ii. p. 619. Note 2. While Mr. Leaf says that "the oldest
parts of the poems tell us nothing " of burial, he accepts XXII. 342, 343 as of
the oldest part. These lines describe cremation, and Mr. Leaf does not think
them borrowed from the "later " VII. 79, 80, but that VII. 79, 80 are " perhaps borrowed " from XXII. 342, 343. It follows that "the oldest parts of
the poems " do tell us of cremation.

and partial mummification ; " the second fact is dubious.
" In the post-Mycenæan 'Dipylon' period, we find
cremation and sepulture practised side by side. In the
interval, therefore, two beliefs have come into conflict.[1]
It seems that the Homeric poems mark this intermediate point. . . ."[2] In that case the Homeric
poems are of one age, or, at least, all of them save
" the original kernel " are of one age, namely, a period
subsequent to the Mycenæan prime, but considerably
prior to the Dipylon period, which exhibits a mixture
of custom ; cremation and inhumation coexisting, without barrows or howes.

We welcome this conclusion, and note that (whatever may be the case with the oldest parts of the poems
which say nothing about funerals) the latest expansions must be of about 1100–1000 B.C. (?). The poem
is so early that it is prior to hero worship and ancestor
worship ; or it might be more judicious to say that the
poem is of an age that did not, officially, practise
ancestor worship, whatever may have occurred in folk-
custom. The Homeric age is one which had outgrown
ancestor and hero worship, and had not, like the age
of the Cyclics, relapsed into it. *Enfin*, unless we
agree with Helbig as to essential variations of custom,
the poems are the work of one age, and that a
brief age, and an age of peculiar customs, cremation
and barrow burial ; and of a religion that stood,
without spirit worship, between the Mycenæan period
and the ninth century.

[1] All conceivable beliefs, we have said, about the dead are apt to coexist.
For every conceivable and some rather inconceivable contemporary Australian
modes of dealing with the dead, see Howitt, *Native Tribes of South-East
Australia* ; Spencer and Gillen, *Northern Tribes of Central Australia*.

[2] Leaf, *Iliad*, vol. ii. p. 622.

That seems as certain as anything in prehistoric times can be, unless we are to say, that after the age of shaft graves and spirit worship came an age of cremation and of no spirit worship ; and that late poets consciously and conscientiously preserved the tradition of *this* period into their own ages of hero worship and inhumation, though they did *not* preserve the tradition of the shaft-grave period. We cannot accept this theory of adherence to stereotyped poetical descriptions, nor can any one consistently adopt it in this case.

The reason is obvious. Mr. Leaf, with many other critics, distinguishes several successive periods of " expansion." In the first stratum we have the remains of " the original kernel." Among these remains is The Slaying of Hector (XXII. 1–404), " with but slight additions." [1] In the Slaying of Hector that hero indicates cremation as the mode of burial. " Give them my body back again, that the Trojans and Trojans' wives grant me my due of fire after my death." Perhaps this allusion to cremation, in the " original kernel " in the Slaying of Hector, may be dismissed as a late borrowing from Book VII. 79, 80, where Hector makes conditions that the fallen hero shall be restored to his friends when he challenges the Achæans to a duel. But whoever knows the curious economy by way of repetition that marks early national epics has a right to regard the allusion to cremation (XXII. 342, 343) as an example of this practice. Compare *La Chancun de Willame*, lines 1041–1058 with lines 1140–1134. In both the dinner of a knight who has been long deprived of food is described in passages containing many iden-

---

[1] Leaf, *Iliad*, vol. ii. p. xi.

tical lines.   The poet, having found his formula, uses
it whenever occasion serves.   There are several other
examples in the same epic.[1]   Repetitions in Homer
need not indicate late additions ; the artifice is part of
the epic as it is of the ballad manner.   If we are
right, cremation is the mode of burial even in "the
original kernel."   Hector, moreover, in the kernel
(XXII. 256–259) makes, *before* his final fight with
Achilles, the same proposal as he makes in his
challenge to a duel (VII. 85 *et seqq.*).   The victor
shall give back the body of the vanquished to his
friends, but how the friends are to bury it Hector
does not say—in this place.   When dying, he does
say (XXII. 342, 343).

In the kernel and all periods of expansion, funeral
rites are described, and in all the method is cremation,
with a howe or a barrow.   Thus the method of cremation had come in as early as the " kernel," The Slaying
of Hector, and as early as the first expansions, and it
lasted till the period of the latest expansions, such as
Books XXIII., XXIV.

But what is the approximate date of the various
expansions of the original poem ?   On that point Mr.
Leaf gives his opinion.   The Making of the Arms
of Achilles (Books XVIII., XIX. 1–39) is, with the
Funeral of Patroclus (XXIII. 1–256), in the second set
of expansions, and is thus two removes later than
the original " kernel." [2]   Now this is the period—the
Making of the Shield for Achilles is, at least, in touch
with the period—of " the eminently free and naturalistic
treatment which we find in the best Mycenæan work,

[1] *Romania*, xxxiv. pp. 245, 246.
[2] Leaf, *Iliad*, vol. ii. p. xii.

in the dagger blades, in the siege fragment, and notably in the Vaphio cups," (which show long-haired men, not men close-cropped, as in the daggers and siege fragment). [1] The poet of the age of the second expansions, then, is at least in touch with the work of the shaft grave and *tholos* ages. He need not be contemporary with that epoch, but " may well have had in his mind the work of artists older than himself." It is vaguely possible that he may have seen an ancient shield of the Mycenæan prime, and may be inspired by that. [2]

Moreover, and still more remarkable, the ordinary Homeric form of cremation and howe-burial is even older than the period which, if not contemporary with, is clearly reminiscent of, the art of the shaft graves. For, in the period of the first expansions (VII. 1-312), the form of burial is cremation, with a barrow or tumulus. [3] Thus Mr. Leaf's opinion might lead us to the conclusion that the usual Homeric form of burial occurs in a period *prior* to an age in which the poet is apparently reminiscent of the work of two early epochs—the epoch of shaft graves and that of *tholos* graves. If this be so, cremation and urn burial in cairns may be nearly as old as the Mycenæan shaft graves, or as old as the *tholos* graves, and they endure into the age of the latest expansions.

We must not press, however, opinions founded on the apparent technical resemblance of the free style and coloured metal work on the shield of Achilles, to the coloured metal work and free design on the daggers of the Mycenæan shaft graves. It is enough for us to note that the passages concerning burial, from the

---

[1] Leaf, *Iliad*, vol. ii. p. 606.   [2] *Ibid.*, vol. ii. pp. 606, 607.
[3] *Ibid.*, vol. ii. p. xi. and pp. 606, 607.

"kernel" itself, and also from the earliest to the latest expansions, are all perfectly harmonious, and of a single age—unless we are convinced by Helbig's objections. That age must have been brief, indeed, for, before it arrives, the period of *tholos* graves, as at Vaphio, must expire, on one hand, while the blending of cremation with inhumation, in the Dipylon age, must have been evolved after the cremation age passed, on the other. That brief intervening age, however, was the age of the *Iliad* and *Odyssey*. This conclusion can only be avoided by alleging that late poets, however recent and revolutionary, carefully copied the oldest epic model of burial, while they innovated in almost every other point, so we are told. We can go no further till we find an unrifled cairn burial answering to Homeric descriptions. We have, indeed, in Thessaly, "a large tumulus which contained a silver urn with burned remains." But the accompanying pottery dated it in the second century B.C.[1]

It is possible enough that all tumuli of the Homeric period have been robbed by grave plunderers in the course of the ages, as the Vikings are said to have robbed the cairns of Sutherlandshire, in which they were not likely to find a rich reward for their labours. A conspicuous howe invites robbery—the heroes of the Saga, like Grettir, occasionally rob a howe—and the fact is unlucky for the Homeric archæologist.

We have now tried to show that, as regards (1) the absence from Homer of new religious and ritual ideas, or of very old ideas revived in Ionia, (2) as concerns

[1] Ridgeway, *Early Age of Greece*, vol. i. p. 491 ; *Journal of Hellenic Studies*, vol. xx. pp. 20–25.

the clear conception of a loose form of feudalism, with an Over-Lord, and (3) in the matter of burial, the *Iliad* and *Odyssey* are self-consistent, and bear the impress of a single and peculiar moment of culture.

The fact, if accepted, is incompatible with the theory that the poets both introduced the peculiar conditions of their own later ages and also, on other occasions, consciously and consistently "archaised." Not only is such archaising inconsistent with the art of an uncritical age, but a careful archaiser, with all the resources of Alexandrian criticism at his command, could not archaise successfully. We refer to Quintus Smyrnæus, author of the *Post Homerica*, in fourteen books. Quintus does his best ; but we never observe in him that *naïf* delight in describing weapons and works of art, and details of law and custom which are so conspicuous in Homer and in other early poets. He does give us Penthesilea's great sword, with a hilt of ivory and silver ; but of what metal was the blade ? We are not told, and the reader of Quintus will observe that, though he knows χάλκος, bronze, as a synonym for weapons, he scarcely ever, if ever, says that a sword or spear or arrow-head was of bronze—a point on which Homer constantly insists. When he names the military metal Quintus usually speaks of iron. He has no interest in the constitutional and legal sides of heroic life, so attractive to Homer.

Yet Quintus consciously archaises, in a critical age, with Homer as his model. Any one who believes that in an uncritical age rhapsodists archaised, with such success as the presumed late poets of the *Iliad* must have done, may try his hand in our critical age, at a ballad in the style of the Border ballads. If he succeeds in producing nothing that will at once mark his work as modern, he will be more successful than any poet who has made the experiment, and more successful than the most ingenious modern forgers of gems, jewels, and terra-cottas. They seldom deceive experts, and, when they do, other experts detect the deceit.

CHAPTER VII

HOMERIC ARMOUR

TESTED by their ideas, their picture of political society, and their descriptions of burial rites, the presumed authors of the alleged expansions of the *Iliad* all lived in one and the same period of culture. But, according to the prevalent critical theory, we read in the *Iliad* not only large "expansions" of many dates, but also briefer interpolations inserted by the strolling reciters or rhapsodists. " Until the final literary redaction had come," says Mr. Leaf—that is about 540 B.C.—" we cannot feel sure that any details, even of the oldest work, were secure from the touch of the latest poet."[1]

Here we are far from Mr. Leaf's own opinion that "the whole scenery of the poems, the details of armour, palaces, dress, decoration . . . had become stereotyped, and formed a foundation which the Epic poet dared not intentionally sap. . . ."[2] We now find[3] that " the latest poet " saps as much as he pleases down to the middle of the sixth century B.C. Moreover, in the middle of the sixth century B.C., the supposed editor employed by Pisistratus made " constant additions of transitional passages," and added many speeches by Nestor, an ancestor of Pisistratus.

Did these very late interlopers, down to the sixth century, introduce modern details into the picture of

---

[1] Leaf, *Iliad*, vol. ii. p. ix.   [2] *Ibid.*, vol. i. p. xv.
[3] *Ibid.*, vol. ii. p. ix.

life ? did they blur the *unus color ?*   We hope to prove that, if they did so at all, it was but slightly.

That the poems, however, with a Mycenæan or sub-Mycenæan basis of actual custom and usage, contain numerous contaminations from the usage of centuries as late as the seventh, is the view of Mr. Leaf, and Reichel and his followers.[1]

Reichel's hypothesis is that the heroes of the original poet had no defensive armour except the great Mycenæan shields ; that the ponderous shield made the use of chariots imperatively necessary ; that, after the Mycenæan age, a small buckler and a corslet superseded the unwieldy shield ; that chariots were no longer used ; that, by the seventh century B.C., a warrior could not be thought of without a breastplate ; and that new poets thrust corslets and greaves into songs both new and old.

How the new poets could conceive of warriors as always in chariots, whereas in practice they knew no war chariots, and yet could *not* conceive of them without corslets which the original poet never saw, is Reichel's secret.   The new poets had in the old lays a plain example to follow.   They did follow it as to chariots and shields ; as to corslets and greaves they reversed it.   Such is the Reichelian theory.

THE SHIELD

As regards armour, controversy is waged over the shield, corslet, and bronze greaves.   In Homer the shield is of leather, plated with bronze, and of bronze is the corslet.   No shields of bronze plating and no

[1] *Homerische Waffen.*   Von Wolfgang Reichel.   Wien, 1901.

bronze corslets have been found in Mycenæan excavations.

We have to ask, do the Homeric descriptions of shields tally with the representations of shields in works of art, discovered in the graves of Mycenæ, Spata in Attica, Vaphio in Sparta, and elsewhere ? If the descriptions in Homer vary from these relics, to what extent do they vary ? and do the differences arise from the fact that the poet describes consistently what he sees in his own age, or are the variations caused by late rhapsodists in the Iron Age, who keep the great obsolete shields and bronze weapons, yet introduce the other military gear of their day, say 800–600 B.C.—gear unknown to the early singers ?

It may be best to inquire, first, what does the poet, or what do the poets, say about shields ? and, next, to examine the evidence of representations of shields in Mycenæan art ; always remembering that the poet does not pretend to live, and beyond all doubt does not live, in the Mycenæan prime, and that the testimony of the tombs is liable to be altered by fresh discoveries.

In *Iliad*, II. 388, the shield (*aspis*) is spoken of as "covering a man about" (ἀμφιβρότη), while, in the heat of battle, the baldric (*telamon*), or belt of the shield, "shall be wet with sweat." The shield, then, is not an Ionian buckler worn on the left arm, but is suspended by a belt, and covers a man, or most of him, just as Mycenæan shields are suspended by belts shown in works of art, and cover the body and legs. This (II. 388) is a general description applying to the shields of all men who fight from chariots. Their great shield answers to the great mediæval shield of the knights of the twelfth century, the "double targe," worn

suspended from the neck by a belt. Such a shield
covers a mounted knight's body from mouth to stirrup
in an ivory chessman of the eleventh to twelfth century A.D.,[1] so also in the Bayeux tapestry,[2] and on seals.
Dismounted men have the same shield (p. 132).

The shield of Menelaus (III. 348) is "equal in all
directions," which we might conceive to mean, mathe-
matically "circular," as the words do mean that. A
shield is said to have "circles," and a spear which
grazes a shield—a shield which was πάντοσ᾽ ἐείση, "every
way equal"—rends both circles, the outer circle of
bronze, and the inner circle of leather (*Iliad*, XX. 273–
281). But the passage is not unjustly believed to be
late ; and we cannot rely on it as proof that Homer knew
circular shields among others. The epithet εὔκυκλος,
"of good circle," is commonly given to the shields, but
does not mean that the shield was circular, we are told,
but merely that it was "made of circular plates."[3] As
for the shield of Menelaus, and other shields described
in the same words, "every way equal," the epithet is
not now allowed to mean "circular." Mr. Leaf, anno-
tating *Iliad*, I. 306, says that this sense is "intolerably
mathematical and prosaic," and translates πάντοσ᾽ ἐείση
as "well balanced on every side." Helbig renders the
epithets in the natural sense, as "circular."[4]

To the rendering "circular" it is objected that a
circular shield of, say, four feet and a half in diameter,
would be intolerably heavy and superfluously wide,
while the shields represented in Mycenæan art are not

[1] *Catalogue of Scottish National Antiquities*, p. 375.
[2] Gautier, *Chanson de Roland*. Seventh edition, pp. 393, 394.
[3] Leaf, *Iliad*, vol. i. p. 573.
[4] Helbig, *Homerische Epos*, p. 315 ; *cf.*, on the other hand, p. 317,
Note 1.

circles, but rather resemble a figure of eight, in some cases, or a section of a cylinder, in others, or, again, a door (Fig. 5, p. 130).

What Homer really meant by such epithets as "equal every way," "very circular," "of a good circle," cannot be ascertained, since Homeric epithets of the shield, which were previously rendered "circular," "of good circle," and so on, are now translated in quite other senses, in order that Homeric descriptions may be made to tally with Mycenæan representations of shields, which are never circular as represented in works of art. In this position of affairs we are unable to determine the shape, or shapes, of the shields known to Homer.

A scholar's rendering of Homer's epithets applied to the shield is obliged to vary with the variations of his theory about the shield. Thus, in 1883, Mr. Leaf wrote, "The poet often calls the shield by names which seem to imply that it was round, and yet indicates that it was large enough to cover the whole body of a man. . . . In descriptions the round shape is always implied." The words which indicated that the shield (or one shield) "really looked like a tower, and really reached from neck to ankles" (in two or three cases), were "received by the poet from the earlier Achæan lays." "But to Homer the warriors appeared as using the later small round shield. His belief in the heroic strength of the men of old time made it quite natural to speak of them as bearing a shield which at once combined the later circular shape and the old heroic expanse. . . ."[1]

Here the Homeric words which naturally mean "circular" or "round" are accepted as meaning "round" or "circular." Homer, it is supposed, in practice only knows the round shields of the later age, 700 B.C., so he calls shields "round," but, obedient to tradition, he conceives of them as very large.

But, after the appearance of Reichel's speculations, the Homeric words for "round" and "circular" have been explained as meaning something else, and Mr. Leaf, in place of maintaining that Homer knew no shields but round shields, now writes (1900), "The small circular shield of later times . . . is equally unknown to Homer, with a very few curious exceptions," which Reichel discovered—erroneously, as we shall later try to show.[1]

Thus does science fluctuate! Now Homer knows in practice none but light round bucklers, dating from about 700 B.C.; again, he does not know them at all, though they were habitually used in the period at which the later parts of his Epic were composed. We shall have to ask, how did small round bucklers come to be unknown to late poets who saw them constantly?

Some scholars, then, believe that the old original poet always described Mycenæan shields, which are of various shapes, but never circular in Mycenæan art. If there are any circular shields in the poems, these, they say, must have been introduced by poets accustomed, in a much later age, to seeing circular bucklers. Therefore Homeric words, hitherto understood as meaning "circular," must now mean something else—even if the reasoning seems circular.

Other scholars believe that the poet in real life saw various types of shields in use, and that some of

---

[1] Leaf, *Iliad*, vol. i. p. 575.

H

them were survivals of the Mycenæan shields, semi-cylindrical, or shaped like figures of 8, or like a door ; others were circular ; and these scholars presume that Homer meant "circular" when he said "circular." Neither school will convert the other, and we cannot decide between them. We do not pretend to be certain as to whether the original poet saw shields of various types, including the round shape, in use, though that is possible, or whether he saw only the Mycenæan types.

As regards size, Homer certainly describes, in several cases, shields very much larger than most which we know for certain to have been common after, say, 700 B.C. He speaks of shields reaching from neck to ankles, and "covering the body of a man about." Whether he was also familiar with smaller shields of various types is uncertain ; he does not explicitly say that any small bucklers were used by the chiefs, nor does he explicitly say that all shields were of the largest type. It is possible that at the time when the Epic was composed various types of shield were being tried, while the vast ancient shield was far from obsolete.

To return to the *size* of the shield. In a feigned tale of Odysseus (*Odyssey*, XIV. 474–477), men in a wintry ambush place their shields over their shoulders, as they lie on the ground, to be a protection against snow. But any sort of shield, large or small, would protect the shoulders of men in a recumbent position. Quite a large shield may seem to be indicated in *Iliad*, XIII. 400–405, where Idomeneus curls up his whole person behind his shield ; he was "hidden" by it. Yet, as any one can see by experiment, a man who crouched low would be protected entirely by a Highland targe of less than thirty inches in diameter, so nothing about the size of the shield is ascertained in this passage.

On a black-figured vase in the British Museum (B. 325) the entire body of a crouching warrior is defended by a large Bœotian buckler, oval, and with *échancrures* in the sides. The same remark applies to *Iliad*, XXII. 273–275. Hector watches the spear of Achilles as it flies ; he crouches, and the spear flies over him. Robert takes this as an " old Mycenæan " dodge—to duck down to the bottom of the shield.[1] The avoidance by ducking can be managed with no shield, or with a common Highland targe, which would cover a man in a crouching posture, as when Glenbucket's targe was peppered by bullets at Clifton (1746), and Cluny shouted " What the devil is this ? " the assailants firing unexpectedly from a ditch. A few moments of experiment, we repeat, prove that a round targe can protect a man in Hector's attitude, and that the Homeric texts here throw no light on the *size* of the shield.

The shield of Hector was of black bull's-hide, and as large and long as any represented in Mycenæan art, so that, as he walked, the rim knocked against his neck and ankles. The shape is not mentioned. Despite its size, he *walked* under it from the plain and field of battle into Troy (*Iliad*, VI. 116–118). This must be remembered, as Reichel[2] maintains that a man could not walk under shield, or only for a short way ; wherefore the war chariot was invented, he says, to carry the fighting man from point to point (Leaf, *Iliad*, vol. i. p. 573).

[1] *Studien zur Ilias*, p. 21.
[2] Reichel, 38, 39. Father Browne (*Handbook*, p. 230) writes, " In *Odyssey*, XIV 475, Odysseus says he slept within the shield." He says "under arms" (*Odyssey*, XIV. 474, but *cf.* XIV. 479).

Mr. Leaf elaborates these points : " Why did not the Homeric heroes ride ? Because no man could carry such a shield on horseback." [1] We reply that men could and did carry such shields on horseback, as we know on the evidence of works of art and poetry of the eleventh to twelfth centuries A.D. Mr. Ridgeway has explained the introduction of chariots as the result of horses too small to carry a heavy and heavily-armed man as a cavalier.

The shield ($\dot{a}\sigma\pi\acute{i}s$), we are told by followers of Reichel, was only worn by princes who could afford to keep chariots, charioteers, and squires of the body to arm and disarm them.   But this can scarcely be true, for all the comrades of Diomede had the shield ($\dot{a}\sigma\pi\acute{i}s$, *Iliad*, X. 152), and the whole host of Pandarus of Troy, a noted bowman, were shield-bearers ($\dot{a}\sigma\pi\iota\sigma\tau\acute{a}\omega\nu$ $\lambda a\hat{\omega}\nu$, *Iliad*, IV. 90), and some of them held their shields ($\sigma\acute{a}\kappa\epsilon a$) in front of Pandarus when he took a treacherous shot at Menelaus (IV. 113).   The whole host could not have chariots and squires, we may presume, so the chariot was not indispensable to the *écuyer* or shield-bearing man.

The objections to this conjecture of Reichel are conspicuous, as we now prove.

No Mycenæan work of art shows us a shielded man in a chariot ; the men with the monstrous shields are always depicted on foot.   The only modern peoples who, to our knowledge, used a leather shield of the Mycenæan size and even of a Mycenæan shape had no horses and chariots, as we shall show.   The ancient Eastern peoples, such as the Khita and Egyptians, who fought from chariots, carried *small* shields of various

[1] *Iliad*, vol. i. p. 573.

forms, as in the well-known picture of a battle between the Khita, armed with spears, and the bowmen of Rameses II., who kill horse and man with arrows from their chariots, and carry no spears ; while the Khita, who have no bows, merely spears, are shot down as they advance.[1] Egyptians and Khita, who fight from chariots, use *small* bucklers, whence it follows that war chariots were not invented, or, at least, were not retained in use, for the purpose of giving mobility to men wearing gigantic shields, under which they could not hurry from point to point. War chariots did not cease to be used in Egypt, when men used small shields.

Moreover, Homeric warriors can make marches under shield, while there is no mention of chariots to carry them to the point where they are to lie in ambush (*Odyssey*, XIV. 470–510). If the shield was so heavy as to render a chariot necessary, would Homer make Hector trudge a considerable distance under shield, while Achilles, under shield, sprints thrice round the whole circumference of Troy ? Helbig notices several other cases of long runs under shield. Either Reichel is wrong, when he said that the huge shield made the use of the war chariot necessary, or the poet is "late"; he is a man who never saw a large shield like Hector's, and, though he speaks of such shields, he thinks that men could walk and run under them. When men did walk or run under shield, or ride, if they ever rode, they would hang it over the left side, like the lion-hunters on the famous inlaid dagger of Mycenæ,[2] or the warrior on the chessman referred to above (p. 111).

Aias, again, the big, brave, stupid Porthos of the

---

[1] Maspero, *Hist. Ancienne*, ii. p. 225.

[2] For the chariots, *cf.* Reichel, *Homerische Waffen*, 120 *ff.* Wien, 1901.

Iliad, has the largest shield of all, "like a tower" (this shield cannot have been circular), and is recognised by his shield. But he never enters a chariot, and, like Odysseus, has none of his own, because both men come from rugged islands, unfit for chariot driving. Odysseus has plenty of shields in his house in Ithaca, as we learn from the account of the battle with the Wooers in the *Odyssey;* yet, in Ithaca, as at Troy, he kept no chariot. Here, then, we have nations who fight from chariots, yet use small shields, and heroes who wear enormous shields, yet never own a chariot. Clearly, the great shield cannot have been the cause of the use of the war chariot, as in the theory of Reichel.

Aias and his shield we meet in *Iliad,* VII. 206–220. " He clothed himself upon his flesh in *all* his armour " (τεύχεα), to quote Mr. Leaf's translation ; but the poet only *describes* his shield : his " towerlike shield of bronze, with sevenfold ox-hide, that Tychius wrought him cunningly ; Tychius, the best of curriers, that had his home in Hyle, who made for him his glancing shield of sevenfold hides of stalwart bulls, and overlaid the seven with bronze."

The shield known to Homer then is, in this case, so tall as to resemble a tower, and has bronze plating over bull's hide. By tradition from an age of leather shields the currier is still the shield-maker, though now the shield has metal plating. It is fairly clear that Greek tradition regarded the shield of Aias as of the kind which covered the body from chin to ankles, and resembled a bellying sail, or an umbrella unfurled, and drawn in at the sides in the middle, so as to offer the semblance of two bellies, or of one, pinched in at or near the centre.

This is probable, because the coins of Salamis, where Aias was worshipped as a local hero of great influence, display this shield as the badge of the Æginetan dynasty, claiming descent from Aias. The shield is bossed, or bellied out, with two half-moons cut in the centre, representing the *waist*, or pinched-in part, of the ancient Mycenæan shield ; the same device occurs on a Mycenæan ring from Ægina in the British Museum.[1]

In a duel with Aias the spear of Hector pierced the bronze and six layers of hide on his shield, but stuck in the seventh. The spear of Aias went through the circular (or " every way balanced ") huge shield of Hector, and through his corslet and *chiton*, but Hector had doubled himself up laterally (ἐκλίνθη, VII. 254), and was not wounded. The next stroke of Aias pierced his shield, and wounded his neck ; Hector replied with a boulder that lighted on the centre of the shield of Aias, " on the boss," whether that means a mere ornament or knob, or whether it was the genuine boss—which is disputed. Aias broke in the shield of Hector with another stone ; and the gentle and joyous passage of arms was stopped.

The shield of Agamemnon was of the kind that " cover all the body of a man," and was " every way equal," or " circular." It was plated with twelve circles of bronze, and had twenty ὀμφαλοί, or ornamental knobs of tin, and the centre was of black cyanus (XI. 31–34). There was also a head of the Gorgon, with Fear and Panic. The description is not intelligible, and I do not discuss it.

A man could be stabbed in the middle of the belly, " under his shield " (XI. 424–425), not an easy thing

---

[1] Evans, *Journal of Hellenic Studies*, xiii. 213–216.

to do, if shields covered the whole body to the feet;
but, when a hero was leaping from his chariot (as in
this case), no doubt a spear could be pushed up under
the shield. The ancient Irish romances tell of a *gae
bulg*, a spear held in the warrior's toes, and jerked up
under the shield of his enemy! Shields could be held
up on high, in an attack on a wall garrisoned by archers
(XII. 139), the great Norman shield, also, could be
thus lifted.

The Locrians, light armed infantry, had no shields,
nor bronze helmets, nor spears, but slings and bows
(XIII. 714). Mr. Leaf suspects that this is a piece of
"false archaism," but we do not think that early poets
in an uncritical age are ever archæologists, good or bad.
The poet is aware that some men have larger, some
smaller shields, just as some have longer and some
shorter spears (XIV. 370–377); but this does not prove
that the shields were of different types. A tall man
might inherit the shield of a short father, or *vice versâ*.

A man in turning to fly might trip on the rim of
his shield, which proves how large it was: "it reached
to his feet." This accident of tripping occurred to
Periphetes of Mycenæ, but it might have happened to
Hector, whose shield reached from neck to ankles.[1]

Achilles must have been a large man, for he knew
nobody whose armour would fit him when he lost his
own (though his armour fitted Patroclus), he could,
however, make shift with the tower-like shield of Aias,
he said.

The evidence of the *Iliad*, then, is mainly to the
effect that the heroes carried huge shields, suspended
by belts, covering the body and legs. If Homer means,

---

[1] *Iliad*, XV. 645–646.

Fig. 1.—"THE VASE OF ARISTONOTHOS"

by the epithets already cited, "of good circle" and
"every way equal," that some shields of these vast
dimensions were *circular*, we have one example in early
Greek art which corroborates his description. This is
"the vase of Aristonothos," signed by that painter, and
supposed to be of the seventh century (Fig. 1). On one
side, the companions of Odysseus are boring out the eye
of the Cyclops ; on the other, a galley is being rowed to
the attack of a ship. On the raised deck of the galley
stand three warriors, helmeted and bearing spears.
The artist has represented their shields as covering their
right sides, probably for the purpose of showing their
devices or blazons. *Their* shields are small round bucklers. On the ship are three warriors whose shields,
though circular, *cover the body from chin to ankles,*
as in Homer. One shield bears a bull's head ; the
next has three crosses ; the third blazon is a crab.[1]
Such personal armorial bearings are never mentioned
by Homer. It is not usually safe to argue, from his
silence, that he is ignorant of anything. He never
mentions seals or signet rings, yet they cannot but have
been familiar to his time. Odysseus does not seal the
chest with the Phæacian presents ; he ties it up with a
cunning knot ; there are no rings named among the
things wrought by Hephæstus, nor among the offerings
of the Wooers of Penelope.[2]

But, if we are to admit that Homer knew not rings
and seals, which lasted to the latest Mycenæan times,
through the Dipylon age, to the very late Æginetan
treasure (800 B.C.) in the British Museum, and appear

[1] *Mon. dell. Inst.*, ix. pl. 4.
[2] Helbig citing *Odyssey*, VIII. 445–448 ; *Iliad*, XVIII. 401 ; *Odyssey*,
XVIII. 292–301.

again in the earliest dawn of the classical age and in
a Cyclic poem, it is plain that all the expansionists
lived in one, and that a most peculiar *ringless* age.
This view suits our argument to a wish, but it is not
credible that rings and seals and engraved stones, so
very common in Mycenæan and later times, should
have vanished wholly in the Homeric time. The poet
never mentions them, just as Shakespeare never mentions a thing so familiar to him as tobacco. How often
are finger rings mentioned in the whole mass of Attic
tragic poetry? We remember no example, and instances are certainly rare : Liddell and Scott give none.
Yet the tragedians were, of course, familiar with rings
and seals.

Manifestly, we cannot say that Homer knew no
seals, because he mentions none ; but armorial blazons
on shields could be ignored by no poet of war, if
they existed.

Meanwhile, the shields of the warriors on the vase,
being circular and covering body and legs, answer most
closely to Homer's descriptions. Helbig is reduced to
suggest, first, that these shields are worn by men aboard
ship, as if warriors had one sort of shield when aboard
ship and another when fighting on land, and as if the
men in the other vessel were not equally engaged in
a sea fight. No evidence in favour of such difference
of practice, by sea and land, is offered. Again, Helbig
does not trust the artist, in this case, though the artist
is usually trusted to draw what he sees ; and why should
he give the men in the other ship or boat small bucklers,
genuine, while bedecking the warriors in the adverse
vessel with large, purely imaginary shields ? [1]   It is not

[1] Helbig, *Das Homerische Epos*, ii. pp. 313–314.

in the least "probable," as Helbig suggests, that the artist is shirking the trouble of drawing the figure.

Reichel supposes that round bucklers were novelties when the vase was painted (seventh century), and that the artist did not understand how to depict them.[1] But he depicted them very well as regards the men in the galley, save that, for obvious æsthetic reasons, he chose to assume that the men in the galley were left-handed and wore their shields on their right arms, his desire being to display the blazons of both parties.[2] We thus see, if the artist may be trusted, that shields, which both " reached to the feet " and were circular, existed in his time (the seventh century), so that possibly they may have existed in Homer's time and survived into the age of small bucklers. Tyrtaeus (late seventh century), as Helbig remarks, speaks of " a *wide* shield, covering thighs, shins, breast, and shoulders." [3]

Nothing can be more like the large shields of the vase of Aristonothos. Thus the huge circular shield seems to have been a practicable shield in actual use. If so, when Homer spoke of large circular shields he may have meant large circular shields. On the Dodwell pyxis of 650 to 620 B.C., a man wears an oval shield, covering him from the base of the neck to the ankles. He wears it on his left arm.[4]

Of shields *certainly* small and light, worn by the chiefs, there is not a notice in the *Iliad*, unless there be a hint to that effect in the accounts of heroes running, walking considerable distances, and " stepping lightly "

---

[1] *Homerische Waffen*, p. 47.

[2] See the same arrangement in a Dipylon vase. Baumeister, *Denkmäler*, iii. p. 1945.

[3] *Tyrtaeus*, xi. 23; Helbig, *Das Homerische Epos*, ii. p. 315, Note 2.

[4] Walters, *Ancient Pottery*, p. 316.

under shields, supposed, by the critics, to be of crushing
weight.   In such passages the poet may be carried away
by his own *verve*, or the heroes of ancient times may be
deemed capable of exertions beyond those of the poet's
contemporaries, as he often tells us that, in fact, the old
heroes were.   A poet is not a scientific military writer ;
and in the epic poetry of all other early races very gross
exaggeration is permitted, as in the *Chansons de Geste*, the
old Celtic romances, and, of course, the huge epics of
India.   In Homer " the skill of the poet makes things
impossible convincing," Aristotle says ; and it is a critical error to insist on taking Homer absolutely and
always *au pied de la lettre*.   He seems, undeniably, to
have large body-covering shields present to his mind as
in common use.

Small shields of the Greek historic period are " unknown to Homer," Mr. Leaf says, " with a very few
curious exceptions,"[1] detected by Reichel in Book X. 152,
where Diomede's men sleep with their heads resting on
their shields, whereas a big-bellied Mycenæan shield
rises, he says, too high for a pillow.   But some
Mycenæan shields were perfectly flat ; while, again,
nothing could be more comfortable, as a head-rest, than
the hollow between the upper and lower bulges of the
Mycenæan huge shield.[2]   The Zulu wooden head-rest is
of the same character.   Thus this passage in Book X.
does not prove that small circular shields were known
to Homer, nor does X. 513, 526–530, an obscure text
in which it is uncertain whether Diomede and Odysseus
ride or drive the horses of Rhesus.   They *could* ride, as
every one must see, even though equipped with great
body-covering shields.   True, the shielded hero could

[1] *Iliad*, vol. i. p. 575.   [2] *Ibid*, vol. i. p. 569, fig. 2.

neither put his shield at his back nor in front of him
when he rode ; but he could hang it sidewise, when
it would cover his left side, as in the early Middle
Ages (1060–1160 A.D.).

The taking of the shield from a man's shoulders
(XI. 374) does not prove the shield to be small ; the
shield hung by the belt (*telamon*) from the shoulder.[1]

So far we have the results that Homer seems most
familiar with vast body-covering shields ; that such
shields were suspended by a baldric, not worn on the left
arm ; that they were made of layers of hide, plated with
bronze, and that such a shield as Aias wore must have
been tall, doubtless oblong, "like a tower," possibly it
was semi-cylindrical. Whether the epithets denoting
roundness refer to circular shields or to the *double targe*,
8-shaped, of Mycenæan times is uncertain.

We thus come to a puzzle of unusual magnitude.
If Homer does not know small circular shields, but
refers always to huge shields, whereas, from the eighth
century B.C. onwards, such shields were not in use (disregarding Tyrtaeus, and the vase of Aristonothos on
which they appear conspicuously, and the Dodwell
pyxis), where are we ? Either we have a harmonious
picture of war from a very ancient date of large shields,
or late poets did not introduce the light round buckler
of their own period. Meanwhile they are accused of
introducing the bronze corslets and other defensive
armour of their own period. Defensive armour was
unknown, we are told, in the Mycenæan prime, which,
if true, does not affect the question. Homer did not
live in or describe the Mycenæan prime, with its stone

---

[1] On the other side, see Reichel, *Homerische Waffen*, pp. 40–44. Wien,
1901. We have replied to his arguments above.

arrow-tips. Why did the late poets act so inconsistently? Why were they ignorant of small circular shields, which they saw every day? Or why, if they knew them, did they not introduce them in the poems, which, we are told, they were filling with non-Mycenæan greaves and corslets?

This is one of the dilemmas which constantly arise to confront the advocates of the theory that the *Iliad* is a patchwork of many generations. "Late" poets, if really late, certainly in every-day life knew small parrying bucklers worn on the left arm, and huge body-covering shields perhaps they rarely saw in use. They also knew, and the original poet, we are told, did not know bronze corslets and greaves. The theory of critics is that late poets introduced the bronze corslets and greaves with which they were familiar into the poems, but scrupulously abstained from alluding to the equally familiar small shields. Why are they so recklessly anachronistic and "up-to-date" with the corslets and greaves, and so staunchly but inconsistently conservative about keeping the huge shields?

Mr. Leaf explains thus : "The groundwork of the Epos is Mycenæan, in the arrangement of the house, in the prevalence of copper" (as compared with iron), "and, as Reichel has shown, in armour. Yet in many points the poems are certainly later than the prime, at least, of the Mycenæan age"—which we are the last to deny. "Is it that the poets are deliberately trying to present the conditions of an age anterior to their own? or are they depicting the circumstances by which they are surrounded—circumstances which slowly change during the period of the development of the Epos? Cauer decides for the latter alternative, *the only one which is really conceivable* [1] in an age whose views are in many ways so naïve as the poems themselves prove them to have been." [2]

Here we entirely side with Mr. Leaf. No poet, no painter, no sculptor, in a naïf, uncritical age, ever represents in art anything but what he sees daily in costume, customs, weapons, armour, and ways of life. Mr. Leaf, however, on the other hand, occasionally chides pieces of deliberate archæological pedantry in the poets, in spite of his opinion that they are always "depicting the circumstances by which they are surrounded." But as huge man-covering shields are *not* among the circumstances by which the supposed late poets were surrounded, why do they depict them? Here Mr. Leaf corrects himself, and his argument departs from the statement that only one theory is "conceivable," namely, that the poets depict their own surroundings, and we are introduced to a new proposition. "Or rather we must recognise everywhere a compromise between two opposing principles: the singer, on the one hand, has to be conservatively tenacious of the old material which serves as the substance of his song ; on the other hand, he has to be vivid and actual in the contributions which he himself makes to the common stock." [3]

The conduct of such singers is so weirdly inconsistent as not to be easily credible. But probably they went further, for "it is possible that the allusions" to the corslet "may have been introduced in the course of successive modernisation such as the oldest parts of the *Iliad* seem in many cases to have passed through. But,

---

[1] Then how is the alleged archæology of the poet of Book X. conceivable?
[2] *Classical Review*, ix. pp. 463, 464.
[3] *Ibid.*, ix. pp. 463, 464.

in fact, *Iliad*, XI. 234 is the only mention of a corslet in any of the oldest strata, so far as we can distinguish them, and here Reichel translates *thorex* ' shield.' " [1]

Mr. Leaf's statement we understand to mean that, when the singer or reciter was delivering an *ancient* lay he did not introduce any of the military gear—light round bucklers, greaves, and corslets—with which his audience were familiar. But when the singer delivers a new lay, which he himself has added to " the kernel," then he is " vivid and actual," and speaks of greaves and corslets, though he still cleaves in his new lay to the obsolete chariot, the enormous shield, and, in an age of iron, to weapons of bronze. He is a sadly inconsistent new poet !

Meanwhile, sixteen allusions to the corslet " can be cut out," as probably " some or all these are additions to the text made at a time when it seemed absurd to think of a man in full armour without a corslet." [2] Thus the reciters, after all, did not spare " the old material " in the matter of corslets. The late singers have thus been " conservatively tenacious " in clinging to chariots, weapons of bronze, and obsolete enormous shields, while they have also been " vivid and actual " and " up to date " in the way of introducing everywhere bronze corslets, greaves, and other armour unknown, by the theory, in " the old material which is the substance of their song." By the way, they have not even spared the shield of the old material, for it was of leather or wood (we have no trace of metal plating on the old Mycenæan shields), and the singer, while retaining the size of it, has added a plating of bronze, which we have every reason to suppose that Mycenæan

---

[1] Leaf, *Iliad*, vol. i. p. 578.   [2] *Ibid*, vol. i. p. 577.

shields of the prime did not present to the stone-headed arrow.

This theory of singers, who are at once " conserva-tively tenacious" of the old and impudently radical in pushing in the new, appears to us to be logically untenable. We have, in Chapter I., observed the same inconsistency in Helbig, and shall have occasion to remark again on its presence in the work of that great archæologist. The inconsistency is inseparable from theories of expansion through several centuries. " Many a method," says Mr. Leaf, " has been proposed which, up to a certain point, seemed irresistible, but there has always been a residuum which returned to plague the inventor."[1] This is very true, and our explanation is that no method which starts from the hypothesis that the poems are the product of several centuries will *work*. The "residuum" is the element which cannot be fitted into any such hypothesis. But try the hypothesis that the poems are the product of a single age, and all is harmonious. There is no baffling " residuum." The poet describes the details of a definite age, not that of the Mycenæan bloom, not that of 900–600 A.D.

We cannot, then, suppose that many generations of irresponsible reciters at fairs and public festivals conser-vatively adhered to the huge size of the shield, while alter-ing its material ; and also that the same men, for the sake of being " actual " and up to date, dragged bronze corslets and greaves not only into new lays, but into pas-sages of lays by old poets who had never heard of such things. Consequently, the poetic descriptions of arms and armour must be explained on some other theory.

[1] *Iliad*, vol. ii. p. x.

If the poet, again, as others suppose—Mr. Ridgeway for one—knew such bronze-covered circular shields as are common in central and western Europe of the Bronze Age, why did he sometimes represent them as extending from neck to ankles, whereas the known bronze circular shields are not of more than 2 feet 2 inches to 2 feet 6 inches in diameter?[1] Such a shield, without the wood or leather, weighed 5 lbs. $2\frac{1}{2}$ ozs.,[2] and a strong man might walk or run under it. Homer's shields would be twice as heavy, at least, though, even then, not too heavy for a Hector, or an Aias, or Achilles. I do not see that the round bronze shields of Limerick, Yetholm, Beith, Lincolnshire, and Tarquinii, cited by Mr. Ridgeway, answer to Homer's descriptions of huge shields. They are too small. But it is perfectly possible, or rather highly probable, that in the poet's day shields of various sizes and patterns coexisted.

ARCHÆOLOGY OF THE SHIELDS

Turning to archæological evidence, we find no remains in the graves of the Mycenæan prime of the bronze which covered the ox-hides of Homeric shields, though we do find gold ornaments supposed to have been attached to shields. There is no evidence that the Mycenæan shield was plated with bronze. But if we judge from their shape, as represented in works of Mycenæan art, some of the Mycenæan shields were not of wood, but of hide. In works of art, such as engraved rings and a bronze dagger (Fig. 2) with pictures inlaid

[1] Ridgeway, *Early Age of Greece*, vol. i. pp. 453, 471.
[2] *Ibid.*, vol. i. p. 462.

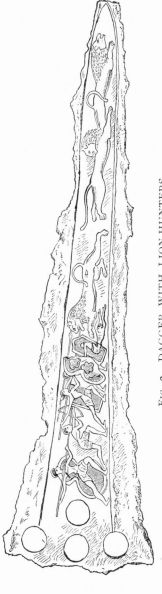

FIG. 2.—DAGGER WITH LION-HUNTERS

in other metals, the shield, covering the whole body,
is of the form of a bellying sail, or a huge umbrella
" up," and pinched at both sides near the centre ; or
is like a door, or a section of a cylinder ; only one
sort of shield resembles a big-bellied figure of **8**.
Ivory models of shields indicate the same figure.[1]
A gold necklet found at Enkomi, in Cyprus, consists
of a line of models of this Mycenæan shield.[2]

There also exists a set of small Mycenæan relics
called Palladia, found at Mycenæ, Spata, and in the
earliest strata of the Acro-
polis at Athens. They re-
semble " two circles joined
together so as to intersect
one another slightly," or
" a long oval pinched in
at the middle." They vary

FIG. 3.

in size from six inches to half an inch, and are of
ivory, glazed ware, or glass. Several such shields
are engraved on Mycenæan gems ; one, in gold, is
attached to a silver vase. The ornamentation shown
on them occurs, too, on Mycenæan shields in works of
art ; in short, these little objects are representations in
miniature of the big double-bellied Mycenæan shield.
Mr. Ernest Gardner concludes that these objects are
the "schematised" reductions of an armed human
figure, only the shield which covered the whole body
is left. They are talismans symbolising an armed
divinity, Pallas or another. A Dipylon vase (Fig. 3)
shows a man with a shield, possibly evolved out
of this kind, much scooped out at the waist, and

---

[1] Schuchardt, *Schliemann's Excavations*, p. 192.
[2] *Excavations in Cyprus*, pl. vii. fig. 604. A. S. Murray, 1900.

reaching from neck to knees.   The shield covers his
side, not his back or front.[1]

One may guess that the original pinch at the waist
of the Mycenæan shield was evolved later into the two
deep scoops to enable the warrior to use his arms more
freely, while the shield, hanging from his neck by a
belt, covered the front of his body.   Fig. 4 shows
shields of 1060–1160 A.D. equally designed to cover

FIG. 4.

body and legs.   Men wore shields, if we believe the
artists of Mycenæ, when lion-hunting, a sport in which
speed of foot is desirable ; so they cannot have been
very weighty.   The shield then was hung over one
side, and running was not so very difficult as if it hung
over back or front (cf. Fig. 2).   The shields sometimes
reach only from the shoulders to the calf of the leg.[2]
The wearer of the largest kind could only be got at by
a sword-stab over the rim into the throat [3] (Fig. 5).

[1] Journal of Hellenic Studies, vol. xiii. pp. 21-24.
[2] Reichel, p. 3, fig. 5, Grave III. at Mycenæ.   [3] Ibid., p. 2, fig. 2.

FIG. 5.—RINGS: SWORDS AND SHIELDS

Some shields of this shape were quite small, if an engraved rock-crystal is evidence ; here the shield is not half so high as an adjacent goat, but it may be a mere decoration to fill the field of the gem.[1]

Other shields, covering the body from neck to feet, were sections of cylinders ; several of these are represented on engraved Mycenæan ring stones or on the gold ; the wearer was protected in front and flank[2] (Fig. 5).

In a " maze of buildings " outside the precincts of the graves of Mycenæ, Dr. Schliemann found fragments of vases much less ancient than the contents of the sepulchres.   There was a large amphora, the " Warrior Vase " (Fig. 6).   The men wear apparently a close-fitting coat of mail over a chiton, which reaches with its fringes half down the thigh.   The shield is circular, with a half-moon cut out at the bottom.   The art is infantile. Other warriors carry long oval shields reaching, at least, from neck to shin.[3]   They wear round leather caps, their enemies have helmets.   On a Mycenæan painted *stêlê*, apparently of the same relatively late period, the costume is similar, and the shield—oval—reaches from neck to knee.[4]   The Homeric shields do not answer to the smaller of these late and ugly representations, while, in their bronze plating, Homeric shields seem to differ from the leather shields of the Mycenæan prime.

Finally, at Enkomi, near Salamis, in Cyprus, an ivory carving (in the British Museum) shows a fighting man whose perfectly circular shield reaches from neck

---

[1] Reichel, p. 3, fig. 7.   [2] *Ibid.*, p. 4, fig. 11, 12 ; p. 1, fig. 1.
[3] Schuchardt, *Schliemann's Excavations*, pp. 279–285.
[4] Ridgeway, vol. i. p. 314.

to knee ; this is one of several figures in which Mr. Arthur Evans finds " a most valuable illustration of the typical Homeric armour."[1] The shield, however, is not so huge as those of Aias, Hector, and Periphetes.

I can only conclude that Homer describes intermediate types of shield, as large as the Mycenæan but plated with bronze, for a reason to be given later. This kind of shield, the kind known to Homer, was not the invention of late poets living in an age of circular bucklers, worn on the left arm, and these supposed late poets never introduce into the epics such bucklers.

What manner of military needs prompted the invention of the great Mycenæan shields which, by Homer's time, were differentiated by the addition of metal plating ?

The process of evolution of the huge Mycenæan shields, and of the Homeric shields covering the body from chin to ankles, can easily be traced. The nature of the attack expected may be inferred from the nature of the defence employed. Body-covering shields were, obviously, at first, *defences against showers of arrows* tipped with stone. " In the earlier Mycenæan times the arrow-head of obsidian alone appears," as in Mycenæan Grave IV. In the upper strata of Mycenæ and in the later tombs the arrow-head is usually of bronze.[2] No man going into battle naked, without body armour, like the Mycenæans (if they had none), could protect himself with a small shield, or even with a

---

[1] *Journal of the Anthropological Institute*, vol. xxx. pp. 209–214, figs. 5, 6, 9.

[2] Tsountas and Manatt, p. 206.

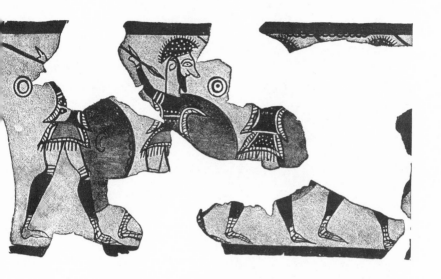

Fig. 6.—FRAGMENTS OF WARRIOR VASE

round buckler of twenty-six inches in diameter, against
the rain of shafts. In a fight, on the other hand, where
man singled out man, and spears were the missiles, and
when the warriors had body armour, or even when
they had not, a small shield sufficed ; as we see among
the spear-throwing Zulus and the spear-throwing aborigines of Australia (unacquainted with bows and arrows),
who mainly use shields scarcely broader than a bat.
On the other hand, the archers of the Algonquins in
their wars with the Iroquois, about 1610, used clubs
and tomahawks but no spears, no missiles but arrows,
and their leather shield was precisely the ἀμφιβρότη
ἀσπίς of Homer, " covering the whole of a man." It
is curious to see, in contemporary drawings (1620),
Mycenæan shields on Red Indian shoulders!

In Champlain's sketches of fights between French
and Algonquins against Iroquois (1610–1620), we
see the Algonquins outside the Iroquois stockade,
which is defended by archers, sheltering under huge
shields shaped like the Mycenæan "tower" shield,
though less cylindrical ; in fact, more like the shield of
the fallen hunter depicted on the dagger of Mycenæ.
These Algonquin shields partially cover the sides as
well as the front of the warrior, who stoops behind
them, resting the lower rim of the shield on the
ground. The shields are oblong and rounded at the
top, much like that of Achilles' in Mr. Leaf's restoration.[1] The sides curve inward. Another shield, oval
in shape and flat, appears to have been suspended
from the neck, and covers an Iroquois brave from
chin to feet. The Red Indian shields, like those of
Mycenæ, were made of leather; usually of buffalo

[1] *Iliad*, vol. ii. p. 605.

hide,[1] good against stone-tipped arrows. The braves
are naked, like the unshielded archers on the Mycenæan
silver vase fragment representing a siege (Fig. 7). The
description of the Algonquin shields by Champlain, when
compared with his drawings, suggests that we cannot
always take artistic representations as exact. In his
designs only a few Algonquins and one Iroquois carry
the huge shields ; the unshielded men are stark naked,
as on the Mycenæan silver vase. But in his text
Champlain says that the Iroquois, like the Algonquins, "carried arrow-proof shields" and "a sort of
armour woven of cotton thread"—Homer's λινοθώρηξ
(*Iliad*, II. 259, 850). These facts appear in only one
of Champlain's drawings [2] (Fig. 8).

These Iroquois and Algonquin shields are the
armour of men exposed, not to spears, but to a hail
of flint-tipped arrows. As spears came in for missiles
in Greek warfare, arrows did not wholly go out, but
the noble warriors preferred spear and sword.[3] Mr.
Ridgeway erroneously says that "no Achæan warrior
employs the bow for war."[4] Teucer, frequently, and
Meriones use the bow ; like Pandarus and Paris, on
the Trojan side, they resort to bow or spear, as occasion serves. Odysseus, in *Iliad*, Book X., is armed
with the bow and arrows of Meriones when acting
as a spy ; in the *Odyssey* his skill as an archer is
notorious, but he would not pretend to equal famous
bowmen of an older generation, such as Heracles
and Eurytus of Œchalia, whose bow he possessed

---

[1] *Les Voyages de Sr. de Champlain*, Paris, 1620, f. 22 : "rondache de
cuir bouili, qui est d'un animal, comme le boufle."

[2] Dix's *Champlain*, p. 113. Appleton, New York, 1903. Laverdière's
Champlain, vol. iv., plate opposite p. 85 (1870).

[3] *Cf.* Archilochus, 3.   [4] *Early Age of Greece*, i. 301.

Fig. 7.—FRAGMENT OF SIEGE VASE

but did not take to Troy.   Philoctetes is his master
in archery.[1]

The bow, however, was little esteemed by Greek
warriors who desired to come to handstrokes, just as
it was despised, to their frequent ruin, by the Scots in
the old wars with England.   Dupplin, Falkirk, Halidon
Hill and many another field proved the error.

There was much need in Homeric warfare for
protection against heavy showers of arrows.   Mr.
Monro is hardly correct when he says that, in Homer,
" we do not hear of *bodies* of archers, of arrows darken-
ing the air, as in descriptions of oriental warfare." [2]
These precise phrases are not used by Homer ; but,
nevertheless, arrows are flying thick in his battle pieces.
The effects are not often noticed, because, in Homer,
helmet, shield, corslet, *zoster*, and greaves, as a rule
prevent the shafts from harming the well-born, well-
armed chiefs ; the nameless host, however, fall frequently.   When Hector came forward for a parley
(*Iliad*, III. 79), the Achæans " kept shooting at him
with arrows," which he took unconcernedly.   Teucer
shoots nine men in *Iliad*, VIII. 297–304.   In XI. 85
the shafts (βέλεα) showered and the common soldiers
fell—βέλεα being arrows as well as thrown spears.[3]
Agamemnon and Achilles are as likely, they say, to
be hit by arrow as by spear (XI. 191 ; XXI. 113).
Machaon is wounded by an arrow.   Patroclus meets
Eurypylus limping, with an arrow in his thigh—archer
unknown.[4]   Meriones, though an Achæan paladin,
sends a bronze-headed arrow through the body of
Harpalion (XIII. 650).   The light-armed Locrians are

[1] *Odyssey*, VIII. 219–222.   [2] *Ibid.*, vol. ii. 305.
[3] *Iliad*, IV. 465 ; XVI. 668, 678.   [4] *Iliad*, XI. 809, 810.

all bowmen and slingers (XIII. 716). Acamas taunts the Argives as "bowmen" (XIV. 479). "The war-cry rose on both sides, and the arrows leaped from the bowstrings" (XV. 313). Manifestly the arrows are always on the wing, hence the need for the huge Homeric and Mycenæan shields. Therefore, as the Achæans in Homer wore but flimsy corslets (this we are going to prove), the great body-covering shield of the Mycenæan prime did not go out of vogue in Homer's time, when bronze had superseded stone arrow-heads, but was strengthened by bronze plating over the leather. In a later age the bow was more and more neglected in Greek warfare, and consequently large shields went out, after the close of the Mycenæan age, and round parrying bucklers came into use.

The Greeks appear never to have been great archers, for some vases show even the old heroes employing the "primary release," the arrow nock is held between the thumb and forefinger—an ineffectual release.[1] The archers in early Greek art often stoop or kneel, unlike the erect archers of old England ; the bow is usually small—a child's weapon ; the string is often drawn only to the breast, as by Pandarus in the *Iliad* (IV. 123). By 730 B.C. the release with three fingers, our western release, had become known.[2]

The course of evolution seems to be : (1) the Mycenæan prime of much archery, no body armour (?) ; huge leather "man-covering" shields are used, like those of the Algonquins ; (2) the same shields streng-

---

[1] C. J. Longman, *Archery*. Badminton Series.
[2] Leaf *Iliad*, vol. i. p. 585.

FIG. 8.—ALGONQUIN CORSLET

From Laverdière, *Œuvres de Champlain*,
vol. iv. fol. 4. Quebec, 1870.

thened with metal, light body armour—thin corslets—
and archery is frequent, but somewhat despised (the
Homeric age); (3) the parrying shield of the latest
Mycenæan age (infantry with body armour); (4) the
Ionian hoplites, with body armour and small circular
bucklers.

It appears, then, that the monstrous Mycenæan
shield is a survival of an age when bows and arrows
played the same great part as they did in the wars of
the Algonquins and Iroquois. The celebrated picture
of a siege on a silver vase, of which fragments were
found in Grave IV., shows archers skirmishing; there
is an archer in the lion hunt on the dagger blade;
thirty-five obsidian arrow-heads were discovered in
Grave IV., while "in the upper strata of Mycenæ and
in the later tombs the arrow-head is usually of bronze,
though instances of obsidian still occur." In 1895
Dr. Tsountas found twenty arrow-heads of bronze,
ten in each bundle, in a Mycenæan chamber tomb.
Messrs. Tsountas and Manatt say, "In the Acropolis
graves at Mycenæ . . . the spear - heads were but
few . . . arrow-heads, on the contrary, are comparatively abundant." They infer that "picked men used
shield and spear; the rank and file doubtless fought
simply with bow and sling."[1] The great Mycenæan
shield was obviously evolved as a defence against
arrows and sling-stones flying too freely to be parried
with a small buckler. What other purpose could it
have served? But other defensive armour was needed,
and was evolved, by Homer's men, as also, we shall
see, by the Algonquins and Iroquois. The Algonquins
and Iroquois thus prove that men who thought their

[1] Tsountas and Manatt, 209.

huge shields very efficient, yet felt the desirableness of
the protection afforded by corslets, for they wore, in
addition to their shields, such corslets as they were
able to manufacture, made of cotton, and corresponding
to the Homeric λινοθώρηξ.[1]

Mr. Leaf, indeed, when reviewing Reichel, says that
"the use of the Mycenæan shield is inconsistent with
that of the metal breastplate;" the shield "covers the
wearer in a way which makes a breastplate an useless
encumbrance ; or rather, it is ignorance of the breastplate which alone can explain the use of such fright-
fully cumbrous gear as the huge shield." [2]

But the Algonquins and Iroquois wore such breastplates as they could manufacture, though they also
used shields of great size, suspended, in Mycenæan
fashion, from the neck and shoulder by a *telamon* or
belt. The knights of the eleventh century A.D., in
addition to very large shields, wore ponderous hauberks or byrnies, as we shall prove presently. As this

---

[1] In the interior of some shields, perhaps of all, were two κανόνες (VIII. 193;
XIII. 407). These have been understood as meaning a brace through which the
left arm went, and another brace which the left hand grasped. Herodotus
says that the Carians first used shield grips, and that previously shields were
suspended by belts from the neck and left shoulder (Herodotus, i. 171). It
would be interesting to know how he learned these facts—perhaps from
Homer ; but certainly the Homeric shield is often described as suspended by
a belt. Mr. Leaf used to explain the κανόνες (XIII. 407) as "serving to attach
the two ends of the baldric to the shield" (*Hellenic Society's Journal*, iv.
291), as does Mr. Ridgeway. But now he thinks that they were two pieces
of wood, crossing each other, and making the framework on which the leather
of the shield was stretched. The hero could grasp the cross-bar, at the centre
of gravity, in his left hand, rest the lower rim of the shield on the ground, and
crouch behind it (XI. 593 ; XIII. 157). In neither passage cited is anything
said about resting the lower rim " on the ground," and in the second passage
the warrior is actually advancing. In this attitude, however—grounding the
lower rim of the great body-covering shield, and crouching behind it—we see
Algonquin warriors of about 1610 in Champlain's drawings of Red Indian
warfare.

[2] *Classical Review*, ix. p. 55. 1895.

combination of great shield with corslet was common and natural, we cannot agree with Mr. Leaf when he says, " it follows that the Homeric warriors wore no metal breastplate, and that all the passages where the θώρηξ is mentioned are either later interpolations or refer to some other sort of armour," which, *ex hypothesi*, would itself be superfluous, given the body-covering shield.

Shields never make corslets superfluous when men can manufacture corslets.

The facts speak for themselves : the largest shields are not exclusive, so to speak, of corslets ; the Homeric warriors used both, just as did Red Indians and the mediæval chivalry of Europe. The use of the ἀσπίς in Homer, therefore, throws no suspicion on the concomitant use of the corslet. The really surprising fact would be if late poets, who knew only small round bucklers, never introduced them into the poems, but always spoke of enormous shields, while they at the same time did introduce corslets, unknown to the early poems which they continued. Clearly Reichel's theory is ill inspired and inconsistent. This becomes plain as soon as we trace the evolution of shields and corslets in ages when the bow played a great part in war. The Homeric bronze-plated shield and bronze corslet are defences of a given moment in military evolution ; they are improvements on the large leather shield of Mycenæan art, but, as the arrows still fly in clouds, the time for the small parrying buckler has not yet come.

By the age of the Dipylon vases with human figures, the shield had been developed into forms unknown to Homer. In Fig. 3 (p. 131) we see one warrior with a fantastic shield, slim at the waist, with

horns, as it were, above and below ; the greater part
of the shield is expended uselessly, covering nothing in
particular.   In form this targe seems to be a burlesque
parody of the figure of 8 Mycenæan shield.   The next
man has a short oblong shield, rather broad for its
length—perhaps a reduction of the Mycenæan door-
shaped shield.   The third warrior has a round buckler.
All these shields are manifestly post-Homeric ; the
first type is the most common in the Dipylon art ;
the third survived in the eighth-century buckler.

Fig. 9.—GOLD CORSLET

CHAPTER VIII

THE BREASTPLATE

No "practicable" breastplates, hauberks, corslets, or any things of the kind have so far been discovered in graves of the Mycenæan prime. A corpse in Grave V. at Mycenæ had, however, a golden breastplate, with oval bosses representing the nipples and with prettily interlaced spirals all over the remainder of the gold (Fig. 9). Another corpse had a plain gold breastplate with the nipples indicated.[1] These decorative corslets of gold were probably funereal symbols of practicable breastplates of bronze, but no such pieces of armour are worn by the fighting-men on the gems and other works of art of Mycenæ, and none are found in Mycenæan graves. But does this prove anything? Leg-guards, broad metal bands clasping the leg below the knee, are found in the Mycenæan shaft graves, but are never represented in Mycenæan art.[2] Meanwhile, bronze corslets are very frequently mentioned in the *Iliad;* "rarely alluded to," says Mr. Leaf,[3] but this must be a slip of the pen. Connected with the breastplate or *thorex* (θώρηξ) is the verb θωρήσσω, θωρήσσεθαι, which means "to arm," or "equip" in general.

The Achæans are constantly styled in the *Iliad* and in the *Odyssey* "*chalkochitones,*" "with bronze chitons." Opponents of the presence of corslets in the original

[1] Schuchardt, *Schliemann's Excavations*, pp. 254-257, fig. 256.
[2] Leaf, *Iliad*, vol. i. p. 575.　　　　　[3] *Iliad*, vol. i. p. 576.

epics have therefore boldly argued that by " bronze chitons " the poet pleasantly alludes to shields. But as the Mycenæans seem scarcely to have worn any *chitons* in battle, as far as we are aware from their art, and are not known to have had any bronze shields, the argument evaporates, as Mr. Ridgeway has pointed out. Nothing can be less like a *chiton* or smock, loose or tight, than either the double-bellied huge shield, the tower-shaped cylindrical shield, or the flat, doorlike shield, covering body and legs in Mycenæan art. " The bronze *chiton*," says Helbig, " is only a poetic phrase for the corslet."

Reichel and Mr. Leaf, however, think that " bronze chitoned " is probably " a picturesque expression . . . and refers to the bronze-covered shield." [1] The breast-plate covered the upper part of the *chiton*, and so might be called a " bronze *chiton*," above all, if it had been evolved, as corselets usually have been, out of a real *chiton*, interwoven with small plates or rings of bronze. The process of evolution might be from a padded linen *chiton* (λινοθώρηξ) worn by Teucer, and on the Trojan side by Amphius (as by nervous Protestants during Oates's "Popish Plot"), to a leathern *chiton*, strengthened by rings, or studs, or scales of bronze, and thence to plates.[2] Here, in this armoured *chiton*, would be an object that a poet might readily call "a *chiton* of bronze." But that, if he lived in the Mycenæan age, when, so far as art shows, *chitons* were not worn at all, or very little, and scarcely ever in battle, and when we know nothing of bronze-plating on shields, the poet should constantly call a monstrous double-bellied leather shield,

[1] Leaf, *Iliad*, i. 578.
[2] Ridgeway, *Early Age of Greece*, vol. i. pp. 309, 310.

or any other Mycenæan type of shield, "*a bronze chiton*," seems almost unthinkable. "A leather cloak" would be a better term for such shields, if cloaks were in fashion. According to Mr. Myres (1899) the "stock line" in the *Iliad*, about piercing a πολυδαίδαλος θώρηξ or corslet, was inserted "to satisfy the practical criticisms of a corslet-wearing age," the age of the later poets, the Age of Iron. But why did not such practical critics object to the constant presence in the poems of bronze weapons, in their age out of date, if they objected to the absence from the poems of the corslets with which they were familiar? Mr. Myres supposes that the line about the πολυδαίδαλος corslet was already old, but had merely meant "many-glittering body clothing"—garments set with the golden discs and other ornaments found in Mycenæan graves. The bronze corslet, he says, would not be "many glittering," but would reflect "a single star of light."[1] Now, first, even if the star were a single star, it would be as "many glittering" when the warrior was in rapid and changeful motion as the star that danced when Beatrix was born. Secondly, if the contemporary corslets of the Iron Age were *not* "many glittering," practical corslet-wearing critics would ask the poet, "why do you call corslets 'many glittering'?" Thirdly, πολυδαίδαλος may surely be translated "a thing of much art," and Greek corslets were incised with ornamental designs. Thus Messrs. Hogarth and Bosanquet report "a very remarkable 'Mycenæan' bronze breastplate" from Crete, which "shows four female draped figures, the two central ones holding a wreath over a bird, below which is a sacred tree. The two outer figures are apparently

[1] *Journal of Hellenic Studies.* 1899.

K

dancing. It is probably a ritual scene, and may help
to elucidate the nature of early Ægean cults."[1]   Here,
apparently, is a genuine Mycenæan bronze breastplate—
πολυδαίδαλος—if that word means " artistically wrought."
Helbig thinks the Epics silent about the gold spangles
on dresses.[2]

Mr. Myres applauds Reichel's theory that *thorex* first
meant a man's chest. If *thorex* means a man's breast,
then *thorex* in a secondary sense, one thinks, would
mean " breastplate," as waist of a woman means,
first, her waist ; next, her blouse (American).   But
Mr. Myres and Reichel say that the secondary sense
of *thorex* is not breastplate but " body clothing," as if
a man were all breast, or wore only a breast covering, whereas Mycenæan art shows men wearing nothing on their breasts, merely drawers or loin-cloths,
which could not be called *thorex*, as they cover the
antipodes of the breast.

The verb θωρήσσεσθαι, the theory runs on, merely
meant "to put on body clothing," which Mycenæans
in works of art, if correctly represented, do not usually
put on ; they fought naked or in bathing drawers.
Surely we might as well argue that a " waistcoat "
might come to mean " body clothing in general," as
that a word for the male breast became, first, a synonym
for the covering of the male buttocks and for apparel
in general, and, next, for a bronze breastplate.   These
arguments appear rather unconvincing,[3] nor does
Mycenæan art instruct us that men went into battle
dressed in body clothing which was thickly set with

---

[1] *Journal of Hellenic Studies*, vol. xx. p. 322.   1899.
[2] Helbig, p. 71.
[3] *Journal of Hellenic Studies*, vol. xx. pp. 149, 150.

many glittering gold ornaments, and was called "a many-glittering *thorex*."

Further, if we follow Reichel and Mr. Leaf, the Mycenæans wore *chitons* and called them *chitons*. They also used bronze-plated shields, though of this we have no evidence. Taking the bronze-plated (?) shield to stand poetically for the *chiton,* the poet spoke of "*the bronze-chitoned Achæans*." But, if we follow Mr. Myres, the Mycenæans also applied the word *thorex* to body clothing at large, in place of the word *chiton;* and when a warrior was transfixed by a spear, they said that his "many-glittering, gold-studded *thorex*," that is, his body clothing in general, was pierced. It does seem simpler to hold that *chiton* meant *chiton;* that *thorex* meant, first, "breast," then "breastplate," whether of linen, or plaited leather, or bronze, and that to pierce a man through his πολυδαίδαλος θώρηξ meant to pierce him through his handsome corslet. No mortal ever dreamt that this was so till Reichel tried to make out that the original poet describes no armour except the large Mycenæan shield and the *mitrê*, and that all corslets in the poems were of much later introduction. Possibly they were, but they had plenty of time wherein to be evolved long before the eighth century, Reichel's date for corslets.

The argument is that a man with a large shield needs no body armour, or uses the shield because he has no body armour.

But the possession and use of a large shield did not in the Middle Ages, or among the Iroquois and Algonquins, make men dispense with corslets, even when the shield was worn, as in Homer, slung round the neck by a *telamon* (*guige* in Old French), belt, or baldric.

We turn to a French *Chanson de Geste—La Chancun de Willem*—of the twelfth century A.D., to judge by the handwriting. One of the heroes, Girard, having failed to rescue Vivien in battle, throws down his weapons and armour, blaming each piece for having failed him. Down goes the heavy lance ; down goes the ponderous shield, suspended by a *telamon : "Ohi grant targe cume peises al col!"* down goes the plated byrnie, *"Ohi grant broine cum me vas apesant!"* [1]

The mediæval warrior has a heavy byrnie as well as a great shield suspended from his neck. It will be remarked also that the Algonquins and Iroquois of the beginning of the seventeenth century, as described by Champlain, give us the whole line of Mycenæan evolution of armour up to a certain point. Not only had they arrow-proof, body-covering shields of buffalo hide, but, when Champlain used his arquebus against the Iroquois in battle, "they were struck amazed that two of their number should have been killed so promptly, seeing that they wore a sort of armour, woven of cotton thread, and carried arrow-proof shields." We have already alluded to this passage, but must add that Parkman, describing from French archives a battle of Illinois against Iroquois in 1680, speaks of "corslets of tough twigs interwoven with cordage." [2] Colden, in his *Five Nations*, writes of the Red Indians as wearing "a kind of cuirass made of pieces of wood joined together." [3]

To the kindness of Mr. Hill Tout I also owe a description of the armour of the Indian tribes of north-

---

[1] *La Chancun de Willame*, lines 716-726.
[2] *Discovery of the Great West*, p. 209. 1869.
[3] Dix, *Champlain*, p. 113, Note 1.

west America, from a work of his own. He says : " For
protective purposes in warfare they employed shields
and coat-armour. The shields varied in form and
material from tribe to tribe. Among the Interior
Salish they were commonly made of wood, which was
afterwards covered with hide. Sometimes they consisted of several thicknesses of hide only. The hides
most commonly used were those of the elk, buffalo, or
bear. After the advent of the Hudson's Bay Co. some
of the Indians used to beat out the large copper kettles
they obtained from the traders and make polished
circular shields of these. In some centres long rect-
angular shields, made from a single or double hide,
were employed. These were often from 4 to 5 feet in
length and from 3 to 4 feet in width—large enough
to cover the whole body. Among the Déné tribes
(Sikanis) the shield was generally made of closely-
woven wicker-work, and was of an ovaloid form (exact
size not given).

" The coat armour *was everywhere used*, and varied in
form and style in almost every centre. There were
two ways in which this was most commonly made.
One of these was the slatted cuirass or corslet, which
was formed of a series of narrow slats of wood set side
by side vertically and fastened in place by interlacings
of raw hide. It went all round the body, being hung
from the shoulders with straps. The other was a kind
of shirt of double or treble elk hide, fastened at the side
with thongs. Another kind of armour, less common
than that just described, was the long elk-hide tunic,
which reached to and even *below the knees and was sleeved
to the elbow.*"

Mr. Hill Tout's minute description, with the other

facts cited, leaves no doubt that even in an early stage, as in later stages of culture, the use of the great shield does not exclude the use of such body armour as the means of the warriors enable them to construct. To take another instance, Pausanias describes the corslets of the neolithic Sarmatæ, which he saw dedicated in the temple of Asclepius at Athens. Corslets these bowmen and users of the lasso possessed, though they did not use the metals. They fashioned very elegant corslets out of horses' hoofs, cutting them into scales like those of a pine cone, and sewing them on to cloth.[1]

Certain small, thin, perforated discs of stone found in Scotland have been ingeniously explained as plates to be strung together on a garment of cloth, a neolithic *chiton*. However this may be, since Iroquois and Algonquins and Déné had some sort of woven, or plaited, or wooden, or buff corslet, in addition to their great shields, we may suppose that the Achæans would not be less inventive. They would pass from the λινοθώρηξ (answering to the cotton corslet of the Iroquois) to a sort of jack or *jaseran* with rings, scales, or plates, and thence to bronze-plate corslets, represented only by the golden breastplates of the Mycenæan grave. Even if the Mycenæans did not evolve the corslet, there is no reason why, in the Homeric times, it should not have been evolved.

For linen corslets, such as Homer mentions, in actual use and represented in works of art we consult Mr. Leaf on *The Armour of Homeric Heroes*.[2] He finds Memnon in a white corslet, on a black-figured vase in the British Museum. There is another white cor-

---

[1] *Pausanias*, i. 21 ; ii. 6.
[2] *Journal of Hellenic Studies*, vol. iv. pp. 82, 83, 85.

sleted Memnon figured in the *Vases Peints* of the Duc de Luynes (plate xii.). Mr. Leaf suggests that the white colour represents " a corslet not of metal but of linen," and cites *Iliad*, II. 529, 530. " Xenophon mentions linen corslets as being worn by the Chalybes" (*Anabasis*, iv. 15). Two linen corslets, sent from Egypt to Sparta by King Amasis, are recorded by Herodotus (ii. 182 ; iii. 47). The corslets were of linen, embroidered in cotton and gold. Such a piece of armour or attire might easily develop into the στρεπτός χιτών of *Iliad*, V. 113, in which Aristarchus appears to have recognised chain or scale armour ; but we find no such object represented in Mycenæan art, which, of course, does not depict Homeric armour or costume, and it seems probable that the bronze corslets mentioned by Homer were plate armour. The linen corslet lasted into the early sixth century B.C. In the poem called *Stasiotica*, Alcæus (No. 5) speaks of his helmets, bronze greaves and corslets of linen (θώρακές τε νέοι λίνω) as a defence against arrows.

Meanwhile a " bronze *chiton* " or corslet would turn spent arrows and spent spears, and be very useful to a warrior whose shield left him exposed to shafts shot or spears thrown from a distance. Again, such a bronze *chiton* might stop a spear of which the impetus was spent in penetrating the shield. But Homeric corslets did not, as a rule, avail to keep out a spear driven by the hand at close quarters, or powerfully thrown from a short distance. Even the later Greek corslets do not look as if they could resist a heavy spear wielded by a strong hand.

I proceed to show that the Homeric corslet did not avail against a spear at close quarters, but could turn an

arrow point (once), and could sometimes turn a spear
which had perforated a shield. So far, and not further,
the Homeric corslet was serviceable. But if a warrior's
breast or back was not covered by the shield, and received a thrust at close quarters, the corslet was pierced
more easily than the pad of paper which was said to
have been used as secret armour in a duel by the Master
of Sinclair (1708).[1] It is desirable to prove this feeble-
ness of the corslet, because the poet often says that
a man was smitten with the spear in breast or back
when unprotected by the shield, without mentioning the
corslet, whence it is argued by the critics that corslets
were not worn when the original lays were fashioned,
and that they have only been sporadically introduced,
in an after age when the corslet was universal, by
"modernising" later rhapsodists aiming at the up-to-
date.

A weak point is the argument that Homer says
back or breast was pierced, without mentioning the
corslet, whence it follows that he knew no corslets.
Quintus Smyrnæus does the same thing. Of course,
Quintus knew all about corslets, yet (Book I. 248, 256,
257) he makes his heroes drive spear or sword through
breast or belly without mentioning the resistance of the
corslet, even when (I. 144, 594) he has assured us
that the victim was wearing a corslet. These facts are
not due to inconsistent interpolation of corslets into
the work of this post-Christian poet Quintus.[2]

Corslets, in Homer, are flimsy ; that of Lycaon,
worn by Paris, is pierced by a spear which has also
perforated his shield, though the spear came only from

---

[1] *Proceedings in Court Marshal held upon John, Master of Sinclair.* Sir
Walter Scott. Roxburghe Club. (Date of event, 1708.)
[2] I find a similar omission in the *Chanson de Roland.*

the weak hand of Menelaus (*Iliad*, III. 357, 358). The arrow of Pandarus whistles through the corslet of Menelaus (IV. 136). The same archer pierces with an arrow the corslet of Diomede (V. 99, 100). The corslet of Diomede, however, avails to stop a spear which has traversed his shield (V. 281). The spear of Idomeneus pierces the corslet of Othryoneus, and the spear of Antilochus perforates the corslet of a charioteer (XIII. 371, 397). A few lines later Diomede's spear reaches the midriff of Hypsenor. No corslet is here mentioned, but neither is the shield mentioned (this constantly occurs), and we cannot argue that Hypsenor wore no corslet, unless we are also to contend that he wore no shield, or a small shield. Idomeneus drives his spear through the " *bronze chiton* " of Alcathöus (XIII. 439, 440). Mr. Leaf reckons these lines "probably an interpolation to turn the linen *chiton*, the rending of which is the sign of triumph, into a bronze corslet." But we ask why, if an editor or rhapsodist went through the *Iliad* introducing corslets, he so often left them out, where the critics detect their absence because they are not mentioned ?

The spear of Idomeneus pierces another feeble corslet over the victim's belly (XIII. 506–508). It is quite a surprise when a corslet does for once avail to turn an arrow (XIII. 586–587). But Aias drives his spear through the corslet of Phorcys, into his belly (XVII. 311–312). Thus the corslet scarcely ever, by itself, protects a hero ; it never protects him against an unspent spear ; even when his shield stands between his corslet and the spear both are sometimes perforated. Yet occasionally the corslet saves a man when the spear has gone through the shield. The poet, therefore, sometimes gives us a man pierced in a part which the corslet covers, without mentioning the flimsy article that could not keep out a spear.

Reichel himself came to see, before his regretted death, that he could not explain away the *thorex* or corslet, on his original lines, as a mere general name for "a piece of armour"; and he inclined to think that jacks, with metal plates sewn on, did exist before the Ionian corslet.[1] The gold breastplates of the Mycenæan graves pointed in this direction. But his general argument is that corslets were interpolated into the old lays by poets of a corslet-wearing age; and Mr. Leaf holds that corslets may have filtered in, " during the course of successive modernisation, such as the oldest parts of the *Iliad* seem in many cases to have passed through,"[2] though the new poets were, for all that, "conservatively tenacious of the old material." We have already pointed out the difficulty.

The poets who did not introduce the new small bucklers with which they were familiar, did stuff the *Iliad* full of corslets unknown, by the theory, to the original poet, but familiar to rhapsodists living centuries later. Why, if they were bent on modernising, did they not modernise the shields? and how, if they modernised unconsciously, as all uncritical poets do, did the shield fail to be unconsciously "brought up to date"? It seems probable that Homer lived at a period when both huge shield and rather feeble corslet were in vogue.

We shall now examine some of the passages in which Mr. Leaf, mainly following Reichel, raises diffi-

---

[1] *Homerische Waffen*, pp. 93–94.   1901.
[2] Leaf, *Iliad*, i. p. 578.

culties about corslets. We do not know their mechanism; they were composed of γύαλα, presumed to be a back-plate and a breastplate. The word *gualon* appears to mean a hollow, or the converse, something convex. We cannot understand the mechanism (see a young man putting on a corslet, on an amphora by Euthymides. Walter, vol. ii. p. 176); but, if late poets, familiar with such corslets, did not understand how they worked, they were very dull men. When their descriptions puzzle us, that is more probably because we are not at the point of view than because poets interpolated mentions of pieces of armour which they did not understand, and therefore cannot have been familiar with, and, in that case, would not introduce.

Mr. Leaf starts with a passage in the *Iliad* (III. 357–360)—it recurs in another case : "Through the bright shield went the ponderous spear, and through the in-wrought" (very artfully wrought, πολυδαιδάλου) "breast-plate it pressed on, and straight beside his flank it rent the tunic, but he swerved and escaped black death." Mr. Leaf says, " It is obvious that, after a spear has passed through a breastplate, there is no longer any possibility for the wearer to bend aside and so to avoid the point. . . ." But I suppose that the wearer, by a motion very natural, doubled up sideways, so to speak, and so the spear merely grazed his flesh. That is what I suppose the poet to intend. The more he knew of corslets, the less would he mention an impos-sible circumstance in connection with a corslet.

Again, in many cases the late poets, by the theory—though it is they who bring the corslets in—leave the corslets out ! A man without shield, helmet, and spear calls himself " naked." Why did not these late poets, it is asked, make him take off his corslet, if he had one, as well as his shield ?   The case occurs in *Iliad*, XXII. 111–113, 124–125.   Hector thinks of laying aside helmet, spear, and shield, and of parleying with Achilles. " But then he will slay me naked," that is, unarmed. " He still had his corslet," the critics say, " so how could he be naked ? or, if he had no corslet, this is a passage uncontaminated by the late poets of the corslet age."   Now certainly Hector *was* wearing a corslet, which he had taken from Patroclus : that is the essence of the story.   He would, however, be " naked " or un- protected if he laid aside helmet, spear, and shield, because Achilles could hit him in the head or neck (as he did), or lightly drive the spear through the corslet, which, we have proved, was no sound defence against a spear at close quarters, though useful against chance arrows, and occasionally against spears spent by tra- versing the shield.

We next learn that no corslet occurs in the *Odyssey*, or in *Iliad*, Book X., called " very late " : Mr. Leaf sug- gests that it is of the seventh century B.C.   But if the *Odyssey* and *Iliad*, Book X., are really very late, their authors and interpolators were perfectly familiar with Ionian corslets.   Why did they leave corslets out, while their predecessors and contemporaries were introducing them all up and down the *Iliad ?*   In fact, in Book X., no prince is regularly equipped ; they have been called up to deliberate in the dead of night, and when two go as spies they wear casual borrowed gear.   It is more important that no corslet is mentioned in Nestor's arms in his tent.   But are we to explain this, and the absence of mention of corslets in the *Odyssey* (where there is little about regular fighting), on the ground that the author of *Iliad*, Book X., and all the many authors and editors of the *Odyssey* happened to be profound archæologists, and, unlike their contemporaries, the later poets and interpolators of the *Iliad*, had formed the theory that corslets were not known at the time of the siege of Troy and therefore must not be mentioned? This is quite incredible. No hypothesis can be more improbable. We cannot imagine late Ionian rhapsodists listening to the *Iliad*, and saying, "These poets of the *Iliad* are all wrong: at the date of the Mycenæan prime, as every educated man knows, corslets were not yet in fashion. So we must have no corslets in the *Odyssey !*"

A modern critic, who thinks this possible, is bringing the practice of archaising poets of the late nineteenth century into the minds of rhapsodists of the eighth century before Christ. Artists of the middle of the sixteenth century always depict Jeanne d'Arc in the armour and costume of their own time, wholly unlike those of 1430. This is the regular rule. Late rhapsodists would not delve in the archæology of the Mycenæan prime. Indeed, one does not see how they could discover, in Asia, that corslets were not worn, five centuries earlier, on the other side of the sea.

We are told that Aias and some other heroes are never spoken of as wearing corslets. But Aias certainly did put on a set of pieces of armour, and did not trust to his shield alone, tower-like as it was. The description runs thus : The Achæans have disarmed, before the duel of Aias and Hector. Aias draws the lucky lot ; he is to meet Hector, and bids the others pray to Zeus "while I clothe me in my armour of battle." While they prayed, Aias "arrayed himself in flashing bronze. And when he had now clothed upon his flesh

all his pieces of armour" (πάντα τεύχη) " he went forth
to fight." If Aias wore only a shield, as on Mr. Leaf's
hypothesis, he could sling it on before the Achæans
could breathe a *pater noster.* His sword he would not
have taken off ; swords were always worn. What, then,
are " all his pieces of armour " ? (VII. 193, 206).

Carl Robert cites passages in which the τεύχεα,
taken from the shoulders, include corslets, and are late
and Ionian, with other passages which are Mycenæan,
with no corslet involved. He adds about twenty more
passages in which τεύχεα include corslets. Among these
references two are from the *Doloneia* (X. 254, 272),
where Reichel finds no mention of corslets. How
Robert can tell τεύχεα, which mean corslets, from τεύχεα,
which exclude corslets, is not obvious. But, at all
events, he does see corslets, as in VII. 122, where
Reichel sees none,[1] and he is obviously right.

It is a strong point with Mr. Leaf that " we never
hear of the corslet in the case of Aias. . . ."[2] Robert,
however, like ourselves, detects the corslet among " *al*
the τεύχεα " which Aias puts on for his duel with Hector
(*Iliad*, VII. 193, 206–207).

In the same Book (VII. 101–103, 122) the same
difficulty occurs. Menelaus offers to fight Hector,
and says, " I will put on my harness " (θωρήξομαι),
and does "put on his fair pieces of armour " (τεύχεα
καλά). Agamemnon forbids him to fight, and his
friends " joyfully take his pieces of armour " (τεύχεα)
" from his shoulders" (*Iliad*, VII. 206–207). They
take off pieces of armour, in the plural, and a shield
cannot be spoken of in the plural ; while the sword

---

[1] Robert, *Studien zur Ilias,* pp. 20–21.
[2] Leaf, *Iliad,* vol. i. p. 576.

would not be taken off—it was worn even in peaceful
costume.

Idomeneus is never named as wearing a corslet, but
he remarks that he has plenty of corslets (XIII. 264);
and in this and many cases opponents of corslets prove
their case by cutting out the lines which disprove it.
Anything may be demonstrated if we may excise whatever passage does not suit our hypothesis. It is impossible to argue against this logical device, especially
when the critic, not satisfied with a clean cut, supposes
that some late enthusiast for corslets altered the prayer
of Thetis to Hephæstus for the very purpose of dragging
in a corslet.[1]   If there is no objection to a line except
that a corslet occurs in it, where is the logic in excising the line because one happens to think that corslets
are later than the oldest parts of the *Iliad*?

Another plan is to maintain that if the poet does
not in any case mention a corslet, there *was* no corslet.
Thus in *Iliad*, V. 99, an arrow strikes Diomede "hard
by the right shoulder, the plate of the corslet." Thirteen
lines later (V. 112, 113) "Sthenelus drew the swift shaft
right through out of Diomede's shoulder, and the blood
darted up through the pliant *chiton*." We do not know
what the word here translated "pliant" ($\sigma\tau\rho\epsilon\pi\tau\acute{o}s$) means,
and Aristarchus seems to have thought it was "a coat
of mail, chain, or scale armour." If so, here is the
corslet, but in this case, if a corslet or jack with inter-
twisted small plates or scales or rings of bronze be
meant, *gualon* cannot mean a large "plate," as it does.
Mr. Ridgeway says, "It seems certain that $\sigma\tau\rho\epsilon\pi\tau\acute{o}s$
$\chi\iota\tau\acute{\omega}\nu$ means, as Aristarchus held, a shirt of mail."[2]

---

[1] Leaf, Note to *Iliad*, xviii. 460, 461.
[2] *Early Age of Greece*, vol. i. p. 306.

Mr. Leaf says just the reverse. As usual, we come to
a deadlock ; a clash of learned opinion. But any one
can see that, in the space of thirteen lines, no poet or
interpolator who wrote V. 112, 113 could forget that
Diomede was said to be wearing a corslet in V. 99 ; and
even if the poet could forget, which is out of the question, the editor of 540 B.C. was simply defrauding his
employer, Pisistratus, if he did not bring a remedy for
the stupid fault of the poet. When this or that hero is
not specifically said to be wearing a corslet, it is usually
because the poet has no occasion to mention it, though,
as we have seen, a man is occasionally smitten, in the
midriff, say, without any remark on the flimsy piece
of mail.

That corslets are usually taken for granted as present by the poet, even when they are not explicitly
named, seems certain. He constantly represents the
heroes as "stripping the pieces of mail" (τεύχεα), when
they have time and opportunity, from fallen foes. If
only the shield is taken, if there is nothing else in the
way of bronze body armour to take, why have we the
plural, τεύχεα ? The corslet, as well as the shield, must
be intended. The stripping is usually "from the
shoulders," and it is "from his shoulders" that Hector
hopes to strip the corslet of Diomede (*Iliad*, VIII. 195)
in a passage, to be sure, which the critics think interpolated. However this may be, the stripping of the
τεύχεα cannot be the mere seizure of the shield, but
must refer to other pieces of armour : "*all* the pieces
of armour." So other pieces of defensive armour
besides the shield are throughout taken for granted.
If they were not there they could not be stripped. It
is the *chitons* that Agamemnon does *something* to, in the

case of two fallen foes (*Iliad*, XI. 100), and Aristarchus thought that these *chitons* were corslets. But the passage is obscure. In *Iliad*, XI. 373, when Diomede strips helmet from head, shield from shoulder, corslet from breast of Agastrophus, Reichel was for excising the corslet, because it was not mentioned when the hero was struck on the hip joint. I do not see that an inefficient corslet would protect the hip joint. To do that, in our eighteenth century cavalry armour, was the business of a *zoster*, as may be seen in a portrait of the Chevalier de St. George in youth. It is a thick ribbed *zoster* that protects the hip joints of the king.

Finally, Mr. Evans observes that the western invaders of Egypt, under Rameses III., are armed, on the monuments, with cuirasses formed of a succession of plates, " horizontal, or rising in a double curve," while the Enkomi ivories, already referred to, corroborate the existence of corslet, *zoster*, and *zoma* as articles of defensive armour.[1] " Recent discoveries," says Mr. Evans, "thus supply a double corroboration of the Homeric tradition which carries back the use of the round shield and the cuirass or θώρηξ to the earlier epic period. . . With such a representation before us, a series of Homeric passages on which Dr. Reichel . . . has exhausted his powers of destructive criticism, becomes readily intelligible." [2]

Homer, then, describes armour *later* than that of the Mycenæan prime, when, as far as works of art show, only a huge leathern shield was carried, though the gold breastplates of the corpses in the grave suggest that corslets existed. Homer's men, on the other hand,

[1] *Journal of Anthropological Institute*, xxx. p. 213.
[2] *Ibid.*, p. 214.

have, at least in certain cases quoted above, large
bronze-plated shields and bronze cuirasses of no great
resisting power, perhaps in various stages of evolution,
from the byrnie with scales or small plates of bronze to
the breastplate and backplate, though the plates for
breast and back certainly appear to be usually worn.

It seems that some critics cannot divest themselves
of the idea that "the original poet" of the "kernel"
was contemporary with them who slept in the shaft
graves of Mycenæ, covered with golden ornaments,
and that for body armour he only knew their monstrous shields. Mr. Leaf writes: "The armour of
Homeric heroes corresponds closely to that of the
Mykenæan age as we learn it from the monuments.
The heroes wore no breastplate ; their only defensive
armour was the enormous Mykenæan shield. . . ."

This is only true if we excise all the passages
which contradict the statement, and go on with Mr.
Leaf to say, "by the seventh century B.C., or thereabouts, the idea of a panoply without a breastplate
had become absurd. By that time the epic poems had
almost ceased to grow ; but they still admitted a few
minor episodes in which the round shield" (where ?)
"and corslet played a part, as well as the interpolation of a certain number of lines and couplets in which
the new armament was mechanically introduced into
narratives which originally knew nothing of it." [1]

On the other hand, Mr. Leaf says that "the small
circular shield of later times is unknown to Homer,"
with "a very few curious exceptions," in which the
shields are not said to be small or circular.[2]

Surely this is rather arbitrary dealing ! We start

[1] *Iliad*, vol. i. p. 568.   [2] *Iliad*, vol. i. p. 575.

from our theory that the original poet described the
armour of "the monuments" though *they* are "of the
prime," while *he* professedly lived long after the prime—
lived in an age when there must have been changes in
military equipment. We then cut out, as of the seventh
century, whatever passages do not suit our theory.
Anybody can prove anything by this method. We
might say that the siege scene on the Mycenæan silver
vase represents the Mycenæan prime, and that, as there
is but one jersey among eight men otherwise stark
naked, we must cut out seven-eighths of the *chitons* in
the *Iliad*, these having been interpolated by late poets
who did not run about with nothing on. We might
call the whole poem late, because the authors know
nothing of the Mycenæan bathing-drawers so common
on the "monuments." The argument compels Mr.
Leaf to assume that a shield can be called τεύχεα, in the
plural, so, in *Iliad*, VII. 122, when the squires of
Menelaus "take the τεύχεα from his shoulders," we are
assured that "the shield (*aspis*) was for the chiefs
alone" (we have seen that all the host of Pandarus
wore shields), "for those who could keep a chariot to
carry them, and squires to assist them in taking off this
ponderous defence" (see VII. 122).[1]

We *do* "see VII. 122," and find that not a *single*
shield, but pieces of gear in the plural number were
taken off Menelaus. The feeblest warrior without any
assistance could stoop his head and put it through the
belt of his shield, as an angler takes off his fishing creel,
and there he was, totally disarmed. No squire was
needed to disarm him, any more than to disarm Girard
in the *Chancun de Willame*. Nobody explains why a

[1] *Iliad*, vol. i. p. 583.

shield is spoken of as a number of things, in the plural, and that constantly, and in lines where, if the poet means a shield, prosody permits him to *say* a shield, θεράποντες ἀπ' ὤμων ἀσπίδ' ἕλοντο.

It really does appear that Reichel's logic, his power of visualising simple things and processes, and his knowledge of the evolution of defensive armour everywhere, were not equal to his industry and classical erudition. Homer seems to describe what he saw : shields, often of great size, made of leather, plated with bronze, and suspended by belts ; and, for body armour, feeble bronze corslets and *zosters*. There is nothing inconsistent in all this : there was no more reason why an Homeric warrior should not wear a corslet as well as a shield than there was reason why a mediæval knight who carried a *targe* should not also wear a hauberk, or why an Iroquois with a shield should not also wear his cotton or wicker-work armour. Defensive gear kept pace with offensive weapons. A big leather shield could keep out stone-tipped arrows ; but as bronze-tipped arrows came in and also heavy bronze-pointed spears, defensive armour was necessarily strengthened ; the shield was plated with bronze, and, if it did not exist before, the bronze corslet was developed.

To keep out stone-tipped arrows was the business of the Mycenæan wooden or leather shield. " Bronze arrow-heads, so common in the *Iliad*, are never found," says Schuchardt, speaking of Schliemann's Mycenæan excavations.[1]

There was thus, as far as arrows went, no reason why Mycenæan shields should be plated with bronze. If the piece of wood in Grave V. was a shield, as

---

[1] Schuchardt, p. 237.

seems probable, what has become of its bronze plates, if it had any ?[1] Gold ornaments, which could only belong to shields,[2] were found, but bronze shield plates never. The inference is certain. The Mycenæan shields of the prime were originally wooden or leather defences against stone-headed arrows. Homer's shields are bronze-plated shields to keep out bronze-headed or even, perhaps, iron-pointed arrows of primitive construction (IV. 123). Homer describes armour based on Mycenæan lines but developed and advanced as the means of attack improved.

Where everything is so natural it seems fantastic to explain the circumstances by the theory that poets in a late age sometimes did and sometimes did not interpolate the military gear of four centuries posterior to the things known by the original singer. These rhapsodists, we reiterate, are now said to be anxiously conservative of Mycenæan detail and even to be deeply learned archæologists.[3] At other times they are said to introduce recklessly part of the military gear of their own age, the corslets, while sternly excluding the bucklers. All depends on what the theory of very late developments of the Epic may happen to demand at this or that moment.

Again, Mr. Leaf informs us that "the first rhapsodies were born in the bronze age, in the day of the ponderous Mycenæan shield ; the last in the iron age, when men armed themselves with breastplate and light round buckler."[4] We cannot guess how he found these things out, for corslets are as common in one "rhapsody" as in another when circumstances call for the

---

[1] Schuchardt, p. 269.
[2] *Ibid.*, p. 237.
[3] Leaf, *Iliad*, vol. ii. p. 629.
[4] *Ibid.*, vol. ii. p. x.

mention of corslets, and are entirely unnamed in the *Odyssey* (save that the Achæans are " bronze-chitoned "), while the *Odyssey* is alleged to be much later than the *Iliad*. As for " the iron age," no " rhapsodist " introduces so much as one iron spear point. It is argued that he speaks of bronze in deference to tradition. Then why does he scout tradition in the matter of greaves and corslets, while he sometimes actually goes behind tradition to find Mycenæan things unknown to the original poets ?

These theories appear too strangely inconsistent ; really these theories cannot possibly be accepted. The late poets, of the theory, are in the iron age, and are, of course, familiar with iron weapons ; yet, in conservative deference to tradition, they keep them absolutely out of their rhapsodies. They are equally familiar with bronze corslets, so, reckless this time of tradition, they thrust them even into rhapsodies which are centuries older than their own day. They are no less familiar with small bucklers, yet they say nothing about them and cling to the traditional body-covering shield.

The source of the inconsistent theories which we have been examining is easily discovered. The scholars who hold these opinions see that several things in the Homeric picture of life are based on Mycenæan facts ; for example, the size of the shields and their suspension by baldrics. But the scholars also do steadfastly believe, following the Wolfian tradition, that there could be no *long* epic in the early period. Therefore the greater part, much the greater part of the *Iliad*, must necessarily, they say, be the work of continuators through several centuries. Critics are fortified in this belief by the discovery of inconsistencies in the Epic,

which, they assume, can only be explained as the result
of a compilation of the patchwork of ages. But as,
on this theory, many men in many lands and ages
made the Epic, their contributions cannot but be
marked by the inevitable changes in manners, customs,
beliefs, implements, laws, weapons, and so on, which
could not but arise in the long process of time. Yet
traces of change in law, religion, manners, and customs
are scarcely, if at all, to be detected ; whence it logically follows that a dozen generations of irresponsible
minstrels and vagrant reciters were learned, conscientious, and staunchly conservative of the archaic tone.
Their erudite conservatism, for example, induced them,
in deference to the traditions of the bronze age, to
describe all weapons as of bronze, though many of the
poets were living in an age of weapons of iron. It also
prompted them to describe all shields as made on the
far-away old Mycenæan model, though they were themselves used to small circular bucklers, with a bracer
and a grip, worn on the left arm.

But at this point the learning and conservatism of
the late poets deserted them, and into their new lays,
also into the old lays, they eagerly introduced many
unwarrantable corslets and greaves — things of the
ninth to seventh centuries. We shall find Helbig stating,
on the same page, that in the matter of usages " the
epic poets shunned, as far as possible, all that was
recent," and also that for fear of puzzling their military
audiences they did the reverse : " they probably kept
account of the arms and armour of their own day." [1]
Now the late poets, on this showing, must have puzzled
warriors who used iron weapons by always speaking of

___
[1] *La Question Mycénienne*, p. 50. *Cf.* Note 1.

bronze weapons. They pleased the critical warriors, on the other hand, by introducing the corslets and greaves which every military man of their late age possessed. But, again, the poets startled an audience which used light bucklers, worn on the left arm, by talking of enormous *targes*, slung round the neck.

All these inconsistencies of theory follow from the assumption that the *Iliad must* be a hotch-potch of many ages. If we assume that, on the whole, it is the work of one age, we see that the poet describes the usages which obtained in his own day. The dead are cremated, not, as in the Mycenæan prime, inhumed. The shield has been strengthened to meet bronze, not stone-tipped, arrows by bronze plates. Corslets and greaves have been elaborated. Bronze, however, is still the metal for swords and spears, and even occasionally for tools and implements, though these are often of iron. In short, we have in Homer a picture of a transitional age of culture ; we have not a medley of old and new, of obsolete and modern. The poets do not describe inhumation, as they should do, if they are conservative archæologists. In that case, though *they* burn, they would have made their heroes bury their dead, as they did at Mycenæ. They do not introduce iron swords and spears, as they must do, if, being late poets, they keep in touch with the armament of their time. If they speak of huge shields only because they are conservative archæologists, then, on the other hand, they speak of corslets and greaves because they are also reckless innovators.

They cannot be both at once. They are depicting a single age, a single "moment in culture." That age is certainly sundered from the Mycenæan prime by the century or two in which changing ideas led to the superseding of burial by burning, or it is sundered from the Mycenæan prime by a foreign conquest, a revolution, and the years in which the foreign conquerors acquired the language of their subjects.

In either alternative, and one or other must be actual, there was time enough for many changes in the culture of the Mycenæan prime to be evolved.   These changes, we say, are represented by the descriptions of culture in the *Iliad*.   That hypothesis explains, simply and readily, all the facts.   The other hypothesis, that the *Iliad* was begun near the Mycenæan prime and was continued throughout four or five centuries, cannot, first, explain how the *Iliad* was *composed*, and, next, it wanders among apparent contradictories and through a maze of inconsistencies.

THE ZOSTER, ZOMA, AND MITRÊ

We are far from contending that it is always possible to understand Homer's descriptions of defensive armour.   But as we have never seen the actual objects, perhaps the poet's phrases were clear enough to his audience and are only difficult to us. I do not, for example, profess to be sure of what happened when Pandarus shot at Menelaus.   The arrow lighted " where the golden buckles of the *zoster* were clasped, and the doubled breastplate met them. So the bitter arrow alighted upon the firm *zoster ;* through the wrought *zoster* it sped, and through the curiously wrought breastplate it pressed on, and through the *mitrê* he wore to shield his flesh, a barrier against darts ; and this best shielded him, yet it passed

on even through this," and grazed the hero's flesh
(*Iliad*, IV. 132 *seq*.).   Menelaus next says that "the
glistering *zoster* in front stayed the dart, and the *zoma*
beneath, and the *mitrê* that the coppersmiths fashioned"
(IV. 185–187).   Then the surgeon, Machaon, "loosed
the glistering *zoster* and the *zoma*, and the *mitrê* beneath that the coppersmiths fashioned" (IV. 215,
216).

Reading as a mere student of poetry I take this to
mean that the corslet was of two pieces, fastening in
the middle of the back and the middle of the front of
a man (though Mr. Monro thinks that the plates met
and the *zoster* was buckled at the side) ; that the *zoster*,
a mailed belt, buckled just above the place where the
plates of the corslet met ; that the arrow went through
the meeting-place of the belt buckles, through the place
where the plates of the corslet met, and then through
the *mitrê*, a piece of bronze armour worn under the
corslet, though the nature of this *mitrê* and of the *zoma*
I do not know.   Was the *mitrê* a separate article or a
continuation of the breastplate, lower down, struck by
a dropping arrow ?

In 1883 Mr. Leaf wrote : " I take it that the *zoma*
means the waist of the cuirass which is covered by the
zoster, and has the upper edge of the *mitrê* or plated
apron beneath it fastened round the warrior's body.
. . . This view is strongly supported by all the archaic
vase paintings I have been able to find."[1]   We see
a "corslet with a projecting rim " ; that rim is called
zoma and holds the *zoster*.   " The hips and upper part
of the thighs were protected either by a belt of leather,
sometimes plated, called the *mitrê*, or else only by the

---

[1] *Journal of Hellenic Studies*, vol. iv. pp. 74, 75.

lower part of the *chiton*, and this corresponds exactly
with Homeric description." [1]

At this time, in days before Reichel, Mr. Leaf
believed in bronze corslets, whether of plates or plated
jacks ; he also believed, we have seen, that the huge
shields, as of Aias, were survivals in poetry ; that
"Homer" saw small round bucklers in use, and supposed that the old warriors were muscular enough to
wear circular shields as great as those in the vase of
Aristonothos, already described. [2]

On the corslet, as we have seen, Mr. Leaf now
writes as a disciple of Reichel. But as to the *mitrê*, he
rejects Helbig's and Mr. Ridgeway's opinion that it was
a band of metal a foot wide in front and very narrow
behind. Such things have been found in Eubœa and
in Italy. Mr. Ridgeway mentions examples from
Bologna, Corneto, Este, Hallstatt, and Hungary. [3] The
zoster is now, in Mr. Leaf's opinion, a "girdle" "holding up the waist-cloth (*zoma*), so characteristic of Mycenæan dress." Reichel's arguments against corslets
"militate just as strongly against the presence of such
a *mitrê*, which is, in fact, just the lower half of a
corslet. . . . The conclusion is that the metallic *mitrê*
is just as much an intruder into the armament of the
Epos as the corslet." The process of evolution was,
Mr. Leaf suggests, first, the abandonment of the huge
shield, with the introduction of small round bucklers
in its place. Then, second, a man naturally felt very
unprotected, and put on "the metallic *mitrê*" of Helbig
(which covered a foot of him in front and three inches

[1] *Journal of Hellenic Studies*, pp. 76, 77.
[2] *Ibid.*, vol. iv. p. 285.
[3] *Early Age of Greece*, p. 311.

behind). "Only as technical skill improved could the
final stage, that of the elaborate cuirass, be attained."

This appears to us an improbable sequence of processes. While arrows were flying thick, as they do fly
in the *Iliad*, men would not reject body-covering shields
for small bucklers while they were still wholly destitute
of body armour. Nor would men arm only their
stomachs when, if they had skill enough to make a
metallic *mitrê*, they could not have been so unskilled
as to be unable to make corslets of some more or less
serviceable type. Probably they began with huge
shields, added the *linothorex* (like the Iroquois cotton
thorex), and next, as a rule, superseded that with the
bronze *thorex*, while retaining the huge shield, because
the bronze *thorex* was so inadequate to its purpose of
defence. Then, when archery ceased to be of so much
importance as coming to the shock with heavy spears,
and as the bronze *thorex* really could sometimes keep
out an arrow, they reduced the size of their shields, and
retained surface enough for parrying spears and meeting point and edge of the sword. That appears to be
a natural set of sequences, but I cannot pretend to
guess how the corslet fastened or what the *mitrê* and
zoster really were, beyond being guards of the stomach
and lower part of the trunk.

HELMETS, GREAVES, SPEARS

No helmets of metal, such as Homer mentions, have
been found in Mycenæan graves. A quantity of boars'
teeth, sixty in all, were discovered in Grave V. and
may have adorned and strengthened leather caps, now
mouldered into dust. An ivory head from Mycenæ

shows a conical cap set with what may be boars' tusks, with a band of the same round the chin, and an earpiece which was perhaps of bronze.[1] Spata and the graves of the lower town of Mycenæ and the Enkomi ivories show similar headgear.[2]

This kind of cap set with boars' tusks is described in *Iliad*, Book X., in the account of the hasty arraying of two spies in the night of terror after the defeat and retreat to the ships. The Trojan spy, Dolon, also wears a leather cap. The three spies put on no corslets, as far as we can affirm, their object being to remain inconspicuous and unburdened with glittering bronze greaves and corslets. The Trojan camp was brilliantly lit up with fires, and there may have been a moon, so the less bronze the better. In these circumstances alone the heroes of the *Iliad* are unequipped, *certainly*, with bronze helmets, corslets, and bronze greaves.[3]

The author of Book X. is now regarded as a precise archæologist, who knew that corslets and bronze helmets were not used in Agamemnon's time, but that leather caps with boars' tusks were in fashion ; while again, as we shall see, he is said to know nothing about heroic costume (*cf. The Doloneia*). As a fact, he has to describe an incident which occurs nowhere else in Homer, though it may often have occurred in practice —a hurried council during a demoralised night, and the hasty arraying of two spies, who wish to be light-footed and inconspicuous. The author's evidence as to the leather cap and its garnishing of boars' tusks

1 Tsountas and Manatt, pp. 196, 197.
2 Evans, *Journal of the Anthropological Institute*, xxx. pp. 209–215.
3 *Iliad*, X. 255–265.

testifies to a survival of such gear in an age of bronze battle - helmets, not to his own minute antiquarian research.

GREAVES

Bronze greaves are not found, so far, in Mycenæan tombs in Greece, and Reichel argued that the original Homer knew none. The greaves, κνημῖδες, " were gaiters of stuff or leather " ; the one mention of bronze greaves is stuff and nonsense interpolated (VII. 41). But why did men who were interpolating bronze corslets freely introduce bronze so seldom, if at all, as the material of greaves ?

Bronze greaves, however, have been found in a Cypro-Mycenæan grave at Enkomi (Tomb XV.), *accompanied by an early type of bronze dagger,* while bronze greaves adorned with Mycenæan ornament are discovered in the Balkan peninsula at Glassinavç.[1] Thus all Homer's description of arms is here corroborated by archæology, and cannot be cut out by what Mr. Evans calls "the Procrustean method" of Dr. Reichel.

A curious feature about the spear may be noticed. In Book X. while the men of Diomede slept, "their spears were driven into the ground erect on the spikes of the butts" (X. 153). Aristotle mentions that this was still the usage of the Illyrians in his day.[2] Though the word for the spike in the butt (*sauroter*) does not elsewhere occur in the *Iliad*, the practice of sticking the spears erect in the ground during a truce is mentioned in III. 135 : "They lean upon their shields"

---

[1] Evans, *Journal of the Anthropological Institute,* pp. 214, 215, figs. 10, 11.

[2] *Poetica,* 25.

(clearly large high shields), "and the tall spears are planted by their sides." No butt-spikes have been found in graves of the Mycenæan prime. The *sauroter* was still used, or still existed, in the days of Herodotus.[1]

On the whole, Homer does not offer a medley of the military gear of four centuries—that view we hope to have shown to be a mass of inconsistencies—but describes a state of military equipment in advance of that of the most famous Mycenæan graves, but other than that of the late "warrior vase." He is also very familiar with some uses of iron, of which, as we shall see, scarcely any has been found in Mycenæan graves of the central period, save in the shape of rings. Homer never mentions rings of any metal.

[1] Tsountas and Manatt, p. 205 ; Ridgeway, vol. i. pp. 306, 307.

CHAPTER IX

BRONZE AND IRON

TAKING the *Iliad* and *Odyssey* just as they have reached us they give, with the exception of one line, an entirely harmonious account of the contemporary uses of bronze and iron. Bronze is employed in the making of weapons and armour (with cups, ornaments, &c.) ; iron is employed (and bronze is also used) in the making of tools and implements, such as knives, axes, adzes, axles of a chariot (that of Hera ; mortals use an axle tree of oak), and the various implements of agricultural and pastoral life. Meanwhile, iron is a substance perfectly familiar to the poets ; it is far indeed from being a priceless rarity (it is impossible to trace Homeric stages of advance in knowlege of iron), and it yields epithets indicating strength, permanence, and stubborn endurance. These epithets are more frequent in the *Odyssey* and the " later " Books of the *Iliad* than in the " earlier " Books of the *Iliad;* but, as articles made of iron, the *Odyssey* happens to mention only one set of axes, which is spoken of ten times—axes and adzes as a class—and " iron bonds," where " iron " probably means " strong," " not to be broken." [1]

---

[1] In these circumstances, it is curious that Mr. Monro should have written thus : " In Homer, as is well known, iron is rarely mentioned in comparison with bronze, but the proportion is greater in the *Odyssey* (25 iron, 80 bronze) than in the *Iliad*" (23 iron, 279 bronze).—Monro, *Odyssey*, vol. ii. p. 339. These statistics obviously do not prove that, at the date of the composition of the *Odyssey*, the use of iron was becoming more common, or that the use of bronze

The statement of facts given here is much akin to Helbig's account of the uses of bronze and iron in Homer.[1] Helbig writes : " It is notable that in the Epic there is much more frequent mention of iron *implements* than of iron *weapons of war.*" He then gives examples, which we produce later, and especially remarks on what Achilles says when he offers a mass of iron as a prize in the funeral games of Patroclus. The iron, says Achilles, will serve for the purposes of the ploughman and shepherd, "a surprising speech from the son of Peleus, from whom we rather expect an allusion to the military uses of the metal." Of course, if iron weapons were not in vogue while iron was the metal for tools and implements, the words of Achilles are appropriate and intelligible.

The facts being as we and Helbig agree in stating them, we suppose that the Homeric poets sing of the usages of their own time. It is an age when iron, though quite familiar, is not yet employed for armour, or for swords or spears, which must be of excellent temper, without great weight in proportion to their length and size. Iron is only employed in Homer for

was becoming more rare, than when the *Iliad* was put together. Bronze is, in the poems, the military metal : the *Iliad* is a military poem, while the *Odyssey* is an epic of peace ; consequently the *Iliad* is much more copious in references to bronze than the *Odyssey* has any occasion to be. Wives are far more frequently mentioned in the *Odyssey* than in the *Iliad*, but nobody will argue that therefore marriage had recently come more into vogue. Again, the method of counting up references to iron in the *Odyssey* is quite misleading, when we remember that ten out of the twenty references are only *one* reference to one and the same set of iron tools—axes. Mr. Monro also proposed to leave six references to iron in the *Iliad* out of the reckoning, "as all of them are in lines which can be omitted without detriment to the sense." Most of the six are in a recurrent epic formula descriptive of a wealthy man, who possesses iron, as well as bronze, gold, and women. The existence of the formula proves familiarity with iron, and to excise it merely because it contradicts a theory is purely arbitrary.—Monro, *Odyssey*, vol. ii. p. 339.

[1] Helbig, *Das Homerische Epos*, pp. 330, 331. 1887.

M

some knives, which are never said to be used in battle (not even for dealing the final stab, like the mediæval poniard, the *miséricorde*), for axes, which have a short cutting edge, and may be thick and weighty behind the edge, and for the rough implements of the shepherd and ploughman, such as tips of ploughshares, of goads, and so forth.

As far as archæological excavations and discoveries enlighten us, these relative uses of bronze and iron did not exist in the ages of Mycenæan culture which are represented in the *tholos* of Vaphio and the graves, earlier and later, of Mycenæ. Even in the later Mycenæan graves iron is found only in the form of finger rings (iron rings were common in late Greece).[1] Iron was scarce in the Cypro-Mycenæan graves of Enkomi. A small knife with a carved handle had left traces of an iron blade. A couple of lumps of iron, one of them apparently the head of a club, were found in Schliemann's "Burned City" at Hissarlik; for the rest, swords, spear-heads, knives, and axes are all of bronze in the age called "Mycenæan." But we do not know whether iron *implements* may not yet be found in the sepulchres of *Thetes*, and other poor and landless men. The latest discoveries in Minoan graves in Crete exhibit tools of bronze.

Iron, we repeat, is in the poems a perfectly familiar metal. Ownership of "bronze, gold, and iron, which requires much labour" (in the smithying or smelting), appears regularly in the recurrent epic formula for describing a man of wealth.[2] Iron, bronze, slaves, and hides are bartered for sea-borne wine at the siege of

---

[1] Tsountas and Manatt, pp. 72, 146, 165.

[2] *Iliad*, VI. 48; IX. 365-366; X. 379; XI. 133; *Odyssey*, XIV. 324; XXI. 10.

Troy.[1] Athene, disguised as Mentes, is carrying a cargo of iron to Temesa (Tamasus in Cyprus ?), to barter for copper. The poets are certainly not describing an age in which only a man of wealth might indulge in the rare and extravagant luxury of an iron ring: iron was a common commodity, like cattle, hides, slaves, bronze, and other such matters. Common as it was, Homer never once mentions its use for defensive armour, or for swords and spears.

Only in two cases does Homer describe any *weapon* as of iron. There is to be sure the "iron," the knife with which Antilochus fears Achilles will cut his own throat.[2] But no knife is ever used as a weapon of war: knives are employed in cutting the throats of victims (see *Iliad*, III. 271 and XXIII. 30); the knife is said to be of iron, in this last passage; also Patroclus uses the knife to cut the arrow-head out of the flesh of a wounded friend.[3] It is the *knife* of Achilles that is called " the iron," and on "the iron" perish the cattle in *Iliad*, XXIII. 30. Mr. Leaf says that by "the usual use, the metal" (iron) "is confined to tools of small size."[4] This is incorrect; the *Odyssey* speaks of *great axes* habitually made of iron.[5] But we do find a knife of bronze, that of Agamemnon, used in sacrificing victims; at least so I infer from *Iliad*, III. 271–292.

The only two specimens of *weapons* named by Homer as of iron are one arrow-head, used by Pandarus,[6] and one mace, borne, before Nestor's time, by Areithöus. To fight with an iron mace was an amiable and apparently unique eccentricity of Areithöus, and caused his death. On account of his peculiar practice he was

[1] *Iliad*, VII. 472–475. [2] *Iliad*, XVIII. 34.
[3] *Iliad*, XI. 844. [4] Leaf, *Iliad*, xxiii. 30, Note.
[5] *Odyssey*, IX. 391. [6] *Iliad*, IV. 123.

named "The Maceman." [1]   The case is mentioned by
Nestor as curious and unusual.

Mr. Leaf gets rid of this solitary iron *casse tête* in a
pleasant way.   Since he wrote his *Companion to the Iliad*,
1902, he has become converted, as we saw, to the theory,
demolished by Mr. Monro, Nutzhorn, and Grote, and
denounced by Blass, that the origin of our Homer is
a text edited by some literary retainer of Pisistratus of
Athens (about 560–540 B.C.).   The editor arranged
current lays, " altered " freely, and " wrote in " as much
as he pleased.   Probably he wrote this passage in which
Nestor describes the man of the iron mace, for "the
tales of Nestor's youthful exploits, all of which bear the
mark of late work, are introduced with no special
applicability to the context, but rather with the intention
of glorifying the ancestor of Pisistratus." [2]   If Pisistratus
was pleased with the ancestral portrait, nobody has a
right to interfere, but we need hardly linger over this
hypothesis (*cf.* pp. 281–288).

Iron axes are offered as prizes by Achilles,[3] and we
have the iron axes of Odysseus, who shot an arrow
through the apertures in the blades, at the close of the
Odyssey.   But all these axes, as we shall show, were
not *weapons*, but *peaceful implements*.

As a matter of certain fact the swords and spears
of Homer's warriors are *invariably* said by the poet to
be of bronze, not of iron, in cases where the metal of
the weapons is specified.

Except for an arrow-head (to which we shall return)
and the one iron mace, noted as an eccentricity, no
weapon in Homer is ever said to be of iron.

---

[1] *Iliad*, VII. 141.   [2] *Iliad* (1900), VII. 149, Note.
[3] *Iliad*, XXIII. 850.

The richest men use swords of bronze. Not one chooses to indulge in a sword said to be of iron. The god, Hephæstus, makes a bronze sword for Achilles, whose own bronze sword was lent to Patroclus, and lost by him to Hector.[1] This bronze sword, at least, Achilles uses, after receiving the divine armour of the god. The sword of Paris is of bronze, as is the sword of Odysseus in the *Odyssey*.[2] Bronze is the sword which he brought from Troy, and bronze is the sword presented to him by Euryalus in Phæacia, and bronze is the spear with which he fought under the walls of Ilios.[3] There are other examples of bronze swords, while spears are invariably said to be of bronze, when the metal of the spear is specified.

Here we are on the ground of solid certainty : we see that the Homeric warrior has regularly spear and sword of bronze. If any man used a spear or sword of iron, Homer never once mentions the fact. If the poets, in an age of iron weapons, always spoke of bronze, out of deference to tradition, they must have puzzled their iron-using military patrons.

Thus, as regards weapons, the Homeric heroes are in the age of bronze, like them who slept in the tombs of the Mycenæan age. When Homer speaks of the use of cutting instruments of iron, he is always concerned, except in the two cases given, not with *weapons*, but with *implements*, which really were of iron. The wheel-wright fells a tree " with the iron," that is, with an axe; Antilochus fears that Achilles " will cut his own throat with the iron," that is, with his knife, a thing never used in battle ; the cattle struggle when slain

---

[1] *Iliad*, XVI. 136 ; XIX. 372–373.   [2] *Iliad*, III. 334–335.
[3] *Odyssey*, X. 162, 261–262.

with "the iron," that is, the butcher's knife ; and
Odysseus shoots "through the iron," that is, through
the holes in the blade of the iron axes.[1] Thus Homer
never says that this or that was done "with the iron"
in the case of any but one weapon of war. Pandarus
"drew the bow-string to his breast and *the iron* to the
bow."[2] Whoever wrote that line was writing in an
age, we may think, when arrow-heads were commonly
of iron ; but in Homer, when the metal of the arrow-
head is mentioned, except, in this one case, it is always
bronze. The iron arrow-tip of Pandarus was of an early
type, the shaft did not run into the socket of the arrow-
head ; the tang of the arrow-head, on the other hand,
entered the shaft, and was whipped on with sinew.[3]
Pretty primitive this method, still the iron is an
advance on the uniform bronze of Homer. The
line about Pandarus and the iron arrow-head may
really be early enough, for the arrow-head is of a
primitive kind—socketless—and primitive is the attitude
of the archer : he "drew the arrow to his breast." On
the Mycenæan silver bowl, representing a siege, the
archers draw to the *breast*, in the primitive style, as
does the archer on the bronze dagger with a representation of a lion hunt. The Assyrians and Khita drew
to the ear, as the monuments prove, and so does the
"Cypro-Mycenæan" archer of the ivory draught-box
from Enkomi.[4] In these circumstances we cannot
deny that the poet may have known iron arrow-heads.

We now take the case of axes. We never hear

---

[1] For this peculiar kind of Mycenæan axe with holes in the blade, see
the design of a bronze example from Vaphio in Tsountas and Manatt, *The
Mycenæan Age*, p. 207, fig. 94.

[2] *Iliad*, IV. 123.   [3] *Iliad*, IV. 151.

[4] Evans, *Journal of the Anthropological Institute*, vol. xxx. p. 210.

from Homer of the use of an iron axe in battle, and warlike use of an axe only occurs twice. In *Iliad*, XV. 711, in a battle at and on the ships, "they were fighting with sharp axes and battle-axes" (ἀξίναι) "and with great swords, and spears armed at butt and tip." At and on the ships, men would set hand to whatever tool of cutting edge was accessible. Seiler thinks that only the Trojans used the battle-axe ; perhaps for damaging the ships : he follows the scholiast. 'Aξίνη, however,[1] may perhaps be rendered "battle-axe," as a Trojan, Peisandros, fights with an ἀξίνη, and this is the only place in the *Iliad*, except XV. 711, where the thing is said to be used as a weapon. But it is not an *iron* axe ; it is "of fine bronze." Only one bronze *battle-axe*, according to Dr. Joseph Anderson, is known to have been found in Scotland, though there are many bronze heads of axes which were tools.

Axes (πελεκεῖς) were *implements*, tools of the carpenter, woodcutter, shipwright, and so on ; they were not weapons of war of the Achæans.

As implements they are, with very rare exceptions, of iron. The wheelwright fells trees "with the gleaming iron," iron being a synonym for axe and for knife.[2] In *Iliad*, XIII. 391, the shipwrights cut timber with axes. In *Iliad*, XXIII. 114, woodcutters' axes are employed in tree-felling, but the results are said to be produced ταναήκει χαλχῷ, "by the long-edged bronze," where the word ταναήκης is borrowed from the usual epithet of swords ; "the long edge" is quite inappropriate to a woodcutter's axe. On Calypso's isle Calypso gives to Odysseus a bronze axe for his raft-making. Butcher's

---

[1] *Iliad*, XIII. 611.   [2] *Iliad*, IV. 485.

work is done with an axe.[1] The axes offered by Achilles
as a prize for archers and the axes through which
Odysseus shot are *implements* of iron.[2]

In the *Odyssey*, when the poet describes the process
of tempering iron, we read, " as when a smith dips a
great axe or an adze in chill water, for thus men
temper iron." [3] He is not using iron to make a sword
or spear, but a tool—adze or axe. The poet is perfectly consistent. There are also examples both of
bronze axes and, apparently, of bronze knives. Thus,
though the woodcutter's or carpenter's axe is of bronze
in two passages cited, iron is the usual material of the
axe or adze. Again we saw, when Achilles gives a
mass of iron as a prize in the games, he does not mean
the armourer to fashion it into sword or spear, but says
that it will serve the shepherd or ploughman for
domestic implements,[4] so that the men need not, on
an upland farm, go to the city for iron implements. In
commenting upon this Mr. Leaf is scarcely at the
proper point of view. He says,[5] " the idea of a state
of things when the ploughman and shepherd forge
their own tools from a lump of raw iron has a suspicious appearance of a deliberate attempt to represent
from the inner consciousness an archaic state of civilisation. In Homeric times the χαλκεύς is already
specialised as a worker in metals. . . ." However,
Homer does not say that the ploughman and shepherd
" forge their own tools." A Homeric chief, far from
a town, would have his own smithy, just as the laird of

---

[1] *Iliad*, XVII. 520; *Odyssey*, III. 442–449.
[2] *Iliad*, XXIII. 850; *Odyssey*, XXI. 3, 81, 97.
[3] *Odyssey*, IX. 391–393.
[4] Leaf, *Iliad* (1902), XXIII. line 30, Note.
[5] *Iliad*, XXIII. 835, Note.

Runraurie (now Urrard) had his smithy at the time of the battle of Killicrankie (1689). Mackay's forces left their *impedimenta* "at the laird's smithy," says an eye-witness.[1]

The idea of a late Homeric poet trying to reconstruct from his fancy a prehistoric state of civilisation is out of the question. Even historical novelists of the eighteenth century A.D. scarcely attempted such an effort.

This was the regular state of things in the Highlands during the eighteenth century, when many chiefs, and most of the clans, lived far from any town. But these rural smiths did not make sword-blades, which Prince Charles, as late as 1750, bought on the Continent. The Andrea Ferrara-marked broadsword blades of the clans were of foreign manufacture. The Highland smiths did such rough iron work as was needed for rural purposes. Perhaps the Homeric chief may have sometimes been a craftsman like the heroes of the Sagas, great sword-smiths. Odysseus himself, notably an excellent carpenter, may have been as good a sword-smith, but every hero was not so accomplished.

In searching with microscopes for Homeric discrepancies and interpolations, critics are apt to forget the ways of old rural society.

The Homeric poems, whether composed in one age or throughout five centuries, are thus entirely uniform in allotting bronze as the material for all sorts of warlike gear, down to the solitary battle-axe mentioned ; and iron as the usual metal for heavy tools, knives, carpenters' axes, adzes, and agricultural implements, with the rare exceptions which we have cited in the case of bronze knives and axes. Either this distinction—iron

[1] Napier's *Life of Dundee*, iii. p. 724.

for tools and implements ; bronze for armour, swords, and spears—prevailed throughout the period of the Homeric poets or poet ; or the poets invented such a stage of culture ; or poets, some centuries later, deliberately kept bronze for weapons only, while introducing iron for implements. In that case they were showing archæological conscientiousness in following the presumed earlier poets of the bronze age, the age of the Mycenæan graves.

Now early poets are never studious archæologists. Examining the *Nibelungenlied*, certainly based on old lays and legends which survive in the Edda, we find that the poets of the *Nibelungenlied* introduce chivalrous and Christian manners. They do not archæologise. The poets of the French *Chansons de Geste* (eleventh to thirteenth centuries) bring their own weapons, and even armorial bearings, into the remote age of Charlemagne, which they know from legends and *cantilènes*. Again, the later *remanieurs* of the earliest *Chansons de Geste* modernise the details of these poems. But, *per impossibile*, and for the sake of argument, suppose that the later interpolators and continuators of the Homeric lays *were* antiquarian precisians, or, on the other hand, " deliberately attempted to reproduce from their inner consciousness an archaic state of civilisation." Suppose that, though they lived in an age of iron weapons, they knew, as Hesiod knew, that the old heroes " had warlike gear of bronze, and ploughed with bronze, and there was no black iron." [1]   In that case, why did the later interpolating poets introduce iron as the special material of tools and implements, knives and axes, in an age when they knew that there was no iron ?

[1] Hesiod, *Works and Days*, pp. 250, 251.

Savants such as, by this theory, the later poets of
the full-blown age of iron were, they must have known
that the knives and axes of the old heroes were made
of bronze. In old votive offerings in temples and in
any Mycenæan graves which might be opened, the
learned poets of 800–600 B.C. saw with their eyes
knives and axes of bronze.[1] The knife of Agamemnon
(μάχαιρα), which hangs from his girdle, beside his
sword,[2] corresponds to the knives found in Grave IV.
at Mycenæ ; the handles of these dirks have a ring for
suspension.[3] But these knives, in Mycenæan graves,
are of bronze, and of bronze are the axes in the
Mycenæan deposits and the dagger of Enkomi.[4]
Why, then, did the late poetic interpolators, who knew
that the spears and swords of the old warriors were
of bronze, and who describe them as of bronze, not
know that their knives and axes were also of bronze ?
Why did they describe the old knives and axes as of
iron, while Hesiod knew, and could have told them—
did tell them, in fact—that they were of bronze ?
Clearly the theory that Homeric poets were archæological precisians is impossible. They describe arms
as of bronze, tools usually as of iron, because they
see them to be such in practice.

The poems, in fact, depict a very extraordinary
condition of affairs, such as no poets could invent
and adhere to with uniformity. We are accustomed
in archæology to seeing the bronze sword pass by a
gradual transition into the iron sword ; but, in Homer,
people with abundance of iron never, in any one

---

[1] *Early Age of Greece*, i. 413–416.   [2] *Iliad*, III. 271 ; XIX. 252.
[3] Tsountas and Manatt, p. 204.
[4] *Ibid.*, pp. 145, 207, 208, 256.   Evans, *Journal of the Anthropological
Institute*, vol xxx. p. 214.

specified case, use iron sword blades or spears. The greatest chiefs, men said to be rich in gold and *iron*, always use swords and spears of *bronze* in *Iliad* and *Odyssey*.

The usual process of transition from bronze to iron swords, in a prehistoric European age, is traced by Mr. Ridgeway at Hallstatt, "in the heart of the Austrian Alps," where a thousand old graves have been explored. The swords pass from bronze to iron with bronze hilts, and, finally, are wholly of iron. Weapons of bronze are fitted with iron edges. Axes of iron were much more common than axes of bronze.[1] The axes were fashioned in the old shapes of the age of bronze, were not of the *bipennis* Mycenæan model—the double axe —nor of the shape of the letter D, very thick, with two round apertures in the blade, like the bronze axe of Vaphio.[2] Probably the axes through which Odysseus shot an arrow were of this kind, as Mr. Monro, and, much earlier, Mr. Butcher and I have argued.[3]

At Hallstatt there was the *normal* evolution from bronze swords and axes to iron swords and axes. Why, then, had Homer's men in his time not made this step, seeing that they were familiar with the use of iron ? Why do they use bronze for swords and spears, iron for tools ? The obvious answer is that they could temper bronze for military purposes much better than they could temper iron. Now Mr. Ridgeway quotes Polybius (ii. 30 ; ii. 33) for the truly execrable quality of the iron of the Celtic invaders of Italy as late as

---

[1] *Early Age of Greece*, i. 413-416.

[2] Monro, *Odyssey*, vol. ii. 176.

[3] *Ibid.* (1901), vol. ii. Book XIX. line 572. Note. Butcher and Lang, *Odyssey*, Appendix (1891).

225 B.C. Their swords were as bad as, or worse than,
British bayonets ; they *always* " doubled up." " Their
long iron swords were easily bent, and could only give
one downward stroke with any effect ; but after this the
edges got so turned and the blades so bent that, unless
they had time to straighten them with the foot against
the ground, they could not deliver a second blow." [1]
If the heroes in Homer's time possessed iron as badly
tempered as that of the Celts of 225 B.C., they had every
reason to prefer, as they did, excellent bronze for all
their military weapons, while reserving iron for pacific
purposes. A woodcutter's axe might have any amount
of weight and thickness of iron behind the edge ; not so
a sword blade or a spear point.[2]

In the *Iliad* we hear of swords breaking at the hilt
in dealing a stroke at shield or helmet, a thing most
incident to bronze swords, especially of the early type,
with a thin bronze tang inserted in a hilt of wood,
ivory, or amber, or with a slight shelf of the bronze hilt
riveted with three nails on to the bronze blade.

Lycaon struck Peneleos on the socket of his helmet
crest, " and his sword brake at the hilt." [3] The sword
of Menelaus broke into three or four pieces when he

---

[1] *Early Age of Greece,* vol. i. 408.

[2] Monsieur Salomon Reinach suggests to me that the story of Polybius may
be a myth. Swords and spear-heads in graves are often found doubled up ;
possibly they are thus made *dead,* like the owner, and their spirits are thus set
free to be of use to his spirit. Finding doubled up iron swords in Celtic
graves, the Romans, M. Reinach suggests, may have explained their useless
condition by the theory that they doubled up in battle, leaving their owners
easy victims, and this myth was accepted as fact by Polybius. But he was
not addicted to myth, nor very remote from the events which he chronicles.
Again, though bronze grave-weapons in our Museum are often doubled up,
the myth is not told of the warriors of the age of bronze. We later give
examples of the doubling up, in battle, of Scandinavian iron swords as late
as 1000 A.D.

[3] *Iliad,* XVI. 339.

smote the helmet ridge of Paris.[1]   Iron of the Celtic
sort described by Polybius would have bent, not
broken.   There is no doubt on that head : if Polybius
is not romancing, the Celtic sword of 225 B.C. doubled
up at every stroke, like a piece of hoop iron.   But Mr.
Leaf tells us that, "by primitive modes of smelting,"
iron is made "hard and brittle, like cast iron."   If so,
it would be even less trustworthy for a sword than
bronze.[2]   Perhaps the Celts of 225 B.C. did not smelt
iron by primitive methods, but discovered some process
for making it not hard and brittle, but flabby.

The swords of the Mycenæan graves, we know,
were all of bronze, and, in three intaglios on rings from
the graves, the point, not the edge, is used,[3] once
against a lion, once over the rim of a shield which
covers the whole body of an enemy, and once at too
close quarters to permit the use of the edge.   It does
not follow from these three cases (as critics argue) that
no bronze sword could be used for a swashing blow,
and there are just half as many thrusts as strokes with
the bronze sword in the *Iliad*.[4]   As the poet constantly
dwells on the "long *edge*" of the *bronze* swords and
makes heroes use both point and edge, how can we
argue that Homeric swords were of *iron* and ill fitted
to give point ?   The Highlanders at Clifton (1746)
were obliged, contrary to their common practice, to
use the point against Cumberland's dragoons.   They,
like the Achæans, had heavy cut and thrust swords, but
theirs were of steel.

If the Achæans had thoroughly excellent bronze,

[1] *Iliad*, III. 349, 380.   [2] *Iliad* (1900), Book VI., line 48, Note.
[3] Tsountas and Manatt. p. 199.
[4] Twenty-four cuts to eleven lunges, in the *Iliad*.

and had iron as bad as that of the Celts a thousand
years later, their preference for bronze over iron for
weapons is explained. In Homer the fighters do not
very often come to sword strokes ; they fight mainly
with the spear, except in pursuit, now and then. But
when they do strike, they cleave heads and cut off arms.
They could not do this with bronze rapiers, such as
those with which men give point over the rim of the
shield on two Mycenæan gems. But Mr. Myres writes,
" From the shaft graves (of Mycenæ) onwards there are
two types of swords in the Mycenæan world—one an exaggerated dagger riveted into the front end of the hilt,
the other with a flat flanged tang running the whole
length of the hilt, and covered on either face by ornamental grip plates riveted on. This sword, though still
of bronze, can deal a very effective cut ; and, as the
Mycenæans had no armour for body or head," (?) " the
danger of breaking or bending the sword on a cuirass
or helmet did not arise." [1] The danger did exist in
Homer's time, as we have seen. But a bronze sword,
published by Tsountas and Manatt (*Mycenæan Age*,
p. 199, fig. 88), is emphatically meant to give both
point and edge, having a solid handle—a continuation
of the blade—and a very broad blade, coming to a very
fine point. Even in Grave V. at Mycenæ, we have a
sword blade so massive at the top that it was certainly
capable of a swashing blow.[2] The sword of the
charioteer on the *stêlê* of Grave V. is equally good for
cut and thrust. A pleasanter cut and thrust bronze
sword than the one found at Ialysus no gentleman
could wish to handle.[3]

[1] *Classical Review*, xvi. 72.
[2] Schuchardt, *Schliemann's Excavations*, p. 265, fig. 269.
[3] Furtwängler und Loeschke, *Myk. Va.* Taf. D.

Homer, in any case, says that his heroes used bronze swords, well adapted to strike. If his age had really good bronze, and iron as bad as that of the Celts of Polybius, a thousand years later, their preference of bronze over iron for weapons needs no explanation. If their iron was not so bad as that of the Celts, their military conservatism might retain bronze for weapons, while in civil life they often used iron for implements.

The uniform evidence of the Homeric poems can only be explained on the supposition that men had plenty of iron ; but, while they used it for implements, did not yet, with a natural conservatism, trust life and victory to iron spears and swords. Unluckily, we cannot test the temper of the earliest known iron swords found in Greece, for rust hath consumed them, and I know not that the temper of the Mycenæan bronze swords has been tested against helmets of bronze. I can thus give no evidence from experiment.

There is just one line in Homer which disregards the distinction—iron for implements, bronze for weapons ; it is in *Odyssey*, XVI. 294; XIX. 13. Telemachus is told to remove the warlike harness of Odysseus from the hall, lest the wooers use it in the coming fray. He is to explain the removal by saying that it has been done, " Lest you fall to strife in your cups, and harm each other, and shame the feast, *and this wooing ; for iron of himself draweth a man to him.*" The proverb is manifestly of an age when iron was almost universally used for weapons, and thus was, as in Thucydides, synonymous with all warlike gear ; but throughout the poems no single article of warlike gear is of iron except one eccentric mace and one arrow-head of

primitive type. The line in the *Odyssey* must therefore
be a very late addition ; it may be removed without
injuring the sense of the passage in which it occurs.[1]
If, on the other hand, the line be as old as the oldest
parts of the poem, the author for once forgets his usual
antiquarian precision.

We are thus led to the conclusion that either there
was in early Greece an age when weapons were all of
bronze while implements were often of iron, or that
the poet, or crowd of poets, invented that state of
things. Now early poets never invent in this way ;
singing to an audience of warriors, critical on such a
point, they speak of what the warriors know to be
actual, except when, in a recognised form of decorative
exaggeration, they introduce

> " Masts of the beaten gold
> And sails of taffetie."

Our theory is, then, that in the age when the
Homeric poems were composed iron, though well
known, was on its probation. Men of the sword preferred bronze for all their military purposes, just as
fifteenth-century soldiers found the long-bow and
cross-bow much more effective than guns, or as the
Duke of Wellington forbade the arming of all our men
with rifles in place of muskets . . . for reasons not
devoid of plausibility.

Sir John Evans supposes that, in the seventh century, the Carian and Ionian invaders of Egypt were
still using offensive arms of bronze, not of iron.[2] Sir

---

[1] This fact, in itself, is of course no proof of interpolation. *Cf.* Helbig,
op. cit., p. 331. He thinks the line very late.

[2] *Ancient Bronze Implements*, p. 8 (1881), citing Herodotus, ii. c. 112.
Sir John is not sure that Achæan spear-heads were not of *copper*, for they
twice double up against a shield. *Iliad*, III. 348 ; VII. 259 ; Evans, p. 13.

John remarks that "for a considerable time after the Homeric period, bronze remained in use for offensive weapons," especially for "spears, lances, and arrows." Hesiod, quite unlike his contemporaries, the "later" poets of *Iliad* and *Odyssey*, gives to Heracles an iron helmet and sword.[1] Hesiod knew better, but was not a consistent archaiser. Sir John thinks that as early as 500 or even 600 B.C. iron and steel were in common use for weapons in Greece, but not yet had they altogether superseded bronze battle-axes and spears.[2] By Sir John's showing, iron for offensive weapons superseded bronze very slowly indeed in Greece ; and, if my argument be correct, it had not done so when the Homeric poems were composed. Iron merely served for utensils, and the poems reflect that stage of transition which no poet could dream of inventing.

These pages had been written before my attention was directed to M. Bérard's book, *Les Phéniciens et l'Odyssée* (Paris, 1902). M. Bérard has anticipated and rather outrun my ideas. "I might almost say," he remarks, "that iron is the *popular* metal, native and rustic . . . the shepherd and ploughman can extract and work it without going to the town." The chief's smith could work iron, if he had iron to work, and this iron Achilles gave as a prize. "With rustic methods of working it iron is always impure ; it has 'straws' in it, and is brittle. It may be the metal for peace and for implements. In our fields we see the reaper sit down and repair his sickle. In war is needed a metal less hard, perhaps, but more tough and not so easily broken. You cannot sit down in the field of

---

[1] *Scutum Herculis*, pp. 122–138.   [2] Evans, p. 18.

battle, as in a field of barley, to beat your sword straight. . . ." [1]

So the Celts found, if we believe Polybius.

On the other hand, iron swords did supersede bronze swords in the long run. Apparently they had not done so in the age of the poet, but iron had certainly ceased to be " a precious metal " ; knives and woodcutters' axes are never made of a metal that is precious and rare. I am thus led, on a general view, to suppose that the poems took shape when iron was very well known, but was not yet, as in the " Dipylon " period in Crete, commonly used by sword-smiths.

The ideas here stated are not unlike those of Paul Cauer.[2] I do not, however, find the mentions of iron useful as a test of " early " and " late " lays, which it is his theory that they are. Thus he says :—

(1) Iron is often mentioned as part of a man's personal property, while we are not told how he means to use it. It is named with bronze, gold, and girls. The poet has no definite picture before his eyes ; he is vague about iron. But, we reply, his picture of iron in these passages is neither more nor less definite than his mental picture of the other commodities. He calls iron "hard to smithy," " grey," " dark-hued " ; he knows, in fact, all about it. He does not tell us what the owner is going to do with the gold and the bronze and the girls, any more than he tells us what is to be done with the iron. Such information was rather in the nature of a luxury than a necessity. Every hearer knew the uses of all four commodities. This does not seem to have occurred to Cauer.

---

[1] Bérard, i. 435.
[2] *Grundfrager des Homerkritik*, pp. 183-187. Leipsic, 1895.

(2) Iron is spoken of as an emblem of hard things, as, to take a modern example, in Mr. Swinburne's "armed and iron maidenhood"—said of Atalanta. Hearts are "iron," strength is "iron," flesh is not "iron," an "iron" noise goes up to the heaven of bronze. It may not follow, Cauer thinks, from these phrases that iron was *used* in any way. Men are supposed to marvel at its strange properties; it was "new and rare." I see no ground for this inference.

(3) We have the "iron gates" of Tartarus, and the "iron bonds" in which Odysseus was possibly lying; it does not follow that chains or gates were made of iron any more than that gates were of chrysoprase in the days of St. John.

(4) Next, we have mention of implements, not weapons, of iron—a remarkable trait of culture. Greek ploughs and axes were made of iron before spears and swords were of iron.

(5) We have mention of iron weapons, namely, the unique iron mace of Areithöus and the solitary iron arrow-head of Pandarus, and what Cauer calls the iron swords (more probably knives) of Achilles and others. It is objected to the "iron" of Achilles that Antilochus fears he will cut his throat with it on hearing of the death of Patroclus, while there is no other mention of suicide in the *Iliad*. It does not follow that suicide was unheard of; indeed, Achilles may be thinking of suicide presently, in XVIII. 98, when he says to his mother : "Let me die at once, since it was not my lot to succour my comrade."

(6) We have the iron-making spoken of in Book IX. 393 of the *Odyssey*.

It does not appear to us that the use of iron as an

epithet bespeaks an age when iron was a mysterious thing, known mainly by reputation, "a costly possession." The epithets "iron strength," and so on, may as readily be used in our own age or any other. If iron were at first a "precious" metal, it is odd that Homeric men first used it, as Cauer sees that they did, to make points to ploughshares and "tools of agriculture and handiwork." "Then people took to working iron for weapons." Just so, but we cannot divide the *Iliad* into earlier and later portions in proportion to the various mentions of iron in various Books. These statistics are of no value for separatist purposes. It is impossible to believe that men when they spoke of "iron strength," "iron hearts," "grey iron," "iron hard to smithy," did so because iron was, first, an almost unknown legendary mineral, next, "a precious metal," then the metal of drudgery, and finally the metal of weapons.

The real point of interest is, as Cauer sees, that domestic preceded military uses of iron among the Achæans. He seems, however, to think that the confinement of the use of bronze to weapons is a matter of traditional style.[1] But, in the early days of the waxing epics, tools as well as weapons were, as in Homer they occasionally are, of bronze. Why, then, do the supposed late continuators represent tools, not weapons, as of iron ? Why do they not cleave to the traditional term—bronze—in the case of tools, as the same men do in the case of weapons ?

Helbig offers an apparently untenable explanation

[1] " Nur die Sprache des Dichter hielt an dem Gebrauch der Bronze fest, die in der Jahrhunderten, wahrend deren der Epische Stil erwachsen war, allein geherrscht hatte."

of this fact.   He has proposed an interpretation of the
uses of bronze and iron in the poems entirely different
from that which I offer.[1]   Unfortunately, one can
scarcely criticise his theory without entering again into
the whole question of the construction of the Epics.
He thinks that the origin of the poems dates from
" the Mycenæan period," and that the later continuators
of the poems retained the traditions of that remote age.
Thus they thrice call Mycenæ " golden," though, in
the changed economic conditions of their own period,
Mycenæ could no longer be " golden " ; and I presume
that, if possible, the city would have issued a papyrus
currency without a metallic basis.   However this may
be, " in the description of customs the epic poets did
their best to avoid everything modern."   Here we have
again that unprecedented phenomenon — early poets
who are archæologically precise.

We have first to suppose that the kernel of the *Iliad*
originated in the Mycenæan age, the age of bronze.
We are next to believe that this kernel was expanded
into the actual Epic in later and changed times, but that
the later poets adhered in their descriptions to the
Mycenæan standard, avoiding " everything modern."
That poets of an uncritical period, when treating of the
themes of ancient legend or song, carefully avoid everything modern is an opinion not warranted by the usage
of the authors of the *Chansons de Geste*, of *Beowulf*, and
of the *Nibelungenlied*.   These poets, we must repeat,
invariably introduce in their chants concerning ancient
days the customs, costume, armour, religion, and
weapons of their own time.   Dr. Helbig supposes
that the late Greek poets, however, who added to the

[1] *Sur la Question Mycénienne.*   1896.

Iliad, carefully avoided doing what other poets of uncritical ages have always done.[1]

This is his position in his text (p. 50). In his note 1 to page 50, however, he occupies the precisely contrary position. "The epic poems were chanted, as a rule, in the houses of more or less warlike chiefs. It is, then, *à priori* probable that the later poets took into account the *contemporary* military state of things. Their audience would have been much perturbed (*bien choqués*) if they had heard the poet mention nothing but arms and forms of attack and defence to which they were unaccustomed." If so, when iron weapons came in the poets would substitute iron for bronze, in lays new and old, but they never do. However, this is Helbig's opinion in his note. But in his text he says that the poets, carefully avoiding the con-temporary, "the modern," make the heroes fight, not on horseback, but from chariots. Their listeners, according to his note, must have been *bien choqués,* for there came a time when *they* were not accustomed to war chariots.

Thus the poets who, in Dr. Helbig's *text,* "avoid as far as possible all that is modern," in his *note,* on the same page, "take account of the contemporary state of things," and are as modern as possible where weapons are concerned. "Their audience would be sadly put out" (*bien choqués*) "if they heard talk only of arms . . . to which they were unaccustomed"; talk of large suspended shields, of uncorsleted heroes, and of bronze weapons. They had to endure it, whether they liked it or not, *teste* Reichel. Dr. Helbig seems to speak correctly in his note; in his text his contradictory

---

[1] *La Question Mycénienne,* p. 50.

opinion appears to be wrong. Experience teaches us that the poets of an uncritical age—Shakespeare, for example—introduce the weapons of their own period into works dealing with remote ages. Hamlet uses the Elizabethan rapier.

In his argument on bronze and iron, unluckily, Dr. Helbig deserts the judicious opinions of his note for the opposite theory of his text. His late poets, in the age of iron, always say that the weapons of the heroes are made of bronze.[1] They thus, "as far as possible avoid what is modern." But, of course, warriors of the age of iron, when they heard the poet talk only of weapons of bronze, " *auraient été bien choqués* " (as Dr. Helbig truly says in his note), on hearing of nothing but " *armes auxquels ils n'étaient pas habitués,*"—arms always of bronze.

Though Dr. Helbig in his text is of the opposite opinion, I must agree entirely with the view which he states so clearly in his note. It follows that if a poet speaks invariably of weapons of bronze, he is living in an age when weapons are made of no other material.

In his text, however, Dr Helbig maintains that the poets of later ages "as far as possible avoid everything modern," and, therefore, mention none but bronze weapons. But, as he has pointed out, they *do* mention iron tools and implements. Why do they desert the traditional bronze? Because "it occasionally happened that a poet, when thinking of an entirely new subject, wholly emancipated himself from traditional forms."[2]

The examples given in proof are the offer by Achilles of a lump of iron as the prize for archery—the iron, as we saw, being destined for the manufacture

---

[1] *Op. laud.*, p. 51.   [2] *Op. laud.*, pp. 51, 52.

of pastoral and agricultural implements, in which Dr. Helbig includes the lances of shepherds and plough-men, though the poet never says that they were of iron.[1] There are also the axes through which Odysseus shoots his arrow.[2] "The poet here treated an entirely new subject, in the development of which he had perfect liberty." So he speaks freely of iron. "But," we exclaim, "tools and implements, axes and knives, are not a perfectly new subject!" They were ex-tremely familiar to the age of bronze, the Mycenæan age. Examples of bronze tools, arrow-heads, and im-plements are discovered in excavations on Mycenæan sites. There was nothing new about bronze tools and implements. Men had bronze tips to their plough-shares, bronze knives, bronze axes, bronze arrow-heads before they used iron.

Perhaps we are to understand that feats of archery, non-military contests in bowmanship, are *un sujet tout à fait nouveau :* a theme so very modern that a poet, in singing of it, could let himself go, and dare to speak of iron implements. But where was the novelty? All peoples who use the bow in war practise archery in time of peace. The poet, moreover, speaks of bronze tools, axes and knives, in other parts of the *Iliad ;* neither tools nor bronze tools constitute *un sujet tout à fait nouveau.* There was nothing new in shooting with a bow and nothing new in the existence of axes. Bows and axes were as familiar to the age of stone and to the age of bronze as to the age of iron. Dr. Helbig's explanation, therefore, explains nothing, and, unless a better explanation is offered, we return to the theory,

---

[1] *Iliad*, XXIII. 826, 835; *Odyssey*, XIV. 531 ; XIII. 225.
[2] *Odyssey*, XIX. 587 ; XXI. 3, 81, 97, 114, 127, 138; XXIV. 168, 177 ; *cf.* XXI. 61.

rejected by Dr. Helbig, that implements and tools were often, not always, of iron, while weapons were of bronze in the age of the poet. Dr. Helbig rejects this opinion. He writes : " We cannot in any way admit that, at a period when the socks of the plough, the lance points of shepherds " (which the poet never describes as of iron), " and axe-heads were of iron, warriors still used weapons of bronze."[1] But it is logically possible to admit that this was the real state of affairs, while it is logically impossible to admit that bows and tools were " new subjects " ; and that late poets, when they sang of military gear, " *tenaient compte de l'armement contemporain*," carefully avoiding the peril of bewildering their hearers by speaking of antiquated arms, and, at the same time, spoke of nothing but antiquated arms— weapons of bronze—and of war chariots, to fighting men who did not use war chariots and did use weapons of iron.

These logical contradictions beset all arguments in which it is maintained that " the late poets " are anxious archaisers, and at the same time are eagerly introducing the armour and equipment of their own age. The critics are in the same quandary as to iron and bronze as traps them in the case of large shields, small bucklers, greaves, and corslets. They are obliged to assign contradictory attitudes to their " late poets." It does not seem possible to admit that a poet, who often describes axes as of iron in various passages, does so in his account of a peaceful contest in bowmanship, because contests in bowmanship are *un sujet tout à fait nouveau ;* and so he feels at liberty to describe axes as of iron, while he adheres to bronze as the metal for

[1] *Op. laud.*, p. 53.

weapons. He, or one of the Odyssean poets, had
already asserted (*Odyssey*, IX. 391) that iron *was* the
metal for adzes and axes.

Dr. Helbig's argument [1] does not explain the facts.
The bow of Eurytus and the uses to which Odysseus
is to put it have been in the poet's mind all through
the conduct of his plot, and there is nothing to suggest
that the exploit of bowmanship is a very new lay,
tacked on to the *Odyssey*.

After writing this chapter, I observed that my
opinion had been anticipated by S. H. Naber.[2] " Quod
Herodoti diserto testimonio novimus, Homeri æstate
ferruminatio nondum inventa erat necdum bene noverant
mortales, uti opinor, *acuere* ferrum. Hinc pauperes
homines ubi possunt, ferro utuntur ; sed in plerisque
rebus tum domi tum militiæ imprimis coguntur uti
ære . . . ."

The theory of Mr. Ridgeway as to the relative uses
of iron and bronze is not, by myself, very easily to
be understood. " The Homeric warrior . . . . has
regularly, as we have seen, spear and sword of iron." [3]
As no spear or sword of iron is ever mentioned in the
Iliad or *Odyssey*, as both weapons are always of bronze
when the metal is specified, I have not " seen " that
they are " regularly," or ever, of iron. In proof,
Mr. Ridgeway cites the axes and knives already mentioned—which are not spears or swords, and are sometimes of bronze. He also quotes the line in the *Odyssey*,
" Iron of itself doth attract a man." But if this line
is genuine and original, it does not apply to the state
of things in the *Iliad*, while it contradicts the whole

---

[1] *La Question Mycénienne*, p. 54.

[2] *Quæstiones Homericæ*, p. 60. Amsterdam. Van der Post, 1897.

[3] *Early Age of Greece*, vol. i. p. 301.

Odyssey, in which swords and spears are *always* of bronze when their metal is mentioned. If the line reveals the true state of things, then throughout the *Odyssey*, if not throughout the *Iliad*, the poets when they invariably speak of bronze swords and spears invariably say what they do not mean. If they do this, how are we to know when they mean what they say, and of what value can their evidence on points of culture be reckoned? They may always be retaining traditional terms as to usages and customs in an age when these are obsolete.

If the Achæans were, as in Mr. Ridgeway's theory, a northern people—" Celts "—who conquered with iron weapons a Pelasgian bronze-using Mycenæan people, it is not credible to me that Achæan or Pelasgian poets habitually used the traditional Pelasgian term for the metal of weapons, namely, bronze, in songs chanted before victors who had won their triumph with iron. The traditional phrase of a conquered bronze-using race could not thus survive and flourish in the poetry of an outlandish iron-using race of conquerors.

Mr. Ridgeway cites the *Odyssey*, wherein we are told that " Euryalus, the Phæacian, presented to Odysseus a bronze sword, though, as we have seen " (Mr. Ridgeway has seen), " the usual material for all such weapons is iron. But the Phæacians both belonged to the older race and lived in a remote island, and therefore swords of bronze may well have continued in use in such out-of-the-world places long after iron swords were in use everywhere else in Greece. The man who could not afford iron had to be satisfied with bronze." [1]

---

[1] *Early Age of Greece*, p. 305.

Here the poet is allowed to mean what he says.
The Phæacian sword is really of bronze, with silver
studs, probably on the hilt (*Odyssey*, VIII. 401–407),
which was of ivory.   The " out-of-the-world " islanders
could afford ivory, not iron.   But when the same poet
tells us that the sword which Odysseus brought from
Troy was "a great silver - studded bronze sword"
(*Odyssey*, X. 261, 262), then Mr. Ridgeway does not
allow the poet to mean what he says.   The poet is now
using an epic formula older than the age of iron
swords.

That Mr. Ridgeway adopts Helbig's theory—the poet
says " bronze," by a survival of the diction of the bronze
age, when he means iron—I infer from the following
passage : " *Chalkos* is the name for the older metal, of
which *cutting* weapons were made, and it thus lingered
in many phrases of the Epic dialect ; ' to smite with the
chalkos ' was equivalent to our phrase ' to smite with the
steel.' " [1]   But we certainly do smite with the steel,
while the question is, " *Did* Homer's men smite with
the iron ? "   Homer says not ; he does not merely use
" an epic phrase " " to smite with the *chalkos*," but he
carefully describes swords, spears, and usually arrow-
heads as being of bronze (*chalkos*), while axes, adzes,
and knives are frequently described by him as of
iron.

Mr. Ridgeway has an illustrative argument with
some one, who says : " The dress and weapons of the
Saxons given in the lay of *Beowulf* fitted exactly the
bronze weapons in England, for they had shields, and
spears, and battle-axes, and swords."   If you pointed
out to him that the Saxon poem spoke of these weapons

[1] *Early Age of Greece*, i. 295.

as made of iron, he would say, " I admit that it is a difficulty, but the resemblances are so many that the discrepancies may be jettisoned." [1]

Now, if the supposed controversialist were a Homeric critic, he would not admit any difficulty. He would say, " Yes ; in *Beowulf* the weapons are said to be of iron, but that is the work of the Christian *remanieur*, or *bearbeiter*, who introduced all the Christian morality into the old heathen lay, and who also, not to puzzle his iron-using audience, changed the bronze into iron weapons."

We may prove anything if we argue, now that the poets retain the tradition of obsolete things, now that they modernise as much as they please. Into this method of reasoning, after duly considering it, I am unable to come with enthusiasm, being wedded to the belief that the poets say what they mean. Were it otherwise, did they not mean what they say, their evidence would be of no value ; they might be dealing throughout in terms for things which were unrepresented in their own age. To prove this possible, it would be necessary to adduce convincing and sufficient examples of early national poets who habitually use the terminology of an age long prior to their own in descriptions of objects, customs, and usages.

Meanwhile, it is obvious that my whole argument has no archæological support. We may find " Mycenæan " corslets and greaves, but they are not in cremation burials. No Homeric cairn with Homeric contents has ever been discovered ; and if we did find examples of Homeric cairns, it appears, from the poems, that they would very seldom contain the arms of the dead.

[1] *Ridgeway*, i. 83, 84.

Nowhere, again, do we find graves containing bronze swords and iron axes and adzes. I know nothing nearer in discoveries to my supposed age of bronze weapons and iron tools than a grave of the early iron and geometrical ornament age of Crete—a *tholos* tomb, with a bronze spear-head and a set of iron tools, among others a double axe and a pick of iron. But these were in company with iron swords.[1] To myself the crowning mystery is, what has become of the Homeric tumuli with their contents ? One can but say that only within the last thirty years have we found, or, finding, have recognised Mycenæan burial records. As to the badness of the iron of the North for military purposes, and the probable badness of all early iron weapons, we have testimony two thousand years later than Homer and some twelve hundred years later than Polybius. In the Eyrbyggja Saga (Morris and Maguússon, chap. xxiv.) we read that Steinthor " was girt with a sword that was cunningly wrought ; the hilts were white with silver, and the grip wrapped round with the same, but the strings thereof were gilded." This was a splendid sword, described with the Homeric delight in such things ; but the battle-cry arises, and then " the fair-wrought sword bit not when it smote armour, and Steinthor *must straighten it under his foot.*" Messrs. Morris and Maguússon add in a note : " This is a very common experience in Scandinavian weapons, and for the first time heard of at the battle of Aquæ Sextiæ between Marius and the Teutons."[2] " In the North weapon-smiths who knew how to forge tempered or steel-laminated weapons were, if not unknown, at

1 *Journal of Hellenic Studies*, xix. 320. 1897.
2 The reference is erroneous.

least very rare." When such skill was unknown or rare in Homer's time, nothing was more natural than that bronze should hold its own, as the metal for swords and spears, after iron was commonly used for axes and ploughshares.

CHAPTER X

THE HOMERIC HOUSE

IF the Homeric poems be, as we maintain, the work of a peculiar age, the Homeric house will also, in all likelihood, be peculiar. It will not be the Hellenic house of classical times. Manifestly the dwelling of a military prince in the heroic age would be evolved to meet his needs, which were not the needs of later Hellenic citizens. In time of peace the later Greeks are weaponless men, not surrounded by and entertaining throngs of armed retainers, like the Homeric chief. The women of later Greece, moreover, are in the background of life, dwelling in the women's chambers, behind those of the men, in seclusion. The Homeric women also, at least in the house of Odysseus, have their separate chambers, which the men seem not to enter except on invitation, though the ladies freely honour by their presence the hall of the warriors. The circumstances, however, were peculiar—Penelope being unprotected in the absence of her lord.

The whole domestic situation in the Homeric poems—the free equality of the women, the military conditions, the life of the chiefs and retainers—closely resembles, allowing for differences of climate, that of the rich landowners of early Iceland as described in the sagas. There can be no doubt that the house of the Icelandic chief was analogous to the

O

house of the Homeric prince. Societies remarkably
similar in mode of life were accommodated in dwellings
similarly arranged. Though the Icelanders owned no
Over-Lord, and, indeed, left their native Scandinavia
to escape the sway of Harold Fairhair, yet each
wealthy and powerful chief lived in the manner of a
Homeric "king." His lands and thralls, horses and
cattle, occupied his attention when he did not chance
to be on Viking adventure—"bearing bane to alien
men." He always carried sword and spear, and often
had occasion to use them. He entertained many
guests, and needed a large hall and ample sleeping
accommodation for strangers and servants. His women
were as free and as much respected as the ladies in
Homer ; and for a husband to slap a wife was to run
the risk of her deadly feud. Thus, far away in the
frosts of the north, the life of the chief was like that
of the Homeric prince, and their houses were alike.

It is our intention to use this parallel in the discussion of the Homeric house. All Icelandic chiefs'
houses in the tenth and eleventh centuries were not
precisely uniform in structure and accommodation, and
saga writers of the twelfth and thirteenth centuries,
living more comfortably than their forefathers, sometimes confuse matters by introducing the arrangements
of their own into the tale of past times. But, in
any case, one Icelandic house of the tenth or eleventh
century might differ from another in certain details.
It is not safe, therefore, to argue that difference of
detail in Homer's accounts of various houses means
that the varying descriptions were composed in different
ages. In the *Odyssey* the plot demands that the poet
must enter into domestic details much more freely than

he ever has occasion to do in the *Iliad*. He may mention upper chambers freely, for example ; it will not follow that in the *Iliad* upper chambers do not exist because they are only mentioned twice in that Epic.

It is even more important to note that in the house of Odysseus we have an unparalleled domestic situation. The lady of the house is beset by more than a hundred wooers—"sorning" on her, in the old Scots legal phrase—making it impossible for her to inhabit her own hall, and desirable to keep the women as much as possible apart from the men. Thus the Homeric house of which we know most, that of Odysseus, is a house in a most abnormal condition.

For the sake of brevity we omit the old theory that the Homeric house was practically that of historical Greece, with the men's hall approached by a door from the courtyard ; while a door at the upper end of the men's hall yields direct access to the quarters where the women dwelt apart, at the rear of the men's hall.

That opinion has not survived the essay by Mr. J. L. Myres on the "Plan of the Homeric House."[1] Quite apart from arguments that rest on the ground plans of palaces at Mycenæ and Tiryns, Mr. Myres has proved, by an exact reading of the poet's words, that the descriptions in the *Odyssey* cannot be made intelligible on the theory that the poet has in his mind a house of the Hellenic pattern. But in his essay he hardly touches on any Homeric house except that of Odysseus, in which the circumstances were unusual. A later critic, Ferdinand Noack, has demonstrated that we must take other Homeric houses into consideration.[2]

[1] *Journal of Hellenic Studies*, vol. xx. 128–150.
[2] *Homerische Paläste*. Teubner. Leipzig, 1903.

The præ-Mycenæan house is, according to Mr. Myres, on the whole of the same plan as the Hellenic house of historic days; between these comes the Mycenæan and Homeric house; "so that the Mycenæan house stands out *as an intrusive phenomenon*, of comparatively late arrival *and short of duration* . . ."[1] Noack goes further; he draws a line between the Mycenæan houses on one hand and the houses described by Homer on the other; while he thinks that the "*late* Homeric house," that of the closing Books of the *Odyssey*, is widely sundered from the Homeric house of the *Iliad* and from the houses of Menelaus and Alcinous in earlier Books of the *Odyssey*.[2]

In this case the Iliadic and earlier Odyssean houses are those of a single definite age, neither Mycenæan of the prime, nor Hellenic—a fact which entirely suits our argument. But it is not so certain, that the house of Odysseus is severed from the other Homeric houses by the later addition of an upper storey, as Noack supposes, and of women's quarters, and of separate sleeping chambers for the heads of the family.

The *Iliad*, save in two passages, and earlier Books of the *Odyssey* may not mention upper storeys because they have no occasion, or only rare occasion, to do so; and some houses may have had upper sleeping chambers while others of the same period had not, as we shall prove from the Icelandic parallel.

Mr. Myres's idea of the Homeric house, or, at least, of the house of Odysseus, is that the women had a μέγαρον, or common hall, apart from that of the men, with other chambers. These did not lie to the direct

---

[1] Myres, *Journal of Hellenic Studies*, vol. xx. p. 149.
[2] Noack, p. 73.

rear of the men's hall, nor were they entered by a door that opened in the back wall of the men's hall. Penelope has a chamber, in which she sleeps and does woman's work, upstairs ; her connubial chamber, unoccupied during her lord's absence, is certainly on the ground floor. The women's rooms are severed from the men's hall by a courtyard ; in the courtyard are chambers. Telemachus has his θάλαμος, or chamber, in the men's courtyard. All this appears plain from the poet's words ; and Mr. Myres corroborates, by the ground plans of the palaces of Tiryns and Mycenæ, a point on which Mr. Monro had doubts, as regards Tiryns, while he accepted it for Mycenæ.[1]

Noack[2] does not, however, agree.

There appears to be no doubt that in the centre of the great halls of Tiryns and of Mycenæ, as of the houses in Homer, was the hearth, with two tall pillars on each side, supporting a *louvre* higher than the rest of the roof, and permitting some, at least, of the smoke of the fire to escape. Beside the fire were the seats of the master and mistress of the house, of the minstrel, and of honoured guests. The place of honour was not on a dais at the inmost end of the hall, like the high table in college halls. Mr. Myres holds that in the Homeric house the πρόδομος, or "forehouse," was a chamber, and was not identical with the αἴθουσα, or portico, though he admits that the two words "are used indifferently to describe the sleeping place of a guest."[3] This was the case at Tiryns ; and in the house of the father of Phœnix, in the *Iliad*, the *prodomos*, or forehouse, and the *aethousa*, or portico, are certainly separate things

---

[1] Monro, *Odyssey*, ii. 497 ; *Journal of Hellenic Studies*, xx. 136.
[2] Noack, p. 39.
[3] *Journal of Hellenic Studies*, xx. 144, 155.

(*Iliad*, IX. 473). Noack does not accept the Tiryns evidence for the Homeric house.

On Mr. Myres's showing, the women in the house of Odysseus had distinct and separate quarters into which no man goes uninvited. Odysseus when at home has, with his wife, a separate bedroom; and in his absence Penelope sleeps upstairs, where there are several chambers for various purposes.

Granting that all this is so, how do the pictures of the house given in the final part of the *Odyssey* compare with those in the *Iliad*, and with the accounts of the dwellings of Menelaus and Alcinous in the *Odyssey*? Noack argues that the house of Odysseus is unlike the other Homeric houses, because in these, he reasons, the women have no separate quarters, and the lord and lady of the house sleep in the great hall, and have no other bedroom, while there are no upper chambers in the houses of the *Iliad*, except in two passages dismissed as "late."

If all this be so, then the Homeric period, as regards houses and domestic life, belongs to an age apart, not truly Mycenæan, and still less later Hellenic.

It must be remembered that Noack regards the *Odyssey* as a composite and in parts very late mosaic (a view on which I have said what I think in *Homer and the Epic*). According to this theory (Kirchhoff is the exponent of a popular form thereof) the first Book of the *Odyssey* belongs to "the latest stratum," and is the "copy" of the general "worker-up," whether he was the editor employed by Pisistratus or a laborious amateur. This theory is opposed by Sittl, who makes his point by cutting out, as interpolations, whatever passages do not suit his ideas, and do suit Kirchhoff's—this is the

regular method of Homeric criticism.   The whole cruise
of Telemachus (Book IV.) is also regarded as a late
addition : on this point English scholars hitherto have
been of the opposite opinion.[1]

The method of all parties is to regard repetitions of
phrases as examples of borrowing, except, of course, in
the case of the earliest poet from whom the others
pilfer, and in other cases of prae-Homeric surviving
epic formulæ. Critics then dispute as to which recurrent passage *is* the earlier, deciding, of course, as may
happen to suit their own general theory.   In our opinion
these passages are traditional formulæ, as in our own
old ballads and in the *Chansons de Geste,* and Noack also
takes this view every now and then.   They may well
be older, in many cases, than *Iliad* and *Odyssey* ; or
the poet, having found his own formula, economically
used it wherever similar circumstances occurred.   Such
passages, so considered, are no tests of earlier composition in one place, of later composition in another.

We now look into Noack's theory of the Homeric
house.   Where do the lord and lady sleep ? *Not,* he
says, as Odysseus and Penelope do (when Odysseus
is at home), in a separate chamber (θάλαμος) on the
ground floor, nor, like Gunnar and Halgerda (Njal's
Saga), in an upper chamber.   They sleep μυχῷ δόμου
ὑψηλοῖο ; that is, not in a separate recess in the *house,*
but in a recess of the great *hall,* or μέγαρον.   Thus, in
the hall of Alcinous, the whole space runs from the
threshold to the μυχός, the innermost part (*Odyssey,*
VII. 87–96).   In the hall of Odysseus, the Wooers retreat
to the μυχός, " the innermost part of the hall " (*Odyssey,*
XXII. 270).   " The μυχός, in Homer, never denotes a

[1] *Cf.* Monro, *Odyssey,* vol. ii. 313–317.

separate chamber." [1]   In *Odyssey*, XI. 373, Alcinous says
it is not yet time to sleep ἐν μεγάρῳ, "in the hall."
Alcinous and Arete, his wife, sleep "in the recess of the
lofty δόμος," that is, in the recess of the *hall*, not of "the
house" (*Odyssey*, VII. 346).   The same words are used
of Helen and Menelaus (*Odyssey*, IV. 304).   But
when Menelaus goes forth next morning, he goes ἐκ
θαλάμοιο, "out of his *chamber*" (*Odyssey*, IV. 310).   But
this, says Noack, is a mere borrowing of *Odyssey*, II. 2–5,
where the same words are used of Telemachus, leaving
his chamber, which undeniably was a separate chamber
in the court: Eurycleia lighted him thither at night
(*Odyssey*, I. 428).   In *Odyssey*, IV. 121, Helen enters the
hall "from her fragrant, lofty chamber," so she *had* a
chamber, not in the hall.   But, says Noack, this verse
"is not original."   The late poet of *Odyssey*, IV. has
cribbed it from the early poet who composed *Odyssey*,
XIX. 53.   In that passage Penelope "comes from her
chamber, like Artemis or golden Aphrodite."   Penelope
had a chamber—being "a lone lorn woman," who could
not sleep in a hall where the Wooers sat up late drink-
ing—and the latest poet transfers this chamber to Helen.
But however late and larcenous he may have been, the
poet of IV. 121 certainly did not crib the words of the
poet of XIX. 53, for he says, "Helen came out of her
fragrant, high-roofed chamber."   The *hall* was not precisely "fragrant"!   However, Noack supposes that the
late poet of Book IV. let Helen have a chamber apart,
to lead up to the striking scene of her entry to the hall
where her guests are sitting.   May Helen not even have
a boudoir?   In *Odyssey*, IV. 263, Helen speaks remorse-
fully of having abandoned her "chamber," and husband,

---

[1] Noack, p. 45. *Cf.* Monro, Note to *Odyssey*, XXII. 270.

and child, with Paris ; but the late poet says this, according to Noack, because he finds that he is in for a chamber, so to speak, at all events, as a result of his having previously cribbed the word "chamber" from *Odyssey*, XIX. 53. Otherwise, we presume Helen would have said that she regretted having left "the recess of the lofty hall" where she really did sleep.[1]

The merit of this method of arguing may be left to the judgment of the reader, who will remark that wedded pairs are not described as leaving the hall when they go to bed ; they sleep in "a recess of the lofty house," the innermost part. Is this the same as the "recess of the *hall*," or is it an innermost part of the *house*? Who can be certain ?

The bridal chamber, built so cunningly, with the trunk of a tree for the support of the bed, by Odysseus (*Odyssey*, XXIII. 177-204), is, according to Noack, an exception, a solitary freak of Odysseus. But we may reply that the θάλαμος, the separate chamber, is no freak ; the freak, by knowledge of which Odysseus proves his identity, is the use of the tree in the construction of the bed. *That* was highly original.

That separate chambers are needed for grown-up children, *because* the parents sleep in the hall, is no strong argument. If the parents had a separate chamber, the young people, unless they slept in the hall, would still need their own. The girls, of course, could not sleep in the hall ; and, in the absence of both Penelope and Odysseus from the hall, ever since Telemachus was a baby, Telemachus could have slept there. But it will be replied that the Wooers did not beset the hall, and Penelope did not retire to a separate chamber,

[1] Noack, pp. 47-48

till Telemachus was a big boy of sixteen. Noack argues
that he had a separate chamber, though the hall was
free, *in deference to tradition.*[1]

Where does Noack think that, in a normal Homeric
house, the girls of the family slept? *They* could not
sleep in the hall, and on the two occasions when the *Iliad*
has to mention the chambers of the young ladies they
are "upper chambers," as is natural. But as Noack
wants to prove the house of Odysseus, with its upper
chambers, to be a late peculiar house, he, of course,
expunges the two mentions of girls' upper chambers
in the *Odyssey.* The process is simple and easy.

We find (*Iliad,* XVII. 36) that a son, wedding
in his father's and mother's life-time, has a *thalamos*
built for him, and a μυχός in the *thalamos,* where
he leaves his wife when he goes to war. This
dwelling of grown-up married children, as in the
case of the sons of Priam, has a θάλαμος, or δῶμα,
and a courtyard—is a house, in fact (*Iliad,* VI. 316).
Here we seem to distinguish the bed-chamber from
the δῶμα, which is the hall. Noack objects that
when Odysseus fumigates his house, after slaying the
Wooers, he thus treats the μέγαρον, *and* the δῶμα, *and*
the courtyard. Therefore, Noack argues, the μέγαρον,
or hall, is one thing; the δῶμα is another. Mr. Monro
writes, "δῶμα usually means μέγαρον," and he supposes
a slip from another reading, θάλαμον for μέγαρον, which
is not satisfactory. But if δῶμα here be not equivalent
to μέγαρον, what room can it possibly be? Who was
killed in another place? what place therefore needed
purification except the hall and courtyard? No other
places needed purifying; there is therefore clearly a

[1] Noack, p. 49.

defect in the lines which cannot be used in the argument.

Noack, in any case, maintains that Paris has but one place to live in by day and to sleep in by night— his θάλαμος. There he sleeps, eats, and polishes his weapons and armour. There Hector finds him looking to his gear ; Helen and the maids are all there (*Iliad*, VI. 321–323). Is this quite certain ? Are Helen and the maids in the *thalamos*, where Paris is polishing his corslet and looking to his bow, or in an adjacent room ? If not in another room, why, when Hector is in the room talking to Paris, does Helen ask him to "come in"? (*Iliad*, VI. 354). He *is* in, is there another room whence she can hear him ?

The minuteness of these inquiries is tedious !

In *Iliad*, III. 125, Iris finds Helen "in the hall" weaving. She summons her to come to Priam on the gate. Helen dresses in outdoor costume, and goes forth "from the chamber," θάλαμος (III. 141–142). Are hall and chamber the same room, or did not Helen *dress* "in the chamber"? In the same Book (III. 174) she repents having left the θάλαμος of Menelaus, not his hall : the passage is not a repetition in words of her speech in the *Odyssey*.

The gods, of course, are lodged like men. When we find that Zeus has really a separate sleeping chamber, built by Hephæstus, as Odysseus has (*Iliad*, XIV. 166–167), we are told that this is a late interpolation. Mr. Leaf, who has a high opinion of this scene, "the Beguiling of Zeus," places it in the "second expansions"; he finds no "late Odyssean" elements in the language. In *Iliad*, I. 608–611, Zeus "departed to his couch " ; he seems not to have stayed and slept in the hall.

Here a quaint problem occurs. Of all late things in the *Odyssey* the latest is said to be the song of Demodocus about the loves of Ares and Aphrodite in the house of Hephæstus.[1] We shall show that this opinion is far from certainly correct. Hephæstus sets a snare round the bed in his *thalamos*, and catches the guilty lovers. Now, was his *thalamos*, or bed-room, also his dining-room ? If so, the author of the song, though so "late," knows what Noack knows, and what the poets who assign sleeping chambers to wedded folks do not know, namely, that neither married gods nor married men have separate bed-rooms. This is plain, for he makes Hephæstus stand at the front door of his house, and shout to the gods to come and see the sinful lovers.[2] They all come and look on *from the front door* (*Odyssey*, VIII. 325), which leads into the μέγαρον, the hall. If the lovers are in bed in the hall, then hall and bedroom are all one, and the terribly late poet who made this lay knows it, though the late poets of the *Odyssey* and *Iliad* do not.

It would appear that the author of the lay is not "late," as we shall prove in another case.

Noack, then, will not allow man or god to have a separate wedding chamber, nor women, before the late parts of the *Odyssey*, to have separate quarters, except in the house of Odysseus. Women's chambers do not exist in the Homeric house.[3] If so, how remote is the true Homeric house from the house of historical Greece !

[1] *Odyssey*, VIII. 266–300.   [2] *Ibid.*, VI. 304–305.
[3] Noack, p. 50.

As for upper chambers, those of the daughter of the house (*Iliad*, II. 514 ; XVI. 184), both passages are "late," as we saw (Noack, p. 56). In the *Odyssey* Penelope both sleeps and works at the shroud in an upper chamber. But the whole arrangement of upper chambers as women's apartments is as late, says Noack, as the time of the poets and "redactors" (whoever they may have been) of the *Odyssey*, XXI., XXII., XXIII.[1] At the earliest these Books are said to be of the eighth century B.C. Here the late poets have their innings at last, and do modernise the Homeric house.

To prove the absence of upper rooms in the *Iliad* we have to abolish II. 514, where Astyoche meets her divine lover in her upper chamber, and XVI. 184, where Polymêlê celebrates her amour with Hermes "in the upper chambers." The places where these two passages occur, *Catalogue* (Book II.) and the *Catalogue of the Myrmidons* (Book XVI.) are, indeed, both called "late," but the author of the latter knows the early law of bride-price, which is supposed to be unknown to the authors of "late" passages in the *Odyssey* (XVI. 190).

Stated briefly, such are the ideas of Noack. They leave us, at least, with permission to hold that the whole of the Epics, except Books XXI., XXII., and XXIII. of the *Odyssey*, bear, as regards the house, the marks of a distinct peculiar age, coming between the period of Mycenæ and Tiryns on one hand and the eighth century B.C. on the other.

This is the point for which we have contended, and this suits our argument very well, though we are sorry to see that *Odyssey*, Books XXI., XXII., and XXIII., are no older than the eighth century B.C. But

[1] Noack, p. 68.

we have not been quite convinced that Helen had not her separate chamber, that Zeus had not his separate chamber, and that the upper chambers of the daughters of the house in the *Iliad* are " late." Where, if not in upper chambers, did the young princesses repose? Again, the marked separation of the women in the house of Odysseus may be the result of Penelope's care in unusual circumstances, though she certainly would not build a separate hall for them. There are over a hundred handsome young scoundrels in her house all day long and deep into the night; she would, vainly, do her best to keep her girls apart.

It stands to reason that young girls of princely families would have bedrooms in the house, not in the courtyard—bedrooms out of the way of enterprising young men. What safer place could be found for them than in upper chambers, as in the *Iliad*? But, if their lovers were gods, we know that none "can see a god coming or going against his will." The arrangements of houses may and do vary in different cases in the same age.

As examples we turn to the parallel afforded by the Icelandic sagas and their pictures of houses of the eleventh century B.C. The present author long ago pointed out the parallel of the houses in the sagas and in Homer.[1] He took his facts from Dasent's translation of the Njal Saga (1861, vol. i. pp. xcviii., ciii., with diagrams). As far as he is aware, no critic looked into the matter till Mr. Monro (1901), being apparently unacquainted with Dasent's researches, found similar lore in works by Dr. Valtyr Gudmundsson.[2] The roof

[1] *The House.* Butcher and Lang. Translation of the *Odyssey.*
[2] Monro, *Odyssey*, vol. ii. pp. 491–495; *cf.* Gudmundsson, *Der Islandske Bolig i Fristats Tiden*, 1894; *cf.* Dasent, *Oxford Essays*, 1858.

of the hall is supported by four rows of columns, the
two inner rows are taller, and between them is the
hearth, with seats of honour for the chief guests and
the lord.   The fire was in a kind of trench down the
hall ; and in very cold weather, we learn from Dasent,
long fires could be lit through the extent of the hall.
The chief had a raised seat ; the guests sat on benches.
The high seats were at the centre ; not till later times
on the dais, as in a college hall.   The tables were
relatively small, and, as in Homer, could be removed
after a meal.   The part of the hall with the dais in later
days was partitioned off as a *stofa* or parlour.   In early
times cooking was done in the hall.

Dr. Gudmundsson, if I understand him, varies from
Dasent in some respects.   I quote an abstract of his
statement.

"About the year 1000 houses generally consisted of,
at least, four rooms ; often a fifth was added, the so-
called bath-room.   The oldest form for houses was
that of one long line or row of separate rooms united
by wooden or clay corridors or partitions, and each
covered with a roof.   Later, this was considered un-
practical, and they began building some of the houses
or rooms behind the others, which facilitated the access
from one to another, and diminished the number of
outer doors and corridors.

"Towards the latter part of the tenth century the
skaal was used as common sleeping-room for the whole
family, including servants and serfs ; it was fitted up
in the same way as the hall.   Like this, it was divided
in three naves by rows of wooden pillars ; the middle
floor was lower than that of the two side naves.   In
these were placed the so-called *saet* or bed-places, not

running the whole length of the *skaal* from gable to gable, but sideways, filling about a third part. Each *saet* was enclosed by broad, strong planks joined into the pillars, but not nailed on, so they might easily be taken out. These planks, called *sattestokke*, could also be turned sideways and' used as benches during the day ; they were often beautifully carved, and consequently highly valued.

" When settling abroad the people took away with them these planks, and put them up in their new home as a symbol of domestic happiness. The *saet* was occupied by the servants of the farm as sleeping-rooms ; generally it was screened by hangings and low panels, which partitioned it off like huge separate boxes, used as beds.

"All beds were filled with hay or straw ; servants and serfs slept on this without any bedclothes, sometimes a sleeping-bag was used, or they covered themselves with deerskins or a mantle. The family had bed-clothes, but only in very wealthy houses were they also provided for the servants. Moveable beds were extremely rare, but are sometimes mentioned. Generally two people slept in each bed.

" In the further end of the *skaal*, facing the door, opened out one or several small bedrooms, destined for the husband with wife and children, besides other members of the family, including guests of a higher standing. These small dormitories were separated by partitions of planks into bedrooms with one or several beds, and shut away from the outer *skaal* either by a sliding-door in the wall or by an ordinary door shutting with a hasp. Sometimes only a hanging covered the opening.

" In some farms were found underground passages, leading from the master's bedside to an outside house, or even as far as a wood or another sheltered place in the neighbourhood, to enable the inhabitants to save themselves during a night attack. For the same reason each man had his arms suspended over his bed.

" *Ildhus* or fire-house was the kitchen, often used besides as a sleeping-room when the farms were very small. This was quite abolished after the year 1000.

" *Buret* was the provision house.

" The bathroom was heated from a stone oven ; the stones were heated red-hot and cold water thrown upon them, which developed a quantity of vapour. As the heat and the steam mounted, the people—men and women—crawled up to a shelf under the roof and remained there as in a Turkish bath.

" In large and wealthy houses there was also a women's room, with a fireplace built low down in the middle, as in the hall, where the women used to sit with their handiwork all day. The men were allowed to come in and talk to them, also beggar-women and other vagabonds, who brought them the news from other places. Towards evening and for meals all assembled together in the hall."

On this showing, people did not sleep in cabins partitioned off the dining-hall, but in the *skaale;* and two similar and similarly situated rooms, one the common dining-hall, the other the common sleeping-hall, have been confused by writers on the sagas.[1] Can there be a similar confusion in the uses of *megaron, doma,* and *domos?*

[1] Gudmundsson, p. 14, Note 1.

In the Eyrbyggja Saga we have descriptions of the
" fire-hall," *skáli* or *eldhús*. " The fire-hall was the common sleeping-room in Icelandic homesteads." Guests
and strangers slept there ; not in the portico, as in
Homer. " Here were the lock-beds." There were
butteries ; one of these was reached by a ladder.
The walls were panelled.[1] Thorgunna had a " berth,"
apparently partitioned off, in the hall.[2] As in Homer
the hall was entered from the courtyard, in which were
separate rooms for stores and other purposes. In the
courtyard also, in the houses of Gunnar of Lithend
and Gisli at Hawkdale, and doubtless in other cases,
were the *dyngjur*, or ladies' chambers, their " bowers "
($\theta\acute{a}\lambda a\mu o\varsigma$, like that of Telemachus in the courtyard),
where they sat spinning and gossiping. The *dyngja*
was originally called *búr*, our " bower " ; the ballads say
" in bower and hall." In the ballad of *Margaret*, her
parents are said to put her in the way of deadly sin
by building her a bower, apparently separate from
the main building ; she would have been safer in an
upper chamber, though, even there, not safe—at least, if
a god wooed her ! It does not appear that all houses
had these chambers for ladies apart from the main
building. You did not enter the main hall in Iceland
from the court directly in front, but by the "man's
door" at the west side, whence you walked through
the porch or outer hall ($\pi\rho\acute{o}\delta o\mu o\varsigma$, $a\ddot{i}\theta ov\sigma a$), in the
centre of which, to the right, were the doors of the hall.
The women entered by the women's door, at the
eastern extremity.

Guests did not sleep, as in Homer, in the *prodomos*, or
the portico—the climate did not permit it—but in one

---

[1] *The Ere Dwellers*, p. 145.   [2] *Ibid.*, 137–140.

or other hall. The hall was wainscotted ; the walls were hung with shields and weapons, like the hall of Odysseus. The heads of the family usually slept in the aisles, in chambers entered through the wainscot of the hall. Such a chamber might be called μυχός ; it was private from the hall though under the same roof. It appears not improbable that some Homeric halls had sleeping places of this kind ; such a μυχός in Iceland seems to have had windows.[1]

Gunnar himself, however, slept with his wife, Hale-gerda, in an upper chamber ; his mother, who lived with him, also had a room upstairs.

In Njal's house, too, there was an upper chamber, wherein the foes of Njal threw fire.[2] But Njal and Bergthora, his wife, when all hope was ended, went into their own bride-chamber in the separate aisle of the hall " and gave over their souls into God's hand." Under a hide they lay ; and when men raised up the hide, after the fire had done its work, "they were unburnt under it. All praised God for that, and thought it was a great token." In this house was a weaving room for the women.[3]

It thus appears that Icelandic houses of the heroic age, as regards structural arrangements, were practically identical with the house of Odysseus, allowing for a separate sleeping-hall, while the differences between that and other Homeric houses may be no more than the differences between various Icelandic dwellings. The parents might sleep in bedchambers off the hall or in upper chambers. Ladies might have bowers in the courtyard or might have none. The

---

[1] *Story of Burnt Njal*, i. 242.   [2] *Ibid.*, ii. 173.
[3] *Ibid.*, ii. 195.

λαύρη—each passage outside the hall—yielded sleeping rooms for servants ; and there were store-rooms behind the passage at the top end of the hall, as well as separate chambers for stores in the courtyard. Mr. Leaf judiciously reconstructs the Homeric house in its "public rooms," of which we hear most, while he leaves the residential portion with "details and limits probably very variable." [1]

Given variability, which is natural and to be expected, and given the absence of detail about the "residential portion" of other houses than that of Odysseus in the poems, it does not seem to us that this house is conspicuously "late," still less that it is the house of historical Greece. Manifestly, in all respects it more resembles the houses of Njal and Gunnar of Lithend in the heroic age of Iceland.

In the house, as in the uses of iron and bronze, the weapons, armour, relations of the sexes, customary laws, and everything else, Homer gives us an harmonious picture of a single and peculiar age. We find no stronger mark of change than in the Odyssean house, if that be changed, which we show reason to doubt.

[1] *Iliad*, vol. i. pp. 586–589, with diagram based on the palace of Tiryns.

CHAPTER XI

NOTES OF CHANGE IN THE "ODYSSEY"

IF the Homeric descriptions of details of life contain anachronisms, points of detail inserted in later progressive ages, these must be peculiarly conspicuous in the *Odyssey*. Longinus regarded it as the work of Homer's advanced life, the sunset of his genius, and nobody denies that it assumes the existence of the *Iliad* and is posterior to that epic. In the *Odyssey*, then, we are to look, if anywhere, for indications of a changed society. That the language of the *Odyssey*, and of four Books of the *Iliad* (IX., X., XXIII., XXIV.), exhibits signs of change is a critical commonplace, but the language is matter for a separate discussion ; we are here concerned with the ideas, manners, customary laws, weapons, implements, and so forth of the Epics.

Taking as a text Mr. Monro's essay, *The Relation of the Odyssey to the Iliad*,[1] we examine the notes of difference which he finds between the twin Epics. As to the passages in which he discovers " borrowing or close imitation of passages " in the *Iliad* by the poet of the *Odyssey*, we shall not dwell on the matter, because we know so little about the laws regulating the repetition of epic formulæ. It is tempting, indeed, to criticise Mr. Monro's list of twenty-four Odyssean " borrowings," and we might arrive at some curious results. For

---

[1] Monro, *Odyssey*, vol. ii. pp. 324, *seqq.*

example, we could show that the *Klôthes,* the spinning
women who "spae" the fate of each new-born child,
are not later, but, as less abstract, are if anything
earlier than "the simple Αἶσα of the *Iliad.*"[1] But our
proof would require an excursion into the beliefs of
savage and barbaric peoples who have their *Klôthes,*
spae-women attending each birth, but who are not
known to have developed the idea of *Aisa* or Fate.

We might also urge that "to send a spear through
the back of a stag" is not, as Mr. Monro thought, "an
improbable feat," and that a man wounded to death as
Leiocritus was wounded, would not, as Mr. Monro
argued, fall backwards. He supposes that the poet of
the *Odyssey* borrowed the forward fall from a passage
in the *Iliad,* where the fall is in keeping. But, to make
good our proof, it might be necessary to spear a human
being in the same way as Leiocritus was speared.[2]

The repetitions of the Epic, at all events, are not the
result of the weakness of a poet who had to steal his
expressions like a schoolboy. They have some other
cause than the indolence or inefficiency of a *cento-*
making undergraduate. Indeed, a poet who used the
many terms in the *Odyssey* which do not occur in the
Iliad was not constrained to borrow from any pre-
decessor.

It is needless to dwell on the Odyssean novelties in
vocabulary, which were naturally employed by a poet
who had to sing of peace, not of war, and whose epic,
as Aristotle says, is "ethical," not military. The poet's
rich vocabulary is appropriate to his novel subject, that
is all.

---

[1] *Odyssey,* VII. 197; *Iliad,* XX. 127.
[2] Monro, *Odyssey,* vol. ii. pp. 239, 230.

Coming to Religion (1) we find Mr. Leaf assigning to his original *Achilleis*—"the kernel"—the very same religious ideas as Mr. Monro takes to be marks of "lateness" and of advance when he finds them in the *Odyssey!*

In the original oldest part of the *Iliad*, says Mr. Leaf, "the gods show themselves just so much as to let us know what are the powers which control mankind from heaven. . . . Their interference is such as becomes the rulers of the world, not partisans in the battle."[1] It is the later poets of the *Iliad*, in Mr. Leaf's view, who introduce the meddlesome, undignified, and extremely unsportsmanlike gods. The original early poet of the *Iliad* had the nobler religious conceptions.

In that case—the *Odyssey* being later than the original kernel of the *Iliad*—the *Odyssey* ought to give us gods as undignified and unworthy as those exhibited by the later continuators of the *Iliad*.

But the reverse is the case. The gods behave fairly well in Book XXIV. of the *Iliad*, which, we are to believe, is the latest, or nearly the latest, portion. They are all wroth with the abominable behaviour of Achilles to dead Hector (XXIV. 134). They console and protect Priam. As for the *Odyssey*, Mr. Monro finds that in this late Epic the gods are just what Mr. Leaf proclaims them to have been in his old original kernel. "There is now an Olympian concert that carries on something like a moral government of the world. It is very different in the *Iliad*. . . ."[2]

But it was not very different ; it was just the same,

---

[1] Leaf, *Iliad*, vol. ii. pp. xii., xiii.
[2] Monro, *Odyssey*, ii. 335.

in Mr. Leaf's genuine old original germ of the *Iliad*.
In fact, the gods are " very much like you and me."
When their *ichor* is up, they misbehave as we do when
our blood is up, during the fury of war.   When Hector
is dead and when the war is over, the gods give play
to their higher nature, as men do.   There is no difference of religious conception to sever the *Odyssey* from
the later but not from the original parts of the *Iliad*.   It
is all an affair of the circumstances in each case.

The *Odyssey* is calmer, more reflective, more *religious*
than the *Iliad*, being a poem of peace.   The *Iliad*, a
poem of war, is more *mythological* than the *Odyssey;*
the gods in the *Iliad* are excited, like the men, by the
great war and behave accordingly.   That neither
gods nor men show any real sense of the moral
weakness of Agamemnon or Achilles, or of the moral
superiority of Hector, is an unacceptable statement.[1]
Even Achilles and Agamemnon are judged by men
and by the poet according to their own standard
of ethics and of customary law.   There is really no
doubt on this point.   Too much (2) is made of the supposed different views of Olympus—a mountain in Thessaly in the *Iliad;* a snowless, windless, supra-mundane
place in *Odyssey*, V. 41–47.[2]   Of the Odyssean passage
Mr. Merry justly says, " the actual description is not
irreconcilable with the general Homeric picture of
Olympus."   It is " an idealised mountain," and conceptions of it vary, with the variations which are
essential to and inseparable from all mythological
ideas.   As Mr. Leaf says,[3] " heaven, οὐρανος and
Olympus, if not identical, are at least closely con-

---

[1] Monro, *Odyssey*, vol. ii. p. 336.   [2] *Ibid.*, ii. 396.
[3] Note to *Iliad*, V. 750.

nected." In *Iliad*, V. 753, the poet "regarded the summit of Olympus as a half-way stage between heaven and earth," thus "departing from the oldest Homeric tradition, which made the earthly mountain Olympus, and not any aerial region, the dwelling of the gods." But precisely the same confusion of mythical ideas occurs among a people so backward as the Australian south-eastern tribes, whose All Father is now seated on a hill-top and now "above the sky." In *Iliad*, VIII. 25, 26, the poet is again said to have "entirely lost the real Epic conception of Olympus as a mountain in Thessaly," and to "follow the later conception, which removed it from earth to heaven." In *Iliad*, XI. 184, "from heaven" means "from the summit of Olympus, which, though Homer does not identify it with οὐρανος, still, as a mountain, reached into heaven" (Leaf). The poet of *Iliad*, XI. 184, says plainly that Zeus descended "*from heaven*" to Mount Ida. In fact, all that is said of Olympus, of heaven, of the home of the gods, is poetical, is mythical, and so is necessarily subject to the variations of conception inseparable from mythology. This is certain if there be any certainty in mythological science, and here no hard and fast line can be drawn between *Odyssey* and *Iliad*.

(3) The next point of difference is that, "we hear no more of Iris as the messenger of Zeus;" in the *Odyssey*, "the agent of the will of Zeus is now Hermes, as in the Twenty-fourth Book of the *Iliad*," a late "Odyssean" Book. But what does that matter, seeing that *Iliad*, Book VIII., is declared to be one of the latest additions; yet in Book VIII. Iris, not Hermes, is the messenger (VIII. 409–425). If in late times Hermes, not Iris, is

the messenger, why, in a very " late " Book (VIII.) is
Iris the messenger, not Hermes? *Iliad*, Book XXIII.,
is also a late " Odyssean " Book, but here Iris goes on
her messages (XXIII. 199) moved merely by the prayers
of Achilles. In the late Odyssean Book (XXIV.) of the
Iliad, Iris runs on messages from Zeus both to Priam
and to Achilles. If Iris, in " Odyssean " times, had
resigned office and been succeeded by Hermes, why
did Achilles pray, not to Hermes, but to Iris? There
is nothing in the argument about Hermes and Iris.
There is nothing in the facts but the variability of
mythical and poetical conceptions. Moreover, the
conception of Iris as the messenger certainly existed
through the age of the *Odyssey*, and later. In the
Odyssey the beggar man is called " Irus," a male Iris,
because he carries messages ; and Iris does her usual
duty as messenger in the Homeric Hymns, as well as
in the so-called late Odyssean Books of the *Iliad*. The
poet of the *Odyssey* knew all about Iris ; there had arisen no
change of belief ; he merely employed Hermes as messenger, not of the one god, but of the divine Assembly.

(4) Another difference is that in the *Iliad* the wife
of Hephæstus is one of the Graces ; in the *Odyssey* she
is Aphrodite.[1] This is one of the inconsistencies which
are the essence of mythology. Mr. Leaf points out
that when Hephæstus is about exercising his craft, in
making arms for Achilles, Charis " is made wife of
Hephæstus by a more transparent allegory than we
find elsewhere in Homer," whereas, when Aphrodite
appears in a comic song by Demodocus (*Odyssey*, VIII.
266–366), " that passage is later and un-Homeric." [2]

---

[1] Monro, *Odyssey*, vol. ii. p. 336.
[2] Leaf, *Iliad*, vol. ii. p. 246.

Of this we do not accept the doctrine that the lay is un-Homeric. The difference comes to no more than *that;* the accustomed discrepancy of mythology, of story-telling about the gods. But as to the lay of Demodocus being un-Homeric and late, the poet at least knows the regular Homeric practice of the bride-price, and its return by the bride's father to the husband of an adulterous wife (*Odyssey*, VIII. 318, 319). The poet of this lay, which Mr. Merry defends as Homeric, was intimately familiar with Homeric customary law. Now, according to Paul Cauer, as we shall see, other "Odyssean" poets were living in an age of changed law, later than that of the author of the lay of Demodocus. All these so-called differences between *Iliad* and *Odyssey* do not point to the fact that the *Odyssey* belongs to a late and changed period of culture, of belief and customs. There is nothing in the evidence to prove that contention.

There (5) are two references to local oracles in the *Odyssey*, that of Dodona (XIV. 327 ; XIX. 296) and that of Pytho (VIII. 80). This is the old name of Delphi. Pytho occurs in *Iliad*, IX. 404, as a very rich temple of Apollo—the oracle is not named, but the oracle brought in the treasures. Achilles (XVI. 233) prays to Pelasgian Zeus of Dodona, whose priests were thickly tabued, but says nothing of the oracle of Dodona. Neither when in leaguer round Troy, nor when wandering in fairy lands forlorn, had the Achæans or Odysseus much to do with the local oracles of Greece ; perhaps not, in Homer's time, so important as they were later, and little indeed is said about them in either Epic.

(6) "The geographical knowledge shown in the

Odyssey goes beyond that of the *Iliad* . . . especially in regard to Egypt and Sicily." But a poet of a widely wandering hero of Western Greece has naturally more occasion than the poet of a fixed army in Asia to show geographical knowledge. Egyptian Thebes is named, in *Iliad*, IX., as a city very rich, especially in chariots ; while in the *Odyssey* the poet has occasion to show more knowledge of the way to Egypt and of Viking descents from Crete on the coast (*Odyssey*, III. 300 ; IV. 351 ; XIV. 257 ; XVII. 426). Archæology shows that the Mycenæan age was in close commercial relation with Egypt, and that the Mycenæan civilisation extended to most Mediterranean lands and islands, and to Italy and Sicily.[1] There is nothing suspicious, as "late," in the mention of Sicily by Odysseus in Ithaca (*Odyssey*, XX. 383 ; XXIV. 307). In the same way, if the poet of a western poem does not dilate on the Troad and the people of Asia Minor as the poet of the *Iliad* does, that is simply because the scene of the *Iliad* is in Asia and the scene of the *Odyssey* is in the west, when it is not in No Man's land. From the same cause the poet of sea-faring has more occasion to speak of the Phœnicians, great sea-farers, than the poet of the Trojan leaguer.

(7) We know so little about land tenure in Homeric times—and, indeed, early land tenure is a subject so complex and obscure that it is not easy to prove advance towards separate property in the *Odyssey*— beyond what was the rule in the time of the *Iliad*. In the Making of the Arms (XVIII. 541–549) we find many men ploughing a field, and this may have been a common field. But in what sense ? Many ploughs

---

[1] Ridgeway, *Early Age of Greece*, i. 69.

were at work at once on a Scottish runrig field, and each farmer had his own strip on several common fields, but each farmer held by rent, or by rent and services, from the laird. These common fields were not common property. In XII. 422 we have "a common field," and men measuring a strip and quarrelling about the marking-stones, across the "baulk," but it does not follow that they are owners; they may be tenants. Such quarrels were common in Scotland when the runrig system of common fields, each man with his strip, prevailed.[1]

A man had a κλῆρος, or lot (*Iliad*, XV. 448), but what was a "lot"? At first, probably, a share in land periodically shifted—*le partage noir* of the Russian peasants. Kings and men who deserve public gratitude receive a τέμενος, a piece of public land, as Bellerophon did from the Lycians (VI. 194). In the case of Melager such an estate is offered to him, but by whom? Not by the people at large, but by the γέροντες (IX. 574).

Who are the γέροντες? They are not ordinary men of the people; they are, in fact, the gentry. In an age so advanced from tribal conditions as is the Homeric time—far advanced beyond ancient tribal Scotland or Ireland—we conceive that, as in these countries during the tribal period, the γέροντες (in Celtic, the *Flaith*) held *in possession*, if not in accordance with the letter of the law, as *property*, much more land than a single "lot." The Irish tribal freeman had a right to a "lot," redistributed by rotation. Wealth consisted of cattle; and a *bogire*, a man of many kine, let *them* out to tenants. Such a rich man,

---

[1] Grey Graham, *Social Life in Scotland in the Eighteenth Century*, i. 157.

a *flatha*, would, in accordance with human nature, use his influence with kineless dependents to acquire *in possession* several lots, avoid the partition, and keep the lots in possession though not legally in property. Such men were the Irish *flaith*, gentry under the *Ri*, or king, his γέροντες ; each with his *ciniod*, or near kinsmen, to back his cause.

" *Flaith* seems clearly to mean land-owners," or squires, says Sir James Ramsay.[1] If land, contrary to the tribal ideal, came into private hands in early Ireland, we can hardly suppose that, in the more advanced and settled Homeric society, no man but the king held land equivalent in extent to a number of " lots." The γέροντες, the gentry, the chariot-owning warriors, of whom there are hundreds not of kingly rank in Homer (as in Ireland there were many *flaith* to one *Ri*) probably, in an informal but tight grip, held considerable lands. When we note their position in the *Iliad*, high above the nameless host, can we imagine that they did not hold more land than the simple, perhaps periodically shifting, " lot " ? There were " lotless " men (*Odyssey*, XI. 490), lotless *freemen*, and what had become of their lots ? Had they not fallen into the hands of the γέροντες or the *flaith* ?

Mr. Ridgeway in a very able essay[2] holds different opinions. He points out that among a man's possessions, in the *Iliad*, we hear only of personal property and live stock. It is in one passage only in the *Odyssey* (XIV. 211) that we meet with men holding several lots of land ; but *they*, we remark, occur in Crete—an isle, as we know, of very advanced civilisation from of old.

---

[1] *Foundations of England*, i. 16, Note 4.
[2] *Journal of Hellenic Studies*, vi. 319–339.

Mr. Ridgeway also asks whether the lotless men may not be "outsiders," such as are attached to certain villages of Central and Southern India ;[1] or they may answer to the *Fuidhir*, or "broken men," of early Ireland, fugitives from one to another tribe. They would be "settled on the waste lands of a community." If so, they would not be lotless ; they would have new lots.[2]

Laertes, though a king, is supposed to have won his farm by his own labours from the waste (*Odyssey*, XXIV. 207). Mr. Monro says, "the land having thus been won from the wastes (the γῆ ακληρός τε καὶ ἄκτιτος of *H., Ven.* 123), was a τέμενος or separate possession of Laertes." The passage is in the rejected conclusion of the *Odyssey;* and if any man might go and squat in the waste, any man might have a lot, or better than one lot. In *Iliad*, XXIII. 832–835, Achilles says that his offered prize of iron will be useful to a man "whose rich fields are very remote from any town." Teucer and Meriones compete for the prize : probably they had such rich remote fields, not each a mere lot in a common field. These remote fields they are supposed to hold in perpetuity, apart from the τέμενος, which, in Mr. Ridgeway's opinion, reverted, on the death of each holder, to the community, save where kingship was hereditary. Now, if κλῆρος had come to mean "a lot of land," as we say "a building lot," obviously men like Teucer and Meriones had many lots, rich fields, which at death might sometimes pass to their heirs. Thus there was separate landed property in the *Iliad;* but the passage is denounced, though not by Mr. Ridgeway, as "late."

---

[1] Maine, *Village Communities*, p. 127.
[2] *Journal of Hellenic Studies*, vi. 322, 323.

The absence of enclosures (ἕρκος ἀρούρης) proves
nothing about absence of several property in land.
In Scotland the laird's lands were unenclosed till deep
in the eighteenth century.

My own case for land in private *possession*, in
Homeric times, rests mainly on human nature in
such an advanced society. Such *possession* as I plead
for is in accordance with human nature, in a society
so distinguished by degrees of wealth as is the
Homeric.

Unless we are able to suppose that all the gentry
of the *Iliad* held no " rich fields remote from towns,"
each having but one rotatory lot apiece, there is no
difference in Iliadic and Odyssean land tenure, though
we get clearer lights on it in the *Odyssey*.

The position of the man of several lots may have
been indefensible, if the ideal of tribal law were ever
made real, but wealth in growing societies universally
tends to override such law. Mr. Keller [1] justly warns
us against the attempt " to apply universally certain
fixed rules of property development. The passages in
Homer upon which opinions diverge most are isolated
ones, occurring in similes and fragmentary descriptions.
Under such conditions the formulation of theories or
the attempt rigorously to classify can be little more
than an intellectual exercise."

We have not the materials for a scientific knowledge of Homeric real property ; and, with all our
materials in Irish law books, how hard it is for us to
understand the early state of such affairs in Ireland !
But does any one seriously suppose that the knightly
class of the *Iliad*, the chariot-driving gentlemen, held

[1] *Homeric Society*, p. 192. 1902.

no more land—legally or by permitted custom—than
the two Homeric swains who vituperate each other
across a baulk about the right to a few feet of a strip of
a runrig field? Whosoever can believe *that* may also
believe that the practice of adding "lot" to "lot"
began in the period between the finished composition
of the *Iliad* (or of the parts of it which allude to land
tenure) and the beginning of the *Odyssey* (or of the
parts of it which refer to land tenure). The inference
is that, though the fact is not explicitly stated in the
Iliad, there were men who held more "lots" than one
in Iliadic times as well as in the Odyssean times, when,
in a solitary passage of the *Odyssey*, we do hear of such
men in Crete. But whosoever has pored over early
European land tenures knows how dim our knowledge
is, and will not rush to employ his lore in discriminat-
ing between the date of the *Iliad* and the date of the
Odyssey.

Not much proof of change in institutions between
Iliadic and Odyssean times can be extracted from two
passages about the ἕδνα, or bride-price of Penelope.
The rule in both *Iliad* and *Odyssey* is that the wooer
gives a bride-price to the father of the bride, ἕδνα. This
was the rule known even to that painfully late and un-
Homeric poet who made the Song of Demodocus
about the loves of Ares and Aphrodite. In that song
the injured husband, Hephæstus, claims back the
bride-price which he had paid to the father of his
wife, Zeus.[1] This is the accepted custom throughout
the *Odyssey* (VI. 159; XVI. 77; XX. 335; XXI.
162; XV. 17, &c.). So far there is no change of
manners, no introduction of the later practice, a

[1] *Odyssey*, VIII. 318.

dowry given with the bride, in place of a bride-price given to the father by the bridegroom. But Penelope was neither maid, wife, nor widow ; her husband's fate, alive or dead, was uncertain, and her son was so anxious to get her out of the house that he says he offered gifts *with* her (XX. 342). In the same way, to buy back the goodwill of Achilles, Agamemnon offers to give him his daughter without bride-price, and to add great gifts (*Iliad*, IX. 147)—the term for the gifts is μείλια. People, of course, could make their own bargain ; take as much for their daughter as they could get, or let the gifts go from husband to bride, and then return to the husband's home with her (as in Germany in the time of Tacitus, *Germania*, 18), or do that, and throw in more gifts. But in *Odyssey*, II. 53, Tele-machus says that the Wooers shrink from going to the house of Penelope's father, Icarius, who would endow (?) his daughter (ἐεδνώσαιτο). And again (*Odyssey*, I. 277 ; II. 196), her father's folk will furnish a bridal feast, and "array the ἔεδνα, many, such as should accompany a dear daughter." Some critics think that the gifts here are *dowry*, a later institution than bride-price ; others, that the father of the dear daughter merely chose to be generous, and returned the bride-price, or its equivalent, in whole or part.[1] If the former view be correct, these passages in *Odyssey*, I., II. are later than the exceedingly "late" song of Demo-docus. If the latter theory be correct the father is merely showing goodwill, and doing as the Germans did when they were in a stage of culture much earlier than the Homeric.

The position of Penelope is very unstable and legally

---

[1] Merry, *Odyssey*, vol. i. p. 50. Note to Book I. 277.

perplexing. Has her father her marriage? has her son her marriage? is she not perhaps still a married woman with a living husband? Telemachus would give much to have her off his hands, but he refuses to send her to her father's house, where the old man might be ready enough to return the bride-price to her new husband, and get rid of her with honour. For if Telemachus sends his mother away against her will he will have to pay a heavy fine to her father, and to thole his mother's curse, and lose his character among men (*Odyssey*, II. 130–138). The Icelanders of the saga period gave dowries with their daughters. But when Njal wanted Hildigunna for his foster-son, Hauskuld, he offered to give ἔδνα. " I will lay down as much money as will seem fitting to thy niece and thyself," he says to Flosi, "if thou wilt think of making this match."[1]

Circumstances alter cases, and we must be hard pressed to discover signs of change of manners in the *Odyssey* as compared with the *Iliad* if we have to rely on a solitary mention of " men of many lots" in Crete, and on the perplexed proposals for the second marriage of Penelope.[2] We must not be told that the many other supposed signs of change, Iris, Olympus, and the rest, have " cumulative weight." If we have disposed of each individual supposed note of change in beliefs and manners in its turn, then these proofs have, in each case, no individual weight and, cumulatively, are not more ponderous than a feather.

[1] *Story of Burnt Njal*, ii. p. 81.
[2] For the alleged "alteration of old customs" see Cauer, *Grundfragen der Homerkritik*, pp. 193–194.

CHAPTER XII

THE great strength of the theory that the poems are the work of several ages is the existence in them of various strata of languages, earlier and later.

Not to speak of differences of vocabulary, Mr. Monro and Mr. Leaf, with many scholars, detect two strata of earlier and later *grammar* in *Iliad* and *Odyssey*. In the *Iliad* four or five Books are infected by "the later grammar," while the *Odyssey* in general seems to be contaminated. Mr. Leaf's words are : " When we regard the Epos in large masses, we see that we can roughly arrange the inconsistent elements towards one end or the other of a line of development both linguistic and historical. The main division, that of *Iliad* and *Odyssey*, shows a distinct advance along this line ; and the distinction is still more marked if we group with the *Odyssey* four Books of the *Iliad* whose Odyssean physiognomy is well marked. Taking as our main guide the dissection of the plot as shown in its episodes, we find that marks of lateness, though nowhere entirely absent, group themselves most numerously in the later additions . . ." [1] We are here concerned with *linguistic* examples of " lateness." The " four Books whose Odyssean physiognomy" and language seem "well marked," are IX., X., XXIII., XXIV. Here Mr. Leaf,

---

[1] *Iliad*, vol. ii. p. x.

Mr. Monro, and many authorities are agreed. But to these four Odyssean Books of the *Iliad* Mr. Leaf adds *Iliad*, XI. 664–772 : "probably a later addition," says Mr. Monro. "It is notably Odyssean in character," says Mr. Leaf ; and the author "is ignorant of the geography of the Western Peloponnesus. No doubt the author was an Asiatic Greek." [1] The value of this discovery is elsewhere discussed (see *The Interpolations of Nestor*).

The Odyssean notes in this passage of a hundred lines (*Iliad*, XI. 670–762) are the occurrence of "a purely Odyssean word" (677), an Attic form of an epic word, and a "forbidden trochaic cæsura in the fourth foot"; an Odyssean word for carving meat, applied in a *non*-Odyssean sense (688), a verb for "insulting," not elsewhere found in the *Iliad* (though the noun is in the *Iliad*) (695), an Odyssean epithet of the sun, "four times in the *Odyssey*" (735). It is also possible that there is an allusion to a four-horse chariot (699).

These are the proofs of Odyssean lateness.

The real difficulty about Odyssean words and grammar in the *Iliad* is that, if they were in vigorous poetic existence down to the time of Pisistratus (as the Odysseanism of the Asiatic editor proves that they were), and if every rhapsodist could add to and alter the materials at the disposal of the Pisistratean editor at will, we are not told how the fashionable Odysseanisms were kept, on the whole, out of twenty Books of the *Iliad*.

This is a point on which we cannot insist too strongly, as an argument against the theory that, till the middle of the sixth century B.C., the *Iliad* scarcely survived save in the memory of strolling rhapsodists.

[1] *Iliad*, vol. i. pp. 465–466. Note on Book XI. 756.

If that were so, all the Books of the *Iliad* would, in the course of recitation of old and composition of new passages, be equally contaminated with late Odyssean linguistic style. It could not be otherwise ; all the Books would be equally modified in passing through the lips of modern reciters and composers. Therefore, if twenty out of twenty-four Books are pure, or pure in the main, from Odysseanisms, while four are deeply stained with them, the twenty must not only be earlier than the four, but must have been specially preserved, and kept uncontaminated, in some manner inconsistent with the theory that all alike scarcely existed save in the memory or invention of late strolling reciters.

How the twenty Books relatively pure " in grammatical forms, in syntax, and in vocabulary," could be kept thus clean without the aid of written texts, I am unable to imagine. If left merely to human memory and at the mercy of reciters and new poets, they would have become stained with " the defining article "—and, indeed, an employment of the article which startles grammarians, appears even in the eleventh line of the First Book of the *Iliad*.[1]

Left merely to human memory and the human voice, the twenty more or less innocent Books would have abounded, like the *Odyssey*, in ἀμφί with the dative meaning "about," and with ἐξ "in consequence of," and "the extension of the use of εἰ clauses as final and objective clauses," and similar marks of lateness, so interesting to grammarians.[2] But the twenty Books are almost, or quite, inoffensive in these respects.

Now, even in ages of writing, it has been found

[1] *Cf.* Monro and Leaf, on *Iliad*, I. 11-12.
[2] Monro, *Odyssey*, ii. pp. 331-333.

difficult or impossible to keep linguistic novelties and novelties of metre out of old epics. We later refer (*Archæology of the Epic*) to the *Chancun de Willame*, of which an unknown benefactor printed two hundred copies in 1903. Mr. Raymond Weeks, in *Romania*, describes *Willame* as taking a place beside the *Chanson de Roland* in the earliest rank of *Chansons de Geste*. If the text can be entirely restored, the poem will appear as "the most primitive" of French epics of the eleventh and twelfth centuries. But it has passed from copy to copy in the course of generations. The methods of versification change, and, after line 2647, "there are traces of change in the language. The word *ço*, followed by a vowel, hitherto frequent, never again reappears. The vowel *i*, of *li*, nominative masculine of the article" (*li Reis*, "the king"), "never occurs in the text after line 2647. Up to that point it is elided or not at pleasure. . . . There is a progressive tendency towards hiatus. After line 1980 the system of assonance changes. *An* and *en* have been kept distinct hitherto ; this ceases to be the case." [1]

The poem is also notable, like the *Iliad*, for textual repetition of passages, but that is common to all early poetry, which many Homeric critics appear not to understand. In this example we see how apt novelties in grammar and metre are to steal into even written copies of epics, composed in and handed down through uncritical ages ; and we are confirmed in the opinion that the relatively pure and orthodox grammar and metre of the twenty Books must have been preserved by written texts carefully executed. The other four Books, if equally old, were less fortunate. Their

[1] *Romania*, xxxiv. pp. 240–246.

grammar and metre, we learn, belong to a later stratum of language.

These opinions of grammarians are not compatible with the hypothesis that *all* of the *Iliad*, even the "earliest" parts, are loaded with interpolations, forced in at different places and in any age from 1000 B.C. to 540 B.C.; for if that theory were true, the whole of the *Iliad* would equally be infected with the later Odyssean grammar. According to Mr. Monro and Sir Richard Jebb, it is not.

But suppose, on the other hand, that the later Odyssean grammar abounds all through the whole *Iliad*, then that grammar is not more Odyssean than it is Iliadic. The alleged distinction of early Iliadic grammar, late Odyssean grammar, in that case vanishes. Mr. Leaf is more keen than Mr. Monro and Sir Richard Jebb in detecting late grammar in the *Iliad* beyond the bounds of Books IX., X., XXIII., XXIV. But he does not carry these discoveries so far as to make the late grammar no less Iliadic than Odyssean. In Book VIII. of the *Iliad*, which he thinks was only made for the purpose of introducing Book IX.,[1] we ought to find the late Odyssean grammar just as much as we do in Book IX., for it is of the very same date, and probably by one or more of the same authors as Book IX. But we do not find the Odyssean grammar in Book VIII.

Mr. Leaf says, "The peculiar character" of Book VIII. "is easily understood, when we recognise the fact that Book VIII. is intended to serve only as a means for the introduction of Book IX. . . ." which is "late" and "Odyssean." Then Book VIII., intended to introduce Book IX., must be at least as late as Book IX. and

---

[1] *Iliad*, vol. i. p. 332. 1900.

might be expected to be at least as Odyssean, indeed one would think it could not be otherwise. Yet it is not so.

Mr. Leaf's theory has thus to face the difficulty that while the whole *Iliad*, by his view, for more than four centuries, was stuffed with late interpolations, in the course of oral recital through all Greek lands, and was crammed with original "copy" by a sycophant of Pisistratus about 540 B.C., the late grammar concentrated itself in only some four Books. Till some reasonable answer is given to this question—how did twenty Books of the *Iliad* preserve so creditably the ancient grammar through centuries of change, and of recitation by rhapsodists who used the Odyssean grammar, which infected the four other Books, and the whole of the *Odyssey?*—it seems hardly worth while to discuss this linguistic test.

Any scholar who looks at these pages knows all about the proofs of grammar of a late date in the *Odyssey* and the four contaminated Books of the *Iliad*. But it may be well to give a few specimens, for the enlightenment of less learned readers of Homer.

The use of ἀμφί, with the dative, meaning "about," when *thinking* or *speaking* "about" Odysseus or anything else, is peculiar to the *Odyssey*. But how has it not crept into the four Odyssean contaminated Books of the *Iliad?*

περί, with the genitive, "follows verbs meaning to speak or know *about* a person," but only in the *Odyssey*. What preposition follows such verbs in the *Iliad?*

Here, again, we ask: how did the contaminated Books of the *Iliad* escape the stain of περί, with the genitive, after verbs meaning to speak or know? What phrase do they use in the *Iliad* for speaking or asking *about* anybody?

μετά, with the genitive, meaning "among" or "with," comes twice in the *Odyssey* (X. 320; XVI. 140) and thrice in the *Iliad* (XIII. 700; XXI. 458; XXIV. 400); but all these passages in the *Iliad* are disposed of as "late" parts of the poem.

ἐπί, with the accusative, meaning *towards* a person, comes often in the *Iliad;* once in the *Odyssey*. But it comes four times in *Iliad*, Book X., which almost every critic scouts as very "late" indeed. If so, why does the "late" *Odyssey* not deal in this grammatical usage so common in the "late" Book X. of the *Iliad?*

ἐπί, with the accusative, "meaning *extent* (without *motion*)," is chiefly found in the *Odyssey*, and in the *Iliad*, IX., X., XXIV. On consulting grammarians one thinks that there is not much in this.

προτί, with the dative, meaning "in addition to," occurs only once (*Odyssey*, X. 68). If it occurs only once, there is little to be learned from the circumstance.

'Aνά, with the genitive, is only in *Odyssey*, only thrice, always of going on board a ship. There are not many ship-farings in the *Iliad*. Odysseus and his men are not described as going on board their ship, in so many words, in *Iliad*, Book I. The usage occurs in the poem where the incidents of seafaring occur frequently, as is to be expected.[1] It is not worth while to persevere with these tithes of mint and cummin. If "Neglect of Position" be commoner—like "Hiatus in the Bucolic Diæresis"—in the *Odyssey* and in *Iliad*, XXIII., XXIV., why do the failings not beset *Iliad*, IX., X., these being such extremely "late" books? As to the

---

[1] Monro, *Homeric Grammar*. See Index, under *Iliad*, p. 339.

later use of the Article in the *Odyssey* and the Odyssean
Books of the *Iliad*, it appears to us that Book I. of the
Iliad uses the article as it is used in Book X. ; but on
this topic we must refer to a special treatise on the
language of *Iliad*, Book X., which is promised.

Turning to the vocabulary: " words expressive of
civilisation " are bound to be more frequent, as they
are, in the *Odyssey*, a poem of peaceful life, than in a
poem about an army in action, like the *Iliad*. Out of
all this no clue to the distance of years dividing the
two poems can be found. As to words concerning
religion, the same holds good. The *Odyssey* is more
frequently *religious* (see the case of Eumæus) than the
Iliad.

In morals the term δίκαιος is more used in the
Odyssey, also ἀθέμιστος (" just " and " lawless "). But
that is partly because the *Odyssey* has to contrast
civilised ("just") with wild outlandish people—Cyclopes
and Læstrygons, who are " lawless." The *Iliad* has no
occasion to touch on savages ; but, as the ὕβρις of the
Wooers is a standing topic in the *Odyssey* (an ethical
poem, says Aristotle), the word ὕβρις is of frequent
occurrence in the *Odyssey*, in just the same sense as it
bears in *Iliad*, I. 214—the insolence of Agamemnon.
Yet when Achilles has occasion to speak of Agamemnon's
insolence in *Iliad*, Book IX., he does not use the *word* ὕβρις,
though Book IX. is so very " late " and " Odyssean." It
would be easy to go through the words for moral ideas
in the *Odyssey*, and to show that they occur in the
numerous moral situations which do not arise, or arise
much less frequently, in the *Iliad*. There is not difference enough in the moral standard of the two poems
to justify us in assuming that centuries of ethical

progress had intervened between their dates of composition.   If the *Iliad*, again, were really, like the *Odyssey*,
a thing of growth through several centuries, which
overlapped the centuries in which the *Odyssey* grew, the
moral ideas of the *Iliad* and *Odyssey* would necessarily be
much the same, would be indistinguishable.   But, as a
matter of fact, it would be easy to show that the moral
standard of the *Iliad* is higher, in many places, than
the moral standard of the *Odyssey;* and that, therefore,
by the critical hypothesis, the *Iliad* is the later poem of
the twain.   For example, the behaviour of Achilles is
most obnoxious to the moralist in *Iliad*, Book IX.,
where he refuses gifts of conciliation.   But by the
critical hypothesis this is not the fault of the *Iliad*, for
Book IX. is declared to be " late," and of the same date
as late parts of the *Odyssey*.   Achilles is not less open
to moral reproach in his abominable cruelty and im-
piety, as shown in his sacrifice of prisoners of war and
his treatment of dead Hector, in *Iliad*, XXIII., XXIV.
But these Books also are said to be as late as the
Odyssey.

The solitary " realistic " or " naturalistic " passage
in Homer, with which a lover of modern " problem
novels " feels happy and at home, is the story of
Phœnix, about his seduction of his father's mistress at
the request of his mother.   What a charming situation!
But that occurs in an " Odyssean " Book of the *Iliad*,
Book IX. ; and thus Odyssean seems lower, not more
advanced, than Iliadic taste in morals.   To be sure,
the poet disapproves of all these immoralities.

In the *Odyssey* the hero, to the delight of Athene, lies
often and freely and with glee.   The Achilles of the
Iliad hates a liar " like the gates of Hades " ; but he

says so in an "Odyssean" Book (Book IX.), so there were obviously different standards in Odyssean ethics.

As to the *Odyssey* being the work of "a milder age," consider the hanging of Penelope's maids and the abominable torture of Melanthius. There is no torturing in the *Iliad*, for the *Iliad* happens not to deal with treacherous thralls.

Enfin, there is no appreciable moral advance in the *Odyssey* on the moral standard of the *Iliad*. It is rather the other way. Odysseus, in the *Odyssey*, tries to procure poison for his arrow-heads. The person to whom he applies is too moral to oblige him. We never learn that a hero of the *Iliad* would use poisoned arrows. The poet himself obviously disapproves ; in both poems the poet is always on the side of morality and of the highest ethical standard of his age. The standard in both Epics is the same ; in both some heroes fall short of the standard.

To return to linguistic tests, it is hard indeed to discover what Mr. Leaf's opinion of the value of linguistic tests of lateness really is. "It is on such fundamental discrepancies"—as he has found in Books IX., XVI.— "that we can depend, *and on these alone*, when we come to dissect the *Iliad* . . . Some critics have attempted to base their analysis on evidences from language, but I do not think they are sufficient to bear the superstructure which has been raised on them." [1]

He goes on, still placing a low value on linguistic tests alone, to say : "It is on the broad grounds of the construction and motives of the poem, *and not on any merely linguistic considerations*, that a decision must be sought." [2]

---

[1] *Companion*, p. 25.   [2] *Ibid.*, p. x.

But he contradicts these comfortable words when he comes to "the latest expansions," such as Books XXIII., XXIV. "The latest expansions are thoroughly in the spirit of those which precede, *and are only separated from them on account of linguistic evidence*, which definitely classes them with the *Odyssey* rather than the rest of the *Iliad*." [1]

Now as Mr. Leaf has told us that we must depend on " fundamental discrepancies," " on these alone," when we want to dissect the *Iliad*; as he has told us that linguistic tests alone are " not sufficient to bear the superstructure," &c., how can we lop off two Books " only on account of linguistic evidence " ?   It would appear that on this point, as on others, Mr. Leaf has entirely changed his mind.   But, even in the *Companion* (p. 388), he had amputated Book XXIV. for no " fundamental discrepancy," but because of " its close kinship to the *Odyssey*, as in the whole language of the Book."

Here, as in many other passages, if we are to account for discrepancies by the theory of multiplex authorship, we must decide that Mr. Leaf's books are the work of several critics, not of one critic only.   But there is excellent evidence to prove that here we would be mistaken.

Confessedly and regretfully no grammarian, I remain unable, in face of what seem contradictory assertions about the value of linguistic tests, to ascertain what they are really worth, and what, if anything, they really prove.

Mr. Monro allows much for " the long insensible influence of Attic recitation upon the Homeric text ; "

---

[1] *Iliad*, vol. ii. p. xiv.

"many Attic peculiarities may be noted" (so much so that Aristarchus thought Homer must have been an Athenian!). "The poems suffered a gradual and unsystematic because generally unconscious process of modernising, the chief agents in which were the rhapsodists" (reciters in a later democratic age), "who wandered over all parts of Greece, and were likely to be influenced by all the chief forms of literature." [1]

Then, wherefore insist so much on tests of language?

Mr. Monro was not only a great grammarian; he had a keen appreciation of poetry. Thus he was conspicuously uneasy in his hypothesis, based on words and grammar, that the two last Books of the *Iliad* are by a late hand. After quoting Shelley's remark that, in these two Books, "Homer truly begins to be himself," Mr. Monro writes, "in face of such testimony can we say that the Book in which the climax is reached, in which the last discords of the *Iliad* are dissolved in chivalrous pity and regret, is not the work of the original poet, but of some Homerid or rhapsodist?"

Mr. Monro, with a struggle, finally voted for grammar, and other indications of lateness, against Shelley and against his own sense of poetry. In a letter to me of May 1905, Mr. Monro sketched a theory that Book IX. (without which he said that he deemed an *Achilleis* hardly possible) might be a *remanié* representative of an earlier lay to the same general effect. Some Greek Shakespeare, then, treated an older poem on the theme of Book IX. as Shakespeare treated old plays, namely, as a canvas to work over with a master's hand. Probably Mr. Monro would not have

---

[1] Monro, *Homeric Grammar*, pp. 394–396. 1891.

gone so far in the case of Book XXIV., *The Repentance of Achilles.* He thought it in too keen contrast with the brutality of Book XXII. (obviously forgetting that in Book XXIV. Achilles is infinitely more brutal than in Book XXII.), and thought it inconsistent with the refusal of Achilles to grant burial at the prayer of the dying Hector, and with his criminal treatment of the dead body of his chivalrous enemy.   But in Book XXIV. his ferocity is increased.   Mr. Leaf shares Mr. Monro's view ; but Mr. Leaf thinks that a Greek audience forgave Achilles, because he was doing "the will of heaven," and "fighting the great fight of Hellenism against barbarism."[1]   But the Achæans were not Puritans of the sixteenth century !   Moreover, the Trojans are as "Hellenic" as the Achæans.   They converse, clearly, in the same language.   They worship the same gods.   The Achæans cannot regard them (unless on account of the breach of truce, by no Trojan, but an ally) as the Covenanters regarded "malignants," their name for loyal cavaliers, whom they also styled "Amalekites," and treated as Samuel treated Agag. The Achæans to whom Homer sang had none of this sanguinary Pharisaism.

Others must decide on the exact value and import of Odyssean grammar as a test of lateness, and must estimate the probable amount of time required for the development of such linguistic differences as they find in the *Odyssey* and *Iliad.*   In undertaking this task they may compare the literary language of America as it was before 1860 and as it is now.   The language of English literature has also been greatly modified in the last forty years, but our times are actively progressive

[1] Leaf, *Iliad*, vol. ii. p. 429. 1902.

in many directions; linguistic variations might arise more slowly in the Greece of the Epics. We have already shown, in the more appropriate instance of the *Chancun de Willame*, that considerable varieties in diction and metre occur in a single MS. of that poem, a MS. written probably within less than a century of the date of the poem's composition.

We can also trace, in *remaniements* of the *Chanson de Roland*, comparatively rapid and quite revolutionary variations from the oldest—the Oxford—manuscript. Rhyme is substituted for assonance ; the process entails frequent modernisations, and yet the basis of thirteenth-century texts continues to be the version of the eleventh century. It may be worth the while of scholars to consider these parallels carefully, as regards the language and prosody of the Odyssean Books of the *Iliad*, and to ask themselves whether the processes of alteration in the course of transmission, which we know to have occurred in the history of the Old French, may not also have affected the *Iliad*, though why the effect is mainly confined to four Books remains a puzzle. It is enough for us to have shown that if Odyssean varies from Iliadic language, in all other respects the two poems bear the marks of the same age. Meanwhile, a Homeric scholar so eminent as Mr. T. W. Allen, says that " the linguistic attack upon their age " (that of the Homeric poems) " may be said to have at last definitely failed, and archæology has erected an apparently indestructible buttress for their defence." [1]

---

[1] *Classical Review*, May 1906, p. 194.

R

CHAPTER XIII

THE "DOLONEIA"

"ILIAD," BOOK X.

OF all Books in the *Iliad*, Book X., called the *Doloneia*, is most generally scouted and rejected. The Book, in fact, could be omitted, and only a minutely analytic reader would perceive the lacuna. He would remark that in *Iliad*, IX. 65–84, certain military preparations are made which, if we suppress Book X., lead up to nothing, and that in *Iliad*, XIV. 9–11, we find Nestor with the shield of his son, Thrasymedes, while Thrasymedes has his father's shield, a fact not explained, though the poet certainly meant something by it. The explanation in both cases is found in Book X., which may also be thought to explain why the Achæans, so disconsolate in Book IX., and why Agamemnon, so demoralised, so gaily assume the offensive in Book XI. Some ancient critics, Scholiast T and Eustathius, attributed the *Doloneia* to Homer, but supposed it to have been a separate composition of his added to the *Iliad* by Pisistratus. This merely proves that they did not find any necessity for the existence of the *Doloneia*. Mr. Allen, who thinks that "it always held its present place," says, "the *Doloneia* is persistently written down." [1]

To understand the problem of the *Doloneia*, we must

[1] *Classical Review*, May 1906, p. 194.

make a summary of its contents. In Book IX. 65–84,
at the end of the disastrous fighting of Book VIII., the
Achæans, by Nestor's advice, station an advanced guard
of "*the young men*" between the fosse and wall; 700
youths are posted there, under Meriones, the squire of
Idomeneus, and Thrasymedes, the son of Nestor. All
this is preparation for Book X., as Mr. Leaf remarks,[1]
though in any case an advanced guard was needed.
Their business is to remain awake, under arms, in case
the Trojans, who are encamped on the plain, attempt
a night attack. At their station the young men will be
under arms till dawn ; they light fires and cook their
provisions ; the Trojans also surround their own watch-
fires.

The Achæan chiefs then hold council, and Agamemnon sends the embassy to Achilles. The envoys bring
back his bitter answer ; and all men go to sleep in their
huts, deeply discouraged, as even Odysseus avowed.

Here the Tenth Book begins, and it is manifest that
the poet is thoroughly well acquainted with the Ninth
Book. Without the arrangements made in the Ninth
Book, and without the despairing situation of that Book,
his lay is impossible. It will be seen that critics suppose him, alternately, to have "quite failed to realise
the conditions of life of the heroes of whom he sang"
(that is, if certain lines are genuine), and also to be a
peculiarly learned archæologist and a valuable authority
on weapons. He is addicted to introducing fanciful
"touches of heroic simplicity," says Mr. Leaf, and is
altogether a puzzling personage to the critics.

The Book opens with the picture of Agamemnon,
sleepless from anxiety, while the other chiefs, save

[1] *Companion*, p. 174.

Menelaus, are sleeping. He " hears the music of the joyous Trojan pipes and flutes," and sees the reflected glow of their camp-fires, we must suppose, for he could not see the fires themselves through the new wall of his own camp, as critics very wisely remark. He tears out his hair before Zeus ; no one else does so, in the *Iliad*, but no one else is Agamemnon, alone and in despair.

He rises to consult Nestor, throwing a lion's skin over his *chiton*, and grasping a spear. Much noise is made about the furs, such as this lion's pelt, which the heroes, in Book X., throw about their shoulders when suddenly aroused. That sportsmen like the heroes should keep the pelts of animals slain by them for use as coverlets, and should throw on one of the pelts when aroused in a hurry, is a marvellous thing to the critics. They know that fleeces were used for coverlets of beds (IX. 661), and pelts of wild animals, slain by Anchises, cover his bed in the Hymn to Aphrodite.

But the facts do not enlighten critics. Yet no facts could be more natural. A scientific critic, moreover, never reflects that the poet is dealing with an unexampled situation—heroes wakened and called into the cold air in a night of dread, but not called to battle. Thus Reichel says : " The poet knows so little about true heroic costume that he drapes the princes in skins of lions and panthers, like giants. . . . But about a corslet he never thinks." [1]

The simple explanation is that the poet has not hitherto had to tell us about men who are called up, *not* to fight, on a night that must have been chilly. In war they do not wear skins, though Paris, in archer's equip-

[1] Reichel, p. 70.

ment, wears a pard's skin (III. 17). Naturally, the men throw over themselves their fur coverlets ; but Nestor, a chilly veteran, prefers a *chiton* and a wide, double-folded, fleecy purple cloak. The cloak lay ready to his hand, for such cloaks were used as blankets (XXIV. 646 ; *Odyssey*, III. 349, 351 ; IV. 299 ; II. 189). We hear more of such bed-coverings in the *Odyssey* than in the *Iliad*, merely because in the *Odyssey* we have more references to beds and to people in bed. That a sportsman may have (as many folk have now) a fur coverlet, and may throw it over him as a kind of dressing-gown or " bed-gown," is a simple circumstance which bewilders the critical mind and perplexed Reichel.

If the poet knew so little as Reichel supposed his omission of corslets is explained. Living in an age of corslets (seventh century), he, being a literary man, knew nothing about corslets, or, as he is also an acute archæologist, he knew too much ; he knew that they were not worn in the Mycenæan prime, so he did not introduce them. The science of this remarkable ignoramus, in *this* view, accounts for his being aware that pelts of animals were in vogue as coverlets, just as fur dressing-gowns were worn in the sixteenth century, and he introduces them precisely as he leaves corslets out, because he knows that pelts of fur were in use, and that, in the Mycenæan prime, corslets were not worn.

In speaking to Nestor, Agamemnon awakens sympathy : " Me, of all the Achæans, Zeus has set in toil and labour ceaselessly." They are almost the very words of Charlemagne in the *Chanson de Roland* : " *Deus, dist li Reis, si peneuse est ma vie.*" The author of the *Doloneia* consistently conforms to the character of Agamemnon as drawn in the rest of the *Iliad*. He is over-anxious ; he is demoralising in his fits of gloom, but all the burden of the host hangs on him—*si peneuse est ma vie.*

To turn to higher things. Menelaus, too, was awake, anxious about the Argives, who risked their lives in his cause alone. He got up, put on a pard's skin and a bronze helmet (here the poet forgets, what he ought to have known, that no bronze helmets have been found in the Mycenæan graves). Menelaus takes a spear, and goes to look for Agamemnon, whom he finds arming himself beside his ship. He discovers that Agamemnon means to get Nestor to go and speak to the advanced guard, as his son is their commander, and they will obey Nestor. Agamemnon's pride has fallen very low ! He tells Menelaus to waken the other chief with all possible formal courtesy, for, brutally rude when in high heart, at present Agamemnon cowers to everybody. He himself finds Nestor in bed, his *shield*, two spears, and helmet beside him, also his glittering *zoster*. His corslet is not named ; perhaps the poet knew that the *zoster*, or broad metallic belt, had been evolved, but that the corslet had not been invented ; or perhaps he " knows so little about the costume of the heroes " that he is unaware of the existence of corslets. Nestor asks Agamemnon what he wants ; and Agamemnon says that his is a toilsome life, that he cannot sleep, that his knees tremble, and that he wants Nestor to come and visit the outposts.

There is really nothing absurd in this. Napoleon often visited his outposts in the night before Waterloo, and Cromwell rode along his lines all through the night before Dunbar, biting his lips till the blood dropped on his linen bands. In all three cases hostile armies were arrayed within striking distance of each other, and the generals were careworn.

Nestor admits that it is an anxious night, and rather blames Menelaus for not rousing the other chiefs ; but Agamemnon explains and defends his brother. Nestor then puts on the comfortable cloak already described, and picks up a spear, *leaving his shield in his quarters.*

As for Odysseus, he merely throws a shield over his shoulders. The company of Diomede are sleeping with their heads on their shields. Thence Reichel (see " The Shield ") infers that the late poet of Book X. gave them small Ionian round bucklers ; but it has been shown that no such inference is legitimate. Their spears were erect by their sides, fixed in the ground by the *sauroter,* or butt-spike, used by the men of the late " warrior vase " found at Mycenæ. To arrange the spears thus, we have seen, was a point of drill that, in Aristotle's time, survived among the Illyrians.[1] The practice is also alluded to in *Iliad,* III. 135. During a truce " the tall spears are planted by their sides." The poet, whether ignorant or learned, knew that point of war, later obsolete in Greece, but still extant in Illyria.

Nestor aroused Diomede, whose night apparel was the pelt of a lion ; he took his spear, and they came to the outposts, where the men were awake, and kept a keen watch on all movements among the Trojans. Nestor praised them, and the princes, taking Nestor's son, Thrasymedes, and Meriones with them, went out into the open in view of the Trojan camp, sat down, and held a consultation.

Nestor asked if any one would volunteer to go as a spy among the Trojans and pick up intelligence. His

[1] *Poetics,* xxv.

reward will be "a black ewe with her lamb at her foot,"
from their chiefs—"nothing like her for value"—and
he will be remembered in songs at feasts, *or* will be
admitted to feasts and wine parties of the chiefs.[1]
The proposal is very odd; what do the princes
want with black ewes, while at feasts they always
have honoured places?　Can Nestor be thinking of
sending out any brave swift-footed young member
of the outpost party, to whom the reward would be
appropriate?

After silence, Diomede volunteers to go, with a
comrade, though this kind of work is very seldom
undertaken in any army of any age by a chief, and
by his remark about admission to wine parties it is
clear that Nestor was not thinking of a princely spy.
Many others volunteer, but Agamemnon bids Diomede
choose his own companion, with a very broad hint
not to take Menelaus.　*His* death, Agamemnon knows,
would mean the disgraceful return of the host to
Greece; besides he is, throughout the *Iliad*, deeply
attached to his brother.

The poet of Book X., however late, knows the *Iliad*
well, for he keeps up the uniform treatment of the
character of the Over-Lord.　As he knows the *Iliad*
well, how can he be ignorant of the conditions of life
of the heroes?　How can he dream of "introducing
a note of heroic simplicity" (Mr. Leaf's phrase), when
he must be as well aware as we are of the way in
which the heroes lived?　We cannot explain the black
ewes, if meant as a princely reward, but we do not
know everything about Homeric life.

Diomede chooses Odysseus, "whom Pallas Athene

---

[1] Leaf, Note on X. 215.

loveth " ; she was also the patroness of Diomede himself, in Books V., VI.

As they are unarmed—all of the chiefs hastily aroused were unarmed, save for a spear there or a sword here—Thrasymedes gives to Diomede his two-edged sword, *his shield*, and "a helm of bull's hide, without horns or crest, that is called a skull-cap (knapskull), and keeps the heads of strong young men." All the advanced guard were young men, as we saw in Book IX. 77. Obviously, Thrasymedes must then send back to camp, though we are not told it, for another shield, sword, and helmet, as he is to lie all night under arms. We shall hear of the shield later.

Meriones, who is an archer (XIII. 650), lends to Odysseus his bow and quiver and a sword. He also gives him "a helm made of leather ; and with many a thong it was stiffly wrought within, while without the white teeth of a boar of flashing tusks were arrayed, thick set on either side well and cunningly. . . ." Here Reichel perceives that the ignorant poet is describing a piece of ancient headgear represented in Mycenæan art, while the boars' teeth were found by Schliemann, to the number of sixty, in Grave IV. at Mycenæ. Each of them had "the reverse side cut perfectly flat, and with the borings to attach them to some other object." They were "in a veritable funereal armoury." The manner of setting the tusks on the cap is shown on an ivory head of a warrior from Mycenæ.[1]

Reichel recognises that the poet's description in Book X. is excellent, " *ebenso klar als eingehend.*" He publishes another ivory head from Spata, with the same helmet set with boars' tusks.[2]

---

[1] Tsountas and Manatt, 196–197. [2] Reichel, pp. 102–104.

Mr. Leaf decides that this description by the poet, wholly ignorant of heroic costume, as Reichel thinks him, must be " another instance of the archaic and archæologising tendency so notable in Book X."[1]

At the same time, according to Reichel and Mr. Leaf, the poet of Book X. introduces the small round Ionian buckler, thus showing his utter ignorance of the great Mycenæan shield. The ignorance was most unusual and quite inexcusable, for any one who reads the rest of the *Iliad* (which the poet of Book X. knew well) is aware that the Homeric shields were huge, often covering body and legs. This fact the poet of Book X. did not know, in Reichel's opinion.[2]

How are we to understand this poet ? He is such an erudite archæologist that, in the seventh century, he knows and carefully describes a helmet of the Mycenæan prime. Did he excavate it ? and had the leather interior lasted with the felt cap through seven centuries ? Or did he see a sample in an old temple of the Mycenæan prime, or in a museum of his own period ? Or had he heard of it in a lost Mycenæan poem ? Yet, careful as he was, so pedantic that he must have puzzled his seventh-century audience, who never saw such caps, the poet knew nothing of the shields and costumes of the heroes, though he might have found out all that is known about them in the then existing Iliadic lays with which he was perfectly familiar—see his portrait of Agamemnon. He was well aware that corslets were, in Homeric poetry, anachronisms, for he gave Nestor none ; yet he fully believed, in his ignorance, that small Ionian bucklers

[1] *Iliad*, vol. ii. p. 629.
[2] Leaf, *Iliad*, vol. i. p. 575.

(which need the aid of corslets badly) were the only wear among the heroes !

Criticism has, as we often observe, no right to throw the first stone at the inconsistencies of Homer. As we cannot possibly believe that one poet knew so much which his contemporaries did not know (and how, in the seventh century, could he know it ?), and that he also knew so little, knew nothing in fact, we take our own view. The poet of Book X. sings of a fresh topic, a confused night of dread ; of young men wearing the headgear which, he says, young men *do* wear ; of pelts of fur such as suddenly wakened men, roused, but not roused for battle, would be likely to throw over their bodies against the chill air. He describes things of his own day ; things with which he is familiar. He is said to " take quite a peculiar delight in the minute description of dress and weapons." [1] We do not observe that he does describe weapons or shields minutely ; but Homer always loves to describe weapons and costume—scores of examples prove it— and here he happens to be describing such costume as he nowhere else has occasion to mention. By an accident of archæological discovery, we find that there were such caps set with boars' tusks as he introduces. They had survived, for young men on night duty, into the poet's age. We really cannot believe that a poet of the seventh century had made excavations in Mycenæan graves. If he did and put the results into his lay, his audience—not wearing boars' tusks —would have asked, " What nonsense is the man talking ? "

Erhardt, remarking on the furs which the heroes

[1] Leaf, *Iliad*, vol. i. p. 423.

throw over their shoulders when aroused, says that this kind of wrap is very late. It was Peisander who, in the second half of the seventh century, clothed Herakles in a lion's skin. Peisander brought this costume into poetry, and the author of the *Doloneia* knew no better than to follow Peisander.[1] The poet of the *Doloneia* was thus much better acquainted with Peisander than with the Homeric lays, which could' have taught him that a hero would never wear a fur coverlet when aroused—not to fight—from slumber. Yet he knew about leathern caps set with boars' tusks. He must have been an erudite excavator, but, in literature, a reader only of recent minor poetry.

Having procured arms, without corslets (*with* corslets, according to Carl Robert)—whether, if they had none, because the poet knew that corslets were anachronisms, or because spies usually go as lightly burdened as possible—Odysseus and Diomede approach the Trojan camp. The hour is the darkest hour before dawn. They hear, but do not see, a heron sent by Athene as an omen, and pray to the goddess, with promise of sacrifice.

In the Trojan camp Hector has called a council, and asked for a volunteer spy to seek intelligence among the Achæans. He offers no black ewes as a reward, but the best horses of the enemy. This allures Dolon, son of a rich Trojan, " an only son among five sisters," a poltroon, a weak lad, ugly, but swift of foot, and an enthusiastic lover of horses. He asks for the steeds of Achilles, which Hector swears to give him ; and to be lightly clad he takes merely spear and bow and a cap of ferret skin, with the pelt of a wolf for covering. Odysseus sees him approach ; he and Diomede lie down

---

[1] *Die Entstehung der Homerischen Gedichte*, pp. 163-164.

among the dead till Dolon passes, then they chase him towards the Achæan camp and catch him. He offers ransom, which before these last days of the war was often accepted. Odysseus replies evasively, and asks for information. Dolon, thinking that the bitterness of death is past, explains that only the Trojans have watch-fires ; the allies, more careless, have none. At the extreme flank of the host sleep the newly arrived Thracians, under their king, Rhesus, who has golden armour, and "the fairest horses that ever I beheld" (the ruling passion for horses is strong in Dolon), "and the greatest, whiter than snow, and for speed like the winds."

Having learned all that he needs to know, Diomede ruthlessly slays Dolon. Odysseus thanks Athene, and hides the poor spoils of the dead, marking the place. They then creep into the dark camp of the sleeping Thracians, and as Diomede slays them Odysseus drags each body aside, to leave a clear path for the horses, that they may not plunge and tremble when they are led forth, "for they were not yet used to dead men."

No line in Homer shows more intimate knowledge and realisation of horses and of war. Odysseus drives the horses of Rhesus out of the camp with the bow of Meriones ; he has forgotten to take the whip from the chariot. Diomede, having slain King Rhesus asleep, thinks whether he shall lift out the chariot (war chariots were very light) or drag it by the pole ; but Athene warns him to be going. He "springs upon the steeds," and they make for their camp. It is not clearly indicated whether they ride or drive (X., 513, 527–528, 541) ; but, suppose that they ride, are we to conclude that the fact proves "lateness"? The heroes always drive in Homer, but it is inconceivable that they could not ride in cases of necessity, as here, if Diomede has thought it wiser not to bring out the chariot and harness the horses. Riding is mentioned in *Iliad*, XV. 679, in a simile ; again, in a simile, *Odyssey*, V. 371. It is not the custom for heroes to ride ; the chariot is used in war and in travelling, but, when there are horses and no chariot, men could not be so imbecile as not to mount the horses, nor could the poet be so pedantic as not to make them do so.

The shields would cause no difficulty ; they would be slung sideways, like the shields of knights in the early Middle Ages. The pair, picking up Dolon's spoils as they pass, hurry back to the chiefs, where Nestor welcomes them. The others laugh and are encouraged (to encourage them and his audience is the aim of the poet) ; while the pair go to Diomede's quarters, wash off the blood and sweat from their limbs in the sea, and then "enter the polished baths," common in the *Odyssey*, unnamed in the *Iliad*. But on no other occasion in the *Iliad* are we admitted to view this part of heroic toilette. Nowhere else, in fact, do we accompany a hero to his quarters and his tub after the day's work is over. Achilles, however, refuses to wash, after fighting, in his grief for Patroclus, though plenty of water was being heated for the purpose, and it is to be presumed that a bath was ready for the water (*Iliad*, XXIII. 40). See, too, for Hector's bath, XXII. 444.

The two heroes then refresh themselves ; breakfast, in fact, and drink, as is natural. By this time the dawn must have been in the sky, and in Book XI. men are stirring with the dawn.

Such is the story of Book X. The reader may decide as to whether it is " *Very late ; barely Homeric,*" or a late and deliberate piece of burlesque,[1] or whether it is very Homeric, though the whole set of situations —a night of terror, an anxious chief, a nocturnal adventure—are unexampled in the poem.

The poet's audience of warriors must have been familiar with such situations, and must have appreciated the humorous, ruthless treatment of Dolon, the spoiled only brother of five sisters. Mr. Monro admitted that Dolon is Shakespearian, but added, "too Shakespearian for Homer." One may as well say that Agincourt, in *Henry V.,* is "too Homeric for Shakespeare."

Mr. Monro argued that "the Tenth Book comes in awkwardly after the Ninth." Nitzsche thinks just the reverse. The patriotic warrior audience would delight in the *Doloneia* after the anguish of Book IX.; would laugh with Odysseus at the close of his adventure, and rejoice with the other Achæans (X. 505).

"The introductory part of the Book is cumbrous," says Mr. Monro. To *us* it is, if we wish to get straight to the adventure, just as the customary delays in Book XIX., before Achilles is allowed to fight, are tedious to us. But the poet's audience did not necessarily share our tastes, and might take pleasure (as I do) in the curious details of the opening of Book X. The poet was thinking of his audience, not of modern professors.

"We hear no more of Rhesus and his Thracians." Of Rhesus there was no more to hear, and his people probably went home, like Glenbuckie's Stewarts after

[1] Henry, *Classical Review.* March 1906.

the mysterious death of their chief in Arnprior's house of Leny before Prestonpans (1745). Glenbuckie was mysteriously pistolled in the night. " The style and tone is unlike that of the *Iliad*. . . . It is rather akin to comedy of a rough farcical kind." But it was time for " comic relief." If the story of Dolon be comic, it is comic with the practical humour of the sagas. In an isolated nocturnal adventure and massacre we cannot expect the style of an heroic battle under the sunlight. Is the poet not to be allowed to be various, and is the scene of the Porter in *Macbeth*, " in style and tone," like the rest of the drama? (*Macbeth*, Act ii. sc. 3). Here, of course, Shakespeare indulges infinitely more in " comedy of a rough practical kind " than does the author of the *Doloneia*.

The humour and the cruelty do not exceed what is exhibited in many of the *gabes*, or insulting boasts of heroes over dead foes in other parts of the *Iliad* ; such as the taunting comparison of a warrior falling from his chariot to a diver after oysters, or as " one of the Argives hath caught the spear in his flesh, and leaning thereon for a staff, methinks that he will go down within the house of Hades " (XIV. 455–457). The *Iliad*, like the sagas, is rich in this extremely practical humour.

Mr. Leaf says that the Book " must have been composed before the *Iliad* had reached its present form, for it cannot have been meant to follow on Book IX. It is rather another case of a parallel rival to that Book, coupled with it only in the final literary redaction," which Mr. Leaf dates in the middle of the sixth century. " The Book must have been composed before the *Iliad* had reached its present form,"[1] It

[1] *Iliad*, vol. i. p. 424.

is not easy to understand this decision; for, as Mr.
Leaf had previously written, about Book IX. 60–68,
"the posting of the watch is at least not necessary to
the story, and it has a suspicious air of being merely
a preparation for the next Book, which is much later,
and which turns entirely upon a visit to the sentinels."[1]

Now a military audience would not have pardoned
the poet of Book IX. if, in the circumstances of defeat,
with a confident enemy encamped within striking distance, he had not made the Achæans throw forth their
outposts. The thing was inevitable and is not suspicious ; but the poet purposely makes the advanced
guard consist of young men under Nestor's son and
Meriones. He needs them for Book X. Therefore
the poet of Book IX. is the poet of Book X. preparing
his effect in advance ; or the poet of Book X. is a man
who cleverly takes advantage of Book IX., or he composed his poem of "a night of terror and adventure,"
"in the air," and the editor of 540 B.C., having heard
it recited and copied it out, went back to Book IX.
and inserted the advanced guard, under Thrasymedes
and Meriones, to lead up to Book X.

On Mr. Leaf's present theory,[2] Book X., we presume, was meant, *not* to follow Book IX., but to follow
the end of Book VII., being an alternative to Book VIII.
(composed, he says, to lead up to Book IX.) and Book
IX. But Book VII. closes with the Achæan refusal of
the compromise offered by Paris—the restoration of the
property but not of the wife of Menelaus. The Trojans
and Achæans feast all night ; the Trojans feast in the
city. There is therefore no place here for Book X.
after Book VII., and the Achæans cannot roam about

[1] *Companion*, p. 174.   [2] *Iliad*, vol. i. p. 424.

all night, as they are feasting ; nor can Agamemnon be
in the state of anxiety exhibited by him in Book X.

Book X. could not exist without Book IX., and *must*
have been " meant to follow on it." Mr. Leaf sees that,
in his preface to Book IX.,[1] " The placing of sentinels "
(in Book IX. 80, 84) " is needed as an introduction to
Book X. but has nothing to do with this Book " (IX.).
But, we have said, it was inevitable, given the new situation in Book IX. (an Achæan repulse, and the enemy
camped in front), that an advanced guard must be placed,
even if there proved to be no need of their services.
We presume that Mr. Leaf's literary editor, finding that
Book X. existed and that the advanced guard was a
necessity of its action, went back to Book IX. and introduced an advanced guard of young men, with its cap-
tains, Thrasymedes and Meriones. Even after this the
editor had much to do, if Book IX. originally exhibited
Agamemnon as not in terror and despair, as it now does.

We need not throw the burden of all this work
on the editor. As Mr. Leaf elsewhere writes, in a
different mind, the Tenth Book " is obviously adapted
to its present place in the *Iliad*, for it assumes a moment
when Achilles is absent from the field, and when the
Greeks are in deep dejection from a recent defeat.
These conditions are exactly fulfilled by the situation
at the end of Book IX." [2]

This is certainly the case. The Tenth Book could
not exist without the Ninth ; yet Mr. Leaf's new opinion
is that it " cannot have been meant to follow on Book
IX." [3] He was better inspired when he held the precisely opposite opinion.

---

[1] *Iliad*, vol. i. p. 371.   [2] *Companion*, p. 190.
[3] *Iliad*, vol. i. p. 424.

Dr. Adolf Kiene[1] accepts Book XI. as originally composed to fill its present place in the *Iliad*. He points out the despondency of the chiefs after receiving the reply of Achilles, and supposes that even Diomede (IX. 708) only urges Agamemnon to "array before the ships thy folk and horsemen," for *defensive* battle. But, encouraged by the success of the night adventure, Agamemnon next day assumes the offensive. To consider thus is perhaps to consider too curiously. But it is clear that the Achæans have been much encouraged by the events of Book X., especially Agamemnon, whose character, as Kiene observes, is very subtly and consistently treated, and " lies near the poet's heart." This is the point which we keep urging. Agamemnon's care for Menelaus is strictly preserved in Book X.

Nitzsche (1897) writes, " Between Book IX. and Book XI. there is a gap ; that gap the *Doloneia* fills : it must have been composed to be part of the *Iliad*." But he thinks that the *Doloneia* has taken the place of an earlier lay which filled the gap.[2] That the Book is never referred to later in the *Iliad*, even if it be true, is no great argument against its authenticity. For when later references are made to Book IX., they are dismissed as clever late interpolations. If the horses of Rhesus took part, as they do not, in the sports at the funeral of Patroclus, the passage would be called a clever interpolation : in fact, Diomede had better horses, divine horses to run. However, it is certainly remarkable that the interpolation was not made by one of the interpolators of critical theory.

[1] *Die Epen des Homer, Zweiter Theil*, pp. 90-94. Hanover, 1884.
[2] *Die Echtheit der Doloneia*, p. 32. Programme des K. K. Staats Gymnasium zu Marburg, 1877.

Meanwhile there is, we think, a reference to Book X. in Book XIV.[1]

In *Iliad*, XIV. 9–11, we read that Nestor, in his quarters with the wounded Machaon, on the day following the night of Dolon's death, hears the cry of battle and goes out to see what is happening. " He took the well-wrought shield of his son, horse-taming Thrasymedes, which was lying in the hut, all glistening with bronze, *but the son had the shield of his father*."

Why had Thrasymedes the shield of his father ? At about 3 A.M. before dawn the shield of Nestor was lying beside him in his own bedroom (Book X. 76), and at the same moment his son Thrasymedes was on outpost duty, and had his own shield with him (Book IX. 81).

When, then, did father and son exchange shields, and why ? Mr. Leaf says, " It is useless to inquire why father and son had thus changed shields, as the scholiasts of course do."

The scholiasts merely babble. Homer, of course, meant *something* by this exchange of shields, which occurred late in the night of Book IX. or very early in the following day, that of Books XI.–XVI.

Let us follow again the sequence of events. On the night before the day when Nestor had Thrasymedes' shield and Thrasymedes had Nestor's, Thrasymedes was sent out, with shield and all, in command of one of the seven companies of an advanced guard, posted between fosse and wall, in case of a camisade by the Trojans, who were encamped on the plain (IX. 81). With him in command were Meriones and five other

---

[1] This was pointed out to me by Mr. Shewan, to whose great knowledge of Homer I am here much indebted.

young men less notable. They had supplies with
them and whatever was needed : they cooked supper
in bivouac.

In the *Doloneia* the wakeful princes, after inspecting
the advanced guard, go forward within view of the
Trojan ranks and consult. With them they take
Nestor's son, Thrasymedes, and Meriones (X. 196).
The two young men, being on active service, are
armed ; the princes are not. Diomede, having been
suddenly roused out of sleep, with no intention to
fight, merely threw on his dressing-gown, a lion's skin.
Nestor wore a thick, double, purple dressing-gown.
Odysseus had cast his shield about his shoulders. It
was decided that Odysseus and Diomede should enter
the Trojan camp and "prove a jeopardy." Diomede
had no weapon but his spear ; so Thrasymedes, who
is armed as we saw, lends him his bull's-hide cap,
"that keeps the heads of stalwart youths," his sword
(for that of Diomede "was left at the ships "), and his
shield.

Diomede and Odysseus successfully achieve their ad-
venture and return to the chiefs, where they talk with
Nestor ; and then they go to Diomede's hut and drink.
The outposts remain, of course, at their stations.

Meanwhile, Thrasymedes, having lent his shield to
Diomede, has none of his own. Naturally, as he was
to pass the night under arms, he would send to his
father's quarters for the old man's shield, a sword,
and a helmet. He would remain at his post (his men
had provisions) till the general *réveillez* at dawn, and
would then breakfast at his post and go into the fray.
Nestor, therefore, missing his shield, would send round
to Diomede's quarters for the shield of Thrasymedes,

which had been lent overnight to Diomede, would take it into the fight, and would bring it back to his own hut when he carried the wounded Machaon thither out of the battle. When he arms to go out and seek for information, he picks up the shield of Thrasymedes.

Nothing can be more obvious ; the poet, being a man of imagination, not a professor, sees it all, and casually mentions that the son had the father's and the father had the son's shield. His audience, men of the sword, see the case as clearly as the poet does : only we moderns and the scholiasts, almost as modern as ourselves, are puzzled.

It may also be argued, though we lay no stress on it, that in Book XI. 312, when Agamemnon has been wounded, we find Odysseus and Diomede alone together, without their contingents, because they have not separated since they breakfasted together, after returning from the adventure of Book X., and thus they have come rather late to the field. They find the Achæans demoralised by the wounding of Agamemnon, and they make a stand. " What ails us," asks Odysseus, "that we forget our impetuous valour ? " The passage appears to take up the companionship of Odysseus and Diomede, who were left breakfasting together at the end of Book X. and are not mentioned till we meet them again in this scene of Book XI., as if they had just come on the field.

As to the linguistic tests of lateness "there are exceptionally numerous traces of later formation," says Mr. Monro ; while Fick, *tout au contraire*, writes, " clumsy Ionisms are not common, and, as a rule, occur in these parts which on older grounds show themselves to be late interpolations." " The cases of agreement" (between Fick and Mr. Monro), "are few, and the passages thus condemned are not more numerous in the *Doloneia* than in any average book."[1] The six examples of "a post-Homeric use of the article" do not seem so very post-Homeric to an ordinary intelligence—parallels occur in Book I.— and "Perfects in κα from derivative verbs" do not destroy the impression of antiquity and unity which is left by the treatment of character ; by the celebrated cap with boars' tusks, which no human being could archæologically reconstruct in the seventh century ; and by the Homeric vigour in such touches as the horses unused to dead men. As the *Iliad* certainly passed through centuries in which its language could not but be affected by linguistic changes, as it could not escape from *remaniements*, consciously or unconsciously intro- duced by reciters and copyists, the linguistic objections are not strongly felt by us. An unphilological reader of Homer notes that Duntzer thinks the *Doloneia* "older than the oldest portion of the *Odyssey*," while Gemoll thinks that the author of the *Doloneia* was familiar with the *Odyssey*.[2]

Meanwhile, one thing seems plain to us: when the author of Book IX. posted the guards under Thrasymedes, he was deliberately leading up to Book X. ; while the casual remark in Book XIV. about the exchange of shields between father and son, Nestor and Thrasymedes, glances back at Book X. and possibly refers to some lost and more explicit statement.

It is not always remembered that, if things could

---

[1] Jevons, *Journal of Hellenic Studies*, vii. p. 302.
[2] Duntzer, *Homer. Abhanglungen*, p. 324. Gemoll, *Hermes*, xv. 557 *ff*.

drop into the *Iliad*, interpolations, things could also drop out of the *Iliad*, causing *lacunæ*, during the dark backward of its early existence.

If the *Doloneia* be "barely Homeric," as Father Browne holds, this opinion was not shared by the listeners or readers of the sixth century. The vase painters often illustrate the *Doloneia ;* but it does not follow that "the story was fresh" because it was "popular," as Mr. Leaf suggests, and "was treated as public property in a different way" (namely, in a comic way) "from the consecrated early legends" (*Iliad*, II. 424, 425). The sixth century vase painters illustrated many passages in Homer, not the *Doloneia* alone. The "comic way" was the ruthless humour of two strong warriors capturing one weak coward. Much later, wild caricature was applied in vase painting to the most romantic scenes in the *Odyssey*, which were "consecrated" enough.

CHAPTER XIV

THE INTERPOLATIONS OF NESTOR

THAT several of the passages in which Nestor speaks are very late interpolations, meant to glorify Pisistratus, himself of Nestor's line, is a critical opinion to which we have more than once alluded. The first example is in *Iliad*, II. 530–568. This passage " is meant at once to present Nestor as the leading counsellor of the Greek army, and to introduce the coming *Catalogue*." [1] Now the *Catalogue* " originally formed an introduction to the whole Cycle." [2] But, to repeat an earlier observation, surely the whole Cycle was much later than the period of Pisistratus and his sons ; that is, the compilation of the Homeric and Cyclic poems into one body of verse, named "The Cycle," is believed to have been much later.

It is objected that Nestor's advice in this passage, " Separate thy warriors by tribes and clans " (φῦλα, φρήτρας), " is out of place in the last year of the war " ; but this suggestion for military reorganisation may be admitted as a mere piece of poetical perspective, like Helen's description of the Achæan chiefs in Book III., or Nestor may wish to return to an obsolete system of clan regiments. The Athenians had "tribes" and "clans," political institutions, and Nestor's advice is noted as a touch of late Attic influence ; but about the

---

[1] Leaf, *Iliad*, vol. i. p. 70.   [2] *Ibid.*, vol. i. p. 87.

nature and origin of these social divisions we know so
little that it is vain to argue about them.   The advice
of Nestor is an appeal to the clan spirit—a very serviceable military spirit, as the Highlanders have often
proved—but we have no information as to whether it
existed in Achæan times.   Nestor speaks as the aged
Lochiel spoke to Claverhouse before Killiecrankie.
Did the· Athenian army of the sixth century fight in
clan regiments ?   The device seems to belong to an
earlier civilisation, whether it survived in sixth century
Athens or not.   It is, of course, notorious that tribes
and clans are most flourishing among the most backward people, though they were welded into the consti-
tution of Athens.   The passage, therefore, cannot with
any certainty be dismissed as very late, for the words
for " tribe " and " clan " could not be novel Athenian
inventions, the institutions designated being of prehistoric origin.

Nestor shows his tactics again in IV. 303–309, offers
his " inopportune tactical lucubrations, doubtless under
Athenian (Pisistratean) influence."   The poet is here
denied a sense of humour.   That a veteran military
Polonius should talk as inopportunely about tactics as
Dugald Dalgetty does about the sconce of Drumsnab
is an essential part of the humour of the character of
Nestor.   This is what Nestor's critics do not see ; the
inopportune nature of his tactical remarks is the point
of them, just as in the case of the laird of Drum-
thwacket, " that should be."   Scott knew little of
Homer, but coincided in the Nestorian humour by
mere congruity of genius.   The Pisistratidæ must have
been humourless if they did not see that the poet smiled
as he composed Nestor's speeches, glorifying old deeds

of his own and old ways of fighting. He arrays his Pylians with chariots in front, footmen in the rear. In the *Iliad* the princely heroes dismounted to fight, the chariots following close behind them.[1] In the same way during the Hundred Years' War the English knights dismounted and defeated the French chivalry till, under Jeanne d'Arc and La Hire, the French learned the lesson, and imitated the English practice. On the other hand, Egyptian wall-paintings show the Egyptian chariotry advancing in neat lines and serried squadrons. According to Nestor these had of old been the Achæan tactics, and he preferred the old way. Nestor's advice in Book IV. is *not* to dismount or break the line of chariots ; these, he says, were the old tactics : " Even so is the far better way ; thus, moreover, did men of old time lay low cities and walls." There was to be no rushing of individuals from the ranks, no dismounting. Nestor's were not the tactics of the heroes — they usually dismount and do single valiances ; but Nestor, commanding his local contingent, recommends the methods of the old school, οἱ πρότεροι. What can be more natural and characteristic ?

The poet's meaning seems quite clear. He is not flattering Pisistratus, but, with quiet humour, offers the portrait of a vain, worthy veteran. It is difficult to see how this point can be missed ; it never was missed before Nestor's speeches seemed serviceable to the Pisistratean theory of the composition of the *Iliad*. In his first edition Mr. Leaf regarded the interpolations as intended " to glorify Nestor " without reference to Pisistratus, whom Mr. Leaf did not then recognise as the master of a sycophantic editor. The passages are

[1] *Iliad*, XI. 48–56.

really meant to display the old man's habit of glorifying himself and past times. Pisistratus could not feel
flattered by passages intended to exhibit his ancestor as
a conceited and inopportune old babbler. I ventured
in 1896 to suggest that the interpolator was trying to
please Pisistratus, but this was said in a spirit of
mockery.

Of all the characters in Homer that of Nestor is
most familiar to the unlearned world, merely because
Nestor's is a " character part," very broadly drawn.

The third interpolation of flattery to Pisistratus in
the person of Nestor is found in VII. 125–160. The
Achæan chiefs are loath to accept the challenge of
Hector to single combat. Only Menelaus rises and
arms himself, moved by the strong sense of honour
which distinguishes a warrior notoriously deficient in
bodily strength. Agamemnon refuses to let him fight ;
the other peers make no movement, and Nestor rebukes
them. It is entirely in nature that he should fall back
on his memory of a similar situation in his youth ; when
the Arcadian champion, Ereuthalion, challenged any
prince of the Pylians, and when " no man plucked up
heart " to meet him except Nestor himself. Had there
never been any Pisistratus, any poet who created the
part of a worthy and wordy veteran must have made
Nestor speak just as he does speak. Ereuthalion " was
the tallest and strongest of men that I have slain ! " and
Nestor, being what he is, offers copious and interesting
details about the armour of Ereuthalion and about its
former owners. The passage is like those in which the
Icelandic sagamen dwelt lovingly on the history of a
good sword, or the Maoris on the old possessors of an
ancient jade *patu*.

An objection is now taken to Nestor's geography : he is said not to know the towns and burns of his own country. He speaks of the swift stream Keladon, the streams of Iardanus, and the walls of Pheia. Pheia " is no doubt the same as Pheai "[1] (*Odyssey*, XV. 297), " but that was a maritime town not near Arkadia. There is nothing known of a Keladon or Iardanus anywhere near it." Now Didymus (Schol. A) "is said to have read Φήρης for Φεῖας," following Pherekydes.[2] M. Victor Bérard, who has made an elaborate study of Elian topography, says that " Pheia is a cape, not a town," and adopts the reading " Phera," the Pheræ of the journey of Telemachus, in the *Odyssey*. He thinks that the Pheræ of Nestor is the Aliphera of Polybius, and believes that the topography of Nestor and of the journey of Telemachus is correct. The Keladon is now the river or burn of Saint Isidore ; the Iardanus is at the foot of Mount Kaiapha. Keladon has obviously the same sense as the Gaelic Altgarbh, " the rough and brawling stream." Iardanus is also a stream in Crete, and Mr. Leaf thinks it Semitic—" *Yārden*, from *yārad*, to flow "; but the Semites did not give the *Yar* to the *Yarrow* nor to the Australian *Yarra Yarra*.

The country, says M. Bérard, is a network of rivers, burns, and rivulets ; and we cannot have any certainty, we may add, as the same river and burn names recur in many parts of the same country ;[3] many of them, in England, are plainly prae-Celtic.

While the correct geography may, on this showing, be that of Homer, we cannot give up Homer's claim to Nestor's speech. As to Nestor's tale about the armour

[1] Monro, Note on *Odyssey*, XV. 297.
[2] Leaf, *Iliad*, vol. i. 308.
[3] Bérard, *Les Phéniciens et L'Odyssée*, 108–113, 1902.

of Ereuthalion, it is manifest that the first owner of the
armour of Ereuthalion, namely Areïthous, " the Maceman," so called because he had the singularity of fighting
with an iron *casse-tête*, as Nestor explains (VII. 138–140),
was a famous character in legendary history. He appears
"as Prince Areïthous, the Maceman," father (or grandfather ?) of an Areïthous slain by Hector (VII. 8–10).
In Greece, it was not unusual for the grandson to bear
the grandfather's name, and, if the Maceman was grandfather of Hector's victim, there is no chronological
difficulty.   The chronological difficulty, in any case, if
Hector's victim is the son of the Maceman, is not at
all beyond a poetic narrator's possibility of error in
genealogy.   If Nestor's speech is a late interpolation,
if its late author borrowed his vivid account of the
Maceman and his *casse-tête* from the mere word " maceman " in VII. 9, he must be credited with a lively
poetic imagination.

Few or none of these reminiscences of Nestor are
really "inapplicable to the context."   Here the context
demands encouragement for heroes who shun a challenge.   Nestor mentions an "applicable" and apposite
instance of similar want of courage, and, as his character
demands, he is the hero of his own story.   His brag,
or *gabe*, about " he was the tallest and strongest of all
the men I ever slew," is deliciously in keeping, and
reminds us of the college don who said of the Czar,
" he is the nicest emperor I ever met."   The poet is
sketching an innocent vanity ; he is not flattering Pisistratus.

The next case is the long narrative of Nestor to the
hurried Patroclus, who has been sent by Achilles to
bring news of the wounded Machaon (XI. 604–702).

Nestor on this occasion has useful advice to give, namely, that Achilles, if he will not fight, should send his men, under Patroclus, to turn the tide of Trojan victory. But the poet wishes to provide an interval of time and of yet more dire disaster before the return of Patroclus to Achilles. By an obvious literary artifice he makes Nestor detain the reluctant Patroclus with a long story of his own early feats of arms. It is a story of a " hot-trod," so called in Border law ; the Eleians had driven a *creagh* of cattle from the Pylians, who pursued, and Nestor killed the Eleian leader, Itymoneus. The speech is an Achæan parallel to the Border ballad of " Jamie Telfer of the Fair Dodhead," in editing which Scott has been accused of making a singular and most obvious and puzzling blunder in the topography of his own sheriffdom of the Forest. On Scott's showing the scene of the raid is in upper Ettrickdale, not, as critics aver, in upper Teviotdale ; thus the narrative of the ballad would be impossible.[1]

The Pisistratean editor is accused of a similar error. " No doubt he was an Asiatic Greek, completely ignorant of the Peloponnesus." [2]   It is something to know that Pisistratus employed an editor, or that his editor employed a collaborator who was an Asiatic Greek !

Meanwhile, nothing is less secure than arguments based on the *Catalogue*. We have already shown how Mr. Leaf's opinions as to the date and historical merits of the *Catalogue* have widely varied, while M. Bérard appears to have vindicated the topography of Nestor. Of the *Catalogue* Mr. Allen writes, " As a table, according to regions, of Agamemnon's forces it bears every mark

---

[1] In fact both sites on the two Dodburns are impossible ; the fault lay with the ballad-maker, not with Scott.

[2] *Iliad.*   Note to XI. 756, and to the *Catalogue*, II. 615-617.

of venerable antiquity," showing "a state of things which never recurred in later history, and which no one had any interest to invent, or even the means for inventing." He makes a vigorous defence of the *Catalogue*, as regards the dominion of Achilles, against Mr. Leaf.[1] Into the details we need not go, but it is not questions of Homeric topography, obscure as they are, that can shake our faith in the humorous portrait of old Nestor, or make us suppose that the sympathetic mockery of the poet is the sycophantic adulation of the editor to his statesman employer, Pisistratus. If any question may be left to literary discrimination it is the authentic originality of the portrayal of Nestor.

---

[1] *Classical Review*, May 1906, pp. 194–201.

CHAPTER XV

THE COMPARATIVE STUDY OF EARLY EPICS

THOUGH comparison is the method of Science, the comparative study of the national poetry of warlike aristocracies, its conditions of growth and decadence, has been much neglected by Homeric critics. Sir Richard Jebb touched on the theme, and, after devoting four pages to a sketch of Sanskrit, Finnish, Persian, and early Teutonic heroic poetry and saga, decided that "in our country, as in others, we fail to find any true parallel to the case of the Homeric poems. These poems must be studied in themselves, without looking for aid, in this sense, to the comparative method."[1] Part of this conclusion seems to us rather hasty. In a brief manual Sir Richard had not space for a thorough comparative study of old heroic poetry at large. His quoted sources are: for India, Lassen; for France, Mr. Saintsbury's *Short History of French Literature* (sixteen pages on this topic), and a work unknown to me, by "M. Paul"; for Iceland he only quoted *The Encyclopædia Britannica* (Mr. Edmund Gosse); for Germany, Lachmann and Bartsch; for the Finnish *Kalewala*, the *Encyclopædia Britannica* (Mr. Sime and Mr. Keltie); and for England, a *Primer of English Literature* by Mr. Stopford Brooke.

These sources appear less than adequate, and Celtic

---

[1] *Homer*, p. 135.

T

heroic romance is entirely omitted. A much deeper and wider comparative criticism of early heroic national poetry is needed, before any one has a right to say that the study cannot aid our critical examination of the Homeric problem. Many peoples have passed through a stage of culture closely analogous to that of Achæan society as described in the *Iliad* and *Odyssey*. Every society of this kind has had its ruling military class, its ancient legends, and its minstrels who on these legends have based their songs. The similarity of human nature under similar conditions makes it certain that comparison will discover useful parallels between the poetry of societies separated in time and space but practically identical in culture. It is not much to the credit of modern criticism that a topic so rich and interesting has been, at least in England, almost entirely neglected by Homeric scholars.

Meanwhile, it is perfectly correct to say, as Sir Richard observes, that "we fail to find any true parallel to the case of the Homeric poems," for we nowhere find the legends of an heroic age handled by a very great poet—the greatest of all poets—except in the *Iliad* and *Odyssey*. But, on the other hand, the critics refuse to believe that, in the *Iliad* and *Odyssey*, we possess the heroic Achæan legends handled by one great poet. They find a composite by many hands, good and bad, and of many ages, they say; sometimes the whole composition and part of the poems are ascribed to a late *littérateur*. Now to that supposed state of things we do find several "true parallels," in Germany, in Finland, in Ireland. But the results of work by these many hands in many ages are anything but "a true parallel" to the results which lie before us in the *Iliad* and *Odyssey*. Where the processes of composite authorship throughout many ages certainly occur, as in Germany and Ireland, there we find no true parallel to the Homeric poems. It follows that, in all probability, no such processes as the critics postulate produced the *Iliad* and *Odyssey*, for where the processes existed, beyond doubt they failed egregiously to produce the results.

Sir Richard's argument would have been logical if many efforts by many hands, in many ages, in England, Finland, Ireland, Iceland, and Germany did actually produce true parallels to the Achæan epics. They did not, and why not ? Simply because these other races had no Homer. All the other necessary conditions were present, the legendary material, the heroic society, the Court minstrels, all—except the great poet. In all the countries mentioned, except Finland, there existed military aristocracies with their courts, castles, and minstrels, while the minstrels had rich material in legendary history and in myth, and *Märchen*, and old songs. But none of the minstrels was adequate to the production of an English, German, or Irish *Iliad* or *Odyssey*, or even of a true artistic equivalent in France.

We have tried to show that the critics, rejecting a Homer, have been unable to advance any adequate hypothesis to account for the existence of the *Iliad* and *Odyssey*. Now we see that, where such conditions of production as they postulate existed but where there was no great epic genius, they can find no true parallels to the Epics. Their logic thus breaks down at both ends.

It may be replied that in non-Greek lands one condition found in Greek society failed : the succession of a reading age to an age of heroic listeners. But this is not so. In France and Germany an age of readers duly began, but they did not mainly read copies of the old heroic poems. They turned to lyric poetry, as in Greece, and they recast the heroic songs into modern and popular forms in verse and prose, when they took any notice of the old heroic poems at all.

One merit of the Greek epics is a picture of "a certain phase of early civilisation," and that picture is "a naturally harmonious whole," with "unity of impression," says Sir Richard Jebb.[1] Certainly we can find no true parallel, on an Homeric scale, to this "harmonious picture" in the epics of Germany and England or in the early literature of Ireland. Sir Richard, for England, omits notice of *Beowulf;* but we know that *Beowulf,* a long heroic poem, is a mass of anachronisms—a heathen legend in a Christian setting. The hero, that great heathen champion, has his epic filled full of Christian allusions and Christian morals, because the clerical redactor, in Christian England, could not but intrude these things into old pagan legends evolved by the continental ancestors of our race. He had no "painful anxiety," like the supposed Ionic continuators of the Achæan poems (when they are not said to have done precisely the reverse), to preserve harmony of ancient ideas. Such archæological anxieties are purely modern.

If we take the *Nibelungenlied,*[2] we find that it is a thing of many rehandlings, even in existing manuscripts. For example, the Greeks clung to the hexameter in Homer. Not so did the Germans adhere to old metres. The poem that, in the oldest MS., is written in assonances,

---

[1] *Homer,* p. 37.

[2] See chapter on the *Nibelungenlied* in *Homer and the Epic,* pp. 382–404.

in later MSS. is reduced to regular rhymes and is re-
touched in many essential respects. The matter of the
Nibelungenlied is of heathen origin. We see the real
state of heathen affairs in the Icelandic versions of the
same tale, for the Icelanders were peculiar in preserving
ancient lays ; and, when these were woven into a *prose*
saga, the archaic and heathen features were retained.
Had the post-Christian prose author of the *Volsunga
Saga* been a great poet, we might find in his work a
true parallel to the *Iliad*. But, though he preserves the
harmony of his picture of pre-Christian princely life
(save in the savage beginnings of his story), he is not a
poet ; so the true parallel to the Greek epic fails, noble
as is the saga in many passages. In the German
Nibelungenlied all is modernised ; the characters are
Christian, the manners are chivalrous, and *Märchen*
older than Homer are forced into a wandering mediæval
chronicle-poem. The Germans, in short, had no early
poet of genius, and therefore could not produce a true
parallel to *Iliad* or *Odyssey*. The mediæval poets, of
course, never dreamed of archæological anxiety, as the
supposed Ionian continuators are sometimes said to have
done, any more than did the French and late Welsh
handlers of the ancient Celtic Arthurian materials. The
late German *bearbeiter* of the *Nibelungenlied* has no idea
of unity of plot—*enfin*, Germany, having excellent and
ancient legendary material for an epic, but producing
no parallel to *Iliad* and *Odyssey*, only proves how
absolutely essential a Homer was to the Greek epics.

"If any inference could properly be drawn from
the Edda" (the Icelandic collection of heroic lays), says
Sir Richard Jebb, "it would be that short separate
poems on cognate subjects can long exist as a collec-

tion *without* coalescing into such an artistic whole as the
Iliad or the *Odyssey*." [1]

It is our own argument that Sir Richard states.
"Short separate poems on cognate subjects" can certainly co-exist for long anywhere, but they cannot
automatically and they cannot by aid of an editor
become a long epic. Nobody can stitch and vamp
them into a poem like the *Iliad* or *Odyssey*. To produce
a poem like either of these a great poetic genius must
arise, and fuse the ancient materials, as Hephæstus fused
copper and tin, and then cast the mass into a mould of
his own making. A small poet may reduce the legends
and lays into a very inartistic whole, a very inharmonious
whole, as in the *Nibelungenlied*, but a controlling poet,
not a mere redactor or editor, is needed to perform
even that feat.

Where a man who is not a poet undertakes to
produce the coalescence, as Dr. Lönnrot (1835–1849)
did in the case of the peasant, not courtly, lays of
Finland, he "fails to prove that mere combining and
editing can form an artistic whole out of originally
distinct songs, even though concerned with closely
related themes," says Sir Richard Jebb. [2]

This is perfectly true ; much as Lönnrot botched and
vamped the Finnish lays he made no epic out of them.
But, as it is true, how did the late Athenian drudge of
Pisistratus succeed where Lönnrot failed ? "In the
dovetailing of the *Odyssey* we see the work of one mind,"
says Sir Richard. [3] This mind cannot have been the
property of any one but a great poet, obviously, as the
Odyssey is confessedly "an artistic whole." Conse-

[1] *Homer*, p. 133.   [2] *Homer*, p. 134–135.
[3] *Homer*, p. 129.

quently the disintegrators of the *Odyssey*, when they are logical, are reduced to averring that the poem is an exceedingly inartistic whole, a whole not artistic at all. While Mr. Leaf calls it "a model of skilful construction," Wilamowitz Möllendorff denounces it as the work of "a slenderly-gifted botcher," of about 650 B.C., a century previous to Mr. Leaf's Athenian editor.

Thus we come, after all, to a crisis in which mere literary appreciation is the only test of the truth about a work of literature. The *Odyssey* is an admirable piece of artistic composition, or it is the very reverse. Blass, Mr. Leaf, Sir Richard Jebb, and the opinion of the ages declare that the composition is excellent. A crowd of German critics and Father Browne, S.J., hold that the composition is feeble. The criterion is the literary taste of each party to the dispute. Kirchhoff and Wilamowitz Möllendorff see a late bad patchwork, where Mr. Leaf, Sir Richard Jebb, Blass, Wolf, and the verdict of all mankind see a masterpiece of excellent construction. The world has judged: the *Odyssey* is a marvel of construction ; therefore is not the work of a late botcher of disparate materials, but of a great early poet. Yet Sir Richard Jebb, while recognising the *Odyssey* as "an artistic whole" and an harmonious picture, and recognising Lönnrot's failure "to prove that mere combining and editing can form an artistic whole out of originally distinct songs, even though concerned with closely related themes," thinks that Kirchhoff has made the essence of his theory of late combination of distinct strata of poetical material from different sources and periods, in the *Odyssey*, "in the highest degree probable." [1]

[1] *Homer*, p. 131.

It is, of course, possible that Mr. Leaf, who has not edited the *Odyssey*, may now, in deference to his belief in the Pisistratean editor, have changed his opinion of the merits of the poem. If the *Odyssey*, like the *Iliad*, was, till about 540 B.C., a chaos of lays of all ages, variously known in various *répertoires* of the rhapsodists, and patched up by the Pisistratean editor, then of two things one—either Mr. Leaf abides by his enthusiastic belief in the excellency of the composition, or he does not. If he does still believe that the composition of the *Odyssey* is a masterpiece, then the Pisistratean editor was a great master of construction. If he now, on the other hand, agrees with Wilamowitz Möllendorff that the *Odyssey* is cobbler's work, then his literary opinions are unstable.

CHAPTER XVI

HOMER AND THE FRENCH MEDIÆVAL EPICS

SIR RICHARD JEBB remarks, with truth, that " before any definite solution of the Homeric problem could derive scientific support from such analogies" (with epics of other peoples), " it would be necessary to show that the particular conditions under which the Homeric poems appear in early Greece had been reproduced with sufficient closeness elsewhere." [1] Now we can show that the particular conditions under which the Homeric poems confessedly arose were "reproduced with sufficient closeness elsewhere," except that no really great poet was elsewhere present.

This occurred among the Germanic aristocracy, " the Franks of France," in the eleventh, twelfth, and early thirteenth centuries of our era. The closeness of the whole parallel, allowing for the admitted absence in France of a very great and truly artistic poet, is astonishing.

We have first, in France, answering to the Achæan aristocracy, the Frankish noblesse of warriors dwelling in princely courts and strong castles, dominating an older population, owing a practically doubtful fealty to an Over-Lord, the King, passing their days in the chace, in private war, or in revolt against the Over-Lord, and, for all literary entertainment, depending on the

---

[1] *Homer*, pp. 131, 132.

recitations of epic poems by *jongleurs*, who in some cases are of gentle birth, and are the authors of the poems which they recite.

"This national poetry," says M. Gaston Paris, "was born and mainly developed among the warlike class, princes, lords, and their courts. . . . At first, no doubt, some of these men of the sword themselves composed and chanted lays" (like Achilles), "but soon there arose a special class of poets. . . . They went from court to court, from castle. . . . Later, when the townsfolk began to be interested in their chants, they sank a degree, and took their stand in public open places. . . ."[1] In the *Iliad* we hear of no minstrels in camp : in the *Odyssey* a prince has a minstrel among his retainers —Demodocus, at the court of Phæacia; Phemius, in the house of Odysseus. In Ionia, when princes had passed away, rhapsodists recited for gain in market-places and at fairs. The parallel with France is so far complete.

The French national epics, like those of the Achæans, deal mainly with legends of a long past legendary age. To the French authors the greatness and the fortunes of the Emperor Charles and other heroic heads of great Houses provide a theme. The topics of song are his wars, and the prowess and the quarrels of his peers with the Emperor and among themselves. These are seen magnified through a mist of legend ; Saracens are substituted for Gascon foes, and the great Charles, so nobly venerable a figure in the oldest French epic (the *Chanson de Roland, circ.* 1050–1070 in its earliest extant form), is more degraded, in the later epics, than Agamemnon himself. The "machinery" of the gods

---

[1] *Littérature Française au Moyen Age*, pp. 36, 37. 1888.

in Homer is replaced by the machinery of angels, but the machinery of dreams is in vogue, as in the *Iliad* and *Odyssey*. The sources are traditional and legendary.

We know that brief early lays of Charles and other heroes had existed, and they may have been familiar to the French epic poets, but they were not merely patched into the epics. The form of verse is not ballad-like, but a series of *laisses* of decasyllabic lines, each *laisse* presenting one assonance, not rhyme. As time went on, rhyme and Alexandrine lines were introduced, and the old epics were expanded, altered, condensed, *remaniés*, with progressive changes in taste, metre, language, manners, and ways of life.

Finally, an age of Cyclic poems began ; authors took new characters, whom they attached by false genealogies to the older heroes, and they chanted the adventures of the sons of the former heroes, like the Cyclic poet who sang of the son of Odysseus by Circe. All these conditions are undeniably "true parallels" to "the conditions under which the Homeric poems appeared." The only obvious point of difference vanishes if we admit, with Sir Richard Jebb and M. Salomon Reinach, the possibility of the existence of written texts in the Greece of the early iron age.

We do not mean texts prepared for a *reading* public. In France such a public, demanding texts for reading, did not arise till the decadence of the epic. The oldest French texts of their epics are small volumes, each page containing some thirty lines in one column. Such volumes were carried about by the *jongleurs*, who chanted their own or other men's verses. They were not in the hands of readers.[1]

---

[1] *Épopées Françaises*, Léon Gautier, vol. i. pp. 226-228. 1878.

An example of an author-reciter, Jendeus de Brie (he was the maker of the first version of the *Bataille Loquifer*, twelfth century) is instructive. Of Jendeus de Brie it is said that " he wrote the poem, kept it very carefully, taught it to no man, made much gain out of it in Sicily where he sojourned, and left it to his son when he died." Similar statements are made in *Renaus de Montauban* (the existing late version is of the thirteenth century) about Huon de Villeneuve, who would not part with his poem for horses or furs, or for any price, and about other poets.[1]

These early *jongleurs* were men of position and distinction ; their theme was the *gestes* of princes ; they were not under the ban with which the Church pursued vulgar strollers, men like the Greek rhapsodists. Pindar's story that Homer wrote the *Cypria*[2] and gave the copy, as the dowry of his daughter, to Stasinus who married her, could only have arisen in Greece in circumstances exactly like those of Jendeus de Brie. Jendeus lived on his poem by reciting it, and left it to his son when he died. The story of Homer and Stasinus could only have been invented in an age when the possession of the solitary text of a poem was a source of maintenance to the poet. This condition of things could not exist, either when there were no written texts or when such texts were multiplied to serve the wants of a reading public.

Again, a poet in the fortunate position of Jendeus would not teach his Epic in a " school " of reciters unless he were extremely well paid. In later years, after his death, his poem came, through copies good or bad, into circulation.

---

[1] *Épopées Françaises*, *Leon Gautier*, vol. i. p. 215, Note I.
[2] *Pindari Opera*, vol. iii. p. 654. Boeckh.

Late, in the fourteenth and fifteenth centuries, we hear of a "school" of *jongleurs* at Beauvais. In Lent they might not ply their profession, so they gathered at Beauvais, where they could learn *novæ cantilenæ*, new lays. But by that time the epic was decadent and dying.[1]

The audiences of the *jongleurs*, too, were no longer, by that time, what they had been. The rich and great, now, had library copies of the epics ; not small *jongleurs'* copies, but folios, richly illuminated and bound, with two or three columns of matter on each page.[2]

The age of recitations from a text in princely halls was ending or ended ; the age of a reading public was begun. The earlier condition of the *jongleur* who was his own poet, and carefully guarded his copyright in spite of all temptations to permit the copying of his MS., is regarded by Sir Richard Jebb as quite a possible feature of early Greece. He thinks that there was "no wide circulation of writings by numerous copies for a reading public" before the end of the fifth century B.C. As Greek mercenaries could write, and write well, in the seventh to sixth centuries, I incline to think that there may then, and earlier, have been a reading public. However, long before that a man might commit his poems to writing. "Wolf allows that some men did, as early at least as 776 B.C. The verses might never be read by anybody except himself" (the author) " or those to whom he privately bequeathed them" (as Jendeus de Brie bequeathed his poem to his son), " but his end would have been gained." [3]

---

[1] *Épopées Françaises*, Léon Gautier, vol. ii. pp. 174, 175.

[2] *Ibid.*, vol. i. p. 228. See, too, photographs of an illuminated, double-columned library copy in *La Chancun de Willame.* London, 1903.

[3] *Homer*, p. 113.

Recent discoveries as to the very early date of linear
non-Phœnician writing in Crete of course increase the
probability of this opinion, which is corroborated by
the story of the *Cypria*, given as a dowry with the
author's daughter.   Thus "the particular conditions
under which the Homeric poems appeared" *have* "been
reproduced with sufficient closeness" in every respect,
with surprising closeness, in the France of the eleventh
to thirteenth centuries.   The social conditions are the
same ;   the legendary materials are of identical character ;   the method of publication by recitation is
identical ;   the cyclic decadence occurs in both cases,
the *monomanie cyclique*.   In the Greece of Homer we
have the four necessary conditions of the epic, as
found by M. Léon Gautier in mediæval France.   We
have :—

(1) An uncritical age confusing history by legend.

(2) We have a national *milieu* with religious uniformity.

(3) We have poems dealing with—

> "Old unhappy far-off things
> And battles long ago."

(4) We have representative heroes, the Over-Lord,
and his peers or paladins.[1]

It may be added that in Greece, as in France, some
poets adapt into the adventures of their· heroes world-
old *Märchen*, as in the *Odyssey*, and in the cycle of the
parents of Charles.

In the French, as in the Greek epics, we have such
early traits of poetry as the textual repetition of speeches,
and the recurring epithets, "swift-footed Achilles,"
"Charles of the white beard," "blameless heroes"

[1] *Épopées Françaises*, Léon Gautier, vol. i. pp. 6–9.

(however blamable). Ladies, however old, are always
"of the clear face." Thus the technical manners of
the French and Greek epics are closely parallel; they
only differ in the exquisite art of Homer, to which no
approach is made by the French poets.

The French authors of epic, even more than Homer,
abound in episodes much more distracting than those
of the *Iliad*. Of blood and wounds, of course, both the
French and the Greek are profuse: they were writing
for men of the sword, not for modern critics. Indeed,
the battle pieces of France almost translate those of
Homer. The Achæan "does on his goodly corslet";
the French knight "*sur ses espalles son halberc li colad.*"
The Achæan, with his great sword, shears off an arm
at the shoulder. The French knight—

> "*Trenchad le braz,*
> *Parmi leschine sun grant espee li passe.*"

The huge shield of Aias becomes *cele grant targe duble*
in France, and the warriors boast over their slain in
France, as in the *Iliad*. In France, as in Greece, a
favourite epic theme was "The Wrath" of a hero,
of Achilles, of Roland, of Ganelon, of Odysseus and
Achilles wrangling at a feast to the joy of Agamemnon,
"glad that the bravest of his peers were at strife." [1]

Of all the many parallels between the Greek and
French epics, the most extraordinary is the coincidence
between Charles with his peers and Agamemnon with
his princes. The same historical conditions occurred,
at an interval of more than two thousand years.
Agamemnon is the Bretwalda, the Over-Lord, as
Mr. Freeman used to say, of the Achæans: he is the
suzerain. Charles in the French epics holds the same

[1] *Odyssey*, VIII. 75-78.

position, but the French poets regard him in different lights. In the earliest epic, the *Chanson de Roland*, a divinity doth hedge the famous Emperor, whom Jeanne d'Arc styled "St. Charlemagne." He was, in fact, a man of thirty-seven at the date of the disaster of Roncesvaux, where Roland fell (778 A.D.). But in the tradition that has reached the poet of the *chanson* he is a white-bearded warrior, as vigorous as he is venerable. As he rules by advice of his council, he bids them deliberate on the proposals of the Paynim King, Marsile —to accept or refuse them. Roland, the counterpart of Achilles in all respects (Oliver is his Patroclus), is for refusing : Ganelon appears to have the rest with him when he speaks in favour of peace and return to France out of Spain. So, in the *Iliad* (II.), the Achæans lend a ready ear to Agamemnon when he proposes the abandonment of the siege of Troy. Each host, French and Achæan, is heartily homesick.

Ganelon's advice prevailing, it is necessary to send an envoy to the Saracen court. It is a dangerous mission ; other envoys have been sent and been murdered. The Peers, however, volunteer, beginning with the aged Naismes, the Nestor of the Franks. His offer is not accepted, nor are those of Oliver, Roland, and Turpin. Roland then proposes that Ganelon shall be sent ; and hence arises the Wrath of Ganelon, which was the ruin of Roland and the peers who stood by him. The warriors attack each other in speeches of Homeric fury. Charles preserves his dignity, and Ganelon departs on his mission. He deliberately sells himself, and seals the fate of the peers whom he detests: the surprise of the rearguard under Roland, the deadly battle, and the revenge of Charles make up the rest of

the poem. Not even in victory is Charles allowed
repose ; the trumpet again summons him to war. He
is of those whom Heaven has called to endless combat—

> "Their whole lives long to be winding
> Skeins of grievous wars, till every soul of them perish,"

in the words of Diomede.

Such is the picture of the imperial Charles in one
of the oldest of the French epics. The heart of the
poet is with the aged, but unbroken and truly imperial,
figure of St. Charlemagne—wise, just, and brave, a true
" shepherd of the people," regarded as the conqueror
of all the known kingdoms of the world. He is, among
his fierce paladins, like " the conscience of a knight
among his warring members." "The greatness of
Charlemagne has entered even into his name ;" but as
time went on and the feudal princes began the long
struggle against the French king, the poets gratified
their patrons by degrading the character of the Emperor. They created a second type of Charles, and it
is the second type that on the whole most resembles
the Agamemnon of the *Iliad*.

We ask why the widely ruling lord of golden
Mycenæ is so skilfully and persistently represented as
respectable, indeed, by reason of his office, but detest-
able, on the whole, in character ?

The answer is that just as the second type of
Charles is the result of feudal jealousies of the king,
so the character of Agamemnon reflects the princely
hatreds of what we may call the feudal age of Greece.
The masterly portrait of Agamemnon could only have
been designed to win the sympathies of feudal listeners,
princes with an Over-Lord whom they cannot re-
pudiate, for whose office they have a traditional rever-

U

ence, but whose power they submit to with no good will, and whose person and character some of them can barely tolerate.

The unity of the Iliad is an historical unity. The poem deals with what may be called a feudal society, and the attitudes of the Achæan Bretwalda and of his peers are, from beginning to end of the *Iliad* and in every Book of it, those of the peers and king in the later *Chansons de Geste.*

Returning to the decadent Charles of the French epics, we lay no stress on the story of his incest with his sister, Gilain, "whence sprang Roland." The House of Thyestes, whence Agamemnon sprang, is marked by even blacker legends. The scandal is mythical, like the same scandal about the King Arthur, who in romance is so much inferior to his knights, a reflection of feudal jealousies and hatreds. In places the reproaches hurled by the peers at Charles read like paraphrases of those which the Achæan princes cast at Agamemnon. Even Naismes, the Nestor of the French epics, cries : " It is for *you* that we have left our lands and fiefs, our fair wives and our children. . . . But, by the Apostle to whom they pray in Rome, were it not that we should be guilty before God we would go back to sweet France, and thin would be your host." [1] In the lines quoted we seem to hear the voice of the angered Achilles : "We came not hither in our own quarrel, thou shameless one, but to please thee ! But now go I back to Phthia with my ships—the better part." [2]

Agamemnon answers that Zeus is on his side, just

[1] *Chevalerie Ogier*, 1510–1529. *Épopées Françaises*, Léon Gautier, vol. iii. pp. 156–157.
[2] *Iliad*, I. 158–169.

as even the angry Naismes admits that duty to God demands obedience to Charles. There cannot be parallels more close and true than these, between poems born at a distance from each other of more than two thousand years, but born in similar historical conditions.

In *Gui de Bourgogne,* a poem of the twelfth century, Ogier cries, " They say that Charlemagne is the conqueror of kingdoms: they lie, it is Roland who conquers them with Oliver, Naismes of the long beard, and myself. As to Charles, he—eats." Compare Achilles to Agamemnon, " Thou, heavy with wine, with dog's eyes and heart of deer, never hast thou dared to arm thee for war with the host. . . ."[1] It is Achilles or Roland who stakes his life in war and captures cities ; it is Agamemnon or Charles who camps by the wine. Charles, in the *Chanson de Saisnes,* abases himself before Herapois, even more abjectly than Agamemnon in his offer of atonement to Achilles.[2] Charles is as arrogant as Agamemnon : he strikes Roland with his glove, for an uncommanded victory, and then he loses heart and weeps as copiously as the penitent Agamemnon often does when he rues his arrogance.[3]

The poet of the *Iliad* is a great and sober artist. He does not make Agamemnon endure the lowest disgraces which the latest French epiç poets heap on Charles. But we see how close is the parallel between Agamemnon and the Charles of the decadent type. Both characters are reflections of feudal jealousy of the

---

[1] *Iliad,* I. 227, 228. *Gui de Bourgogne,* pp. 37–41.
[2] *Épopées Françaises,* Léon Gautier, vol. iii. p. 158.
[3] *Entrée en Espagne.*

Over-Lord ; both reflect real antique historical conditions, and these were the conditions of the Achæans
in Europe, not of the Ionians in Asia.

The treatment of Agamemnon's character is harmonious throughout. It is not as if in "the original
poem" Agamemnon were revered like St. Charlemagne
in the *Chanson de Roland*, and in the "later" parts of
the *Iliad* were reduced to the contemptible estate of the
Charles of the decadent *Chanson de Geste*. In the *Iliad*
Agamemnon's character is consistently presented from
beginning to end, presented, I think, as it could only
be by a great poet of the feudal Achæan society in
Europe. The Ionians—"democratic to the core," says
Mr. Leaf—would either have taken no interest in the
figure of the Over-Lord, or would have utterly degraded him below the level of the Charles of the latest
Chansons. Or the late rhapsodists, in their irresponsible
lays, would have presented a wavering and worthless
portrait.

The conditions under which the *Chansons* arose
were truly parallel to the conditions under which the
Homeric poems arose, and the poems, French and
Achæan, are also true parallels, except in genius. The
French have no Homer : *carent vate sacro*. It follows
that a Homer was necessary to the evolution of the
Greek epics.

It may, perhaps, be replied to this argument that
our *Iliad* is only a very late *remaniement*, like the fourteenth century *Chansons de Geste*, of something much
earlier and nobler. But in France, in the age of
remaniement, even the versification had changed from
assonance to rhyme, from the decasyllabic line to the
Alexandrine in the decadence, while a plentiful lack of

seriousness and a love of purely fanciful adventures in fairyland take the place of the austere spirit of war. Ladies "in a coming on humour" abound, and Charles is involved with his Paladins in *gauloiseries* of a Rabelaisian cast. The French language has become a new thing through and through, and manners and weapons are of a new sort; but the high seriousness of the *Iliad* is maintained throughout, except in the burlesque battle of the gods: the versification is the stately hexameter, linguistic alterations are present, extant, but inconspicuous. That the armour and weapons are uniform in character throughout we have tried to prove, while the state of society and of religion is certainly throughout harmonious. Our parallel, then, between the French and the Greek national epics appears as perfect as such a thing can be, surprisingly perfect, while the great point of difference in degree of art is accounted for by the existence of an Achæan poet of supreme genius. Not such, certainly, were the composers of the Cyclic poems, men contemporary with the supposed later poets of the *Iliad*.

CHAPTER XVII

CONCLUSION

THE conclusion at which we arrive is that the *Iliad*, as a whole, is the work of one age. That it has reached us without interpolations and *lacunæ* and *remaniements* perhaps no person of ordinary sense will allege. But that the mass of the Epic is of one age appears to be a natural inference from the breakdown of the hypotheses which attempt to explain it as a late mosaic. We have also endeavoured to prove, quite apart from the failure of theories of expansion and compilation, that the *Iliad* presents an historical unity, unity of character, unity of customary law, and unity in its archæology. If we are right, we must have an opinion as to how the Epic was preserved.

If we had evidence for an Homeric school, we might imagine that the Epic was composed by dint of memory, and preserved, like the Sanskrit Hymns of the Rig Veda, and the Hymns of the Maoris, the Zuñis, and other peoples in the lower or middle stage of barbarism, by the exertions and teaching of schools. But religious hymns and mythical hymns—the care of a priesthood—are one thing ; a great secular epic is another. Priests will not devote themselves from age to age to its conservation. It cannot be conserved, with its unity of tone and character, and, on the whole, even of language, by generations of paid strollers, who recite new lays of their own, as well as any old lays that they may remember, which they alter at pleasure.

We are thus driven back to the theory of early written texts, not intended to meet the wants of a reading public, but for the use of the poet himself and of those to whom he may bequeath his work. That this has been a method in which orally published epics were composed and preserved in a non-reading age we have proved in our chapter on the French *Chansons de Geste.* Unhappily, the argument that what was done in mediæval France might be done in sub-Mycenæan Greece, is based on probabilities, and these are differently estimated by critics of different schools. All seems to depend on each individual's sense of what is " likely." In that case science has nothing to make in the matter. Nitzsche thought that writing might go back to the time of Homer. Mr. Monro thought it " probable enough that writing, even if known at the time of Homer, was not used for literary purposes." [1] Sir Richard Jebb, as we saw, took a much more favourable view of the probability of early written texts. M. Salomon Reinach, arguing from the linear written clay tablets of Knossos and from a Knossian cup with writing on it in ink, thinks that there may have existed whole " Minoan " libraries—manuscripts executed on perishable materials, palm leaves, papyrus, or parchment.[2] Mr. Leaf, while admitting that " writing was known in some form through the whole period of epic development," holds that " it is in the highest degree unlikely that it was ever employed to form a standard text of the Epic or any portion of it. . . . At best there

---

[1] *Iliad,* vol. i. p. xxxv.
[2] *L'Anthropologie,* vol. xv. pp. 292, 293.

was a continuous tradition of those portions of the poems which were especially popular. . . ." [1] Father Browne dates the employment of writing for the preservation of the Epic "from the sixth century onwards." [2] He also says that "it is difficult to suppose that the Mycenæans, who were certainly in contact with this form of writing" (the Cretan linear), "should not have used it much more freely than our direct evidence warrants us in asserting." He then mentions the Knossian cup "with writing inscribed on it apparently in pen and ink. . . . The conclusion is that ordinary writing was in use, but that the materials, probably palm leaves, have disappeared." [3]

Why it should be unlikely that a people confessedly familiar with writing used it for the preservation of literature, when we know that even the Red Indians preserve their songs by means of pictographs, while West African tribes use incised characters, is certainly not obvious. Many sorts of prae-Phœnician writing were current during the Mycenæan age in Asia, Egypt, Assyria, and in Cyprus. As these other peoples used writing of their own sort for literary purposes, it is not easy to see why the Cretans, for example, should not have done the same thing. Indeed, Father Browne supposes that the Mycenæans used "ordinary writing," and used it freely. Nevertheless, the Epic was not written, he says, till the sixth century B.C. Cauer, indeed, remarks that "the Finnish epic" existed unwritten till Lönnrot, its Pisistratus, first collected it from oral recitation. [4] But there is not, and never was, any "Finnish epic." There were

[1] *Iliad*, vol. i. pp. xvi., xvii.
[2] *Handbook of Homeric Study*, p. 134.
[3] *Ibid.*, pp. 258, 259.
[4] *Grundfragen der Homerkritik*, p. 94.

cosmogonic songs, as among the Maoris and Zuñis—
songs of the beginnings of things ; there were magical songs, songs of weddings, a song based on the
same popular tale that underlies the legend of the
Argonauts. There were songs of the Culture Hero,
songs of burial and feast, and of labour. Lönnrot
collected these, and tried by interpolations to make an
epic out of them ; but the point, as Comparetti has
proved, is that he failed. There is no Finnish epic,
only a mass of *Volkslieder*. Cauer's other argument,
that the German popular tales, Grimm's tales, were
unwritten till 1812, is as remote from the point at
issue. Nothing can be less like an epic than a volume
of *Märchen*.

As usual we are driven back upon a literary judgment. Is the *Iliad* a patchwork of metrical *Märchen* or
is it an epic nobly constructed ? If it is the former,
writing was not needed ; if it is the latter, in the absence
of Homeric guilds or colleges, only writing can account
for its preservation.

It is impossible to argue against a critic's subjective
sense of what is likely. Possibly that sense is born of
the feeling that the Cretan linear script, for example,
or the Cyprian syllabary, looks very odd and outlandish.
The critic's imagination boggles at the idea of an epic
written in such scripts. In that case his is not the
scientific imagination ; he is checked merely by the
unfamiliar. Or his sense of unlikelihood may be a
subconscious survival of Wolf's opinion, formed by
him at a time when the existence of the many scripts
of the old world was unknown.

Our own sense of probability leads us to the conclusion that, in an age when people could write, people

wrote down the Epic. If they applied their art to literature, then the preservation of the Epic is explained. Written first in a præ-Phœnician script, it continued to be written in the Greek adaptation of the Phœnician alphabet. There was not yet, probably, a reading public, but there were a few clerkly men.

That the Cretans, at least, could write long before the age of Homer, Mr. Arthur Evans has demonstrated by his discoveries. From my remote undergraduate days I was of the opinion which he has proved to be correct, starting, like him, from what I knew about savage pictographs.[1]

M. Reinach and Mr. Evans have pointed out that in this matter tradition joins hands with discovery. Diodorus Siculus, speaking of the Cretan Zeus and probably on Cretan authority, says: "As to those who hold that the Syrians invented letters, from whom the Phœnicians received them and handed them on to the Greeks, . . . and that for this reason the Greeks call letters 'Phœnician,' some reply that the Phœnicians did not *discover* letters, but merely modified (transposed?) the forms of the letters, and that most men use this form of script, and thus letters came to be styled 'Phœnician.'"[2] In fact, the alphabet is a collection of signs of palæolithic antiquity and of vast diffusion.[3]

Thus the use of writing for the conservation of the Epic cannot seem to me to be unlikely, but rather probable; and here one must leave the question, as

[1] *Cretan Pictographs and Præ-Phœnician Script.* London, 1905. *Annual of British School of Athens*, 1900–1901, p. 10. *Journal of Hellenic Studies*, 1897, pp. 327–395.

[2] Diodorus Siculus, v. 74. *L'Anthropologie*, vol. xi. pp. 497–502.

[3] *Origins of the Alphabet.* A. L. *Fortnightly Review*, 1904, pp. 634–645.

the subjective element plays so great a part in every man's sense of what is likely or unlikely. That writing cannot have been used for this literary purpose, that the thing is impossible, nobody will now assert.

My supposition is, then, that the text of the Epic existed in Ægean script till Greece adapted to her own tongue the " Phœnician letters," which I think she did not later than the ninth to eighth centuries; "at the beginning of the ninth century," says Professor Bury.[1] This may seem an audaciously early date, but when we find vases of the eighth to seventh centuries bearing inscriptions, we may infer that a knowledge of reading and writing was reasonably common. When such a humble class of hirelings or slaves as the pot-painters can sign their work, expecting their signatures to be read, reading and writing must be very common accomplishments among the more fortunate classes.

If Mr. Gardner is right in dating a number of incised inscriptions on early pottery at Naucratis before the middle of the seventh century, we reach the same conclusion. In fact, if these inscriptions be of a century earlier than the Abu Simbel inscriptions, of date 590 B.C., we reach 690 B.C. Wherefore, as writing does not become common in a moment, it must have existed in the eighth century B.C. We are not dealing here with a special learned class, but with ordinary persons who could write.[2]

Interesting for our purpose is the verse incised on a Dipylon vase, found at Athens in 1880. It is of an ordinary cream-jug shape, with a neck, a handle, a

[1] *History of Greece*, vol. i. p. 78. 1902.
[2] *The Early Ionic Alphabet : Journal of Hellenic Studies*, vol. vii. pp. 220–239. Roberts, *Introduction to Greek Epigraphy*, pp. 31, 151, 159, 164, 165–167.

spout, and a round belly. On the neck, within a zigzag "geometrical" pattern, is a doe, feeding, and a tall water-fowl. On the shoulder is scratched with a point, in very antique Attic characters running from right to left, ὅς νῦν ὀρχηστῶν πάντων ἀταλώτατα παίζει, τοῦ τόδε. "This is the jug of him who is the most delicately sportive of all dancers of our time." The jug is attributed to the eighth century.[1]

Taking the vase, with Mr. Walters, as of the eighth century, I do not suppose that the amateur who gave it to a dancer and scratched the hexameter was of a later generation than the jug itself. The vase may have cost him sixpence : he would give his friend a *new* vase ; it is improbable that old jugs were sold at curiosity shops in these days, and given by amateurs to artists. The inscription proves that, in the eighth to seventh centuries, at a time of very archaic characters (the Alpha is lying down on its side, the aspirate is an oblong with closed ends and a stroke across the middle, and the Iota is curved at each end), people could write with ease, and would put verse into writing. The general accomplishment of reading is taken for granted.

Reading is also taken for granted by the Gortyn (Cretan) inscription of twelve columns long, *boustrophedon* (running alternately from left to right, and from right to left). In this inscribed code of laws, incised on stone, money is not mentioned in the more ancient part, but fines and prices are calculated in "chalders"

---

[1] Walters, *History of Ancient Pottery*, vol. ii. p. 243 ; Kretschmer, *Griechischen Vasen inschriften*, p. 110, 1894, of the seventh century. H. von Rohden, *Denkmaler*, iii. pp. 1945, 1946 : " Probably dating from the seventh century." Roberts, *op. cit.*, vol. i. p. 74, " at least as far back as the seventh century," p. 75.

and "bolls" (λέβητες and τρίποδες), as in Scotland
when coin was scarce indeed. Whether the law con-
templated the value of the vessels themselves, or, as in
Scotland, of their contents in grain, I know not. The
later inscriptions deal with coined money. If coin
came in about 650 B.C., the older parts of the inscription may easily be of 700 B.C.

The Gortyn inscription implies the power of writing
out a long code of laws, and it implies that persons
about to go to law could read the public inscription,
as we can read a proclamation posted up on a wall, or
could have it read to them.[1]

The alphabets inscribed on vases of the seventh
century (Abecedaria), with "the archaic Greek forms
of every one of the twenty-two Phœnician letters
arranged precisely in the received Semitic order,"
were, one supposes, gifts for boys and girls who were
learning to read, just like our English alphabets on
gingerbread.[2]

Among inscriptions on tombstones of the end of the
seventh century, there is the epitaph of a daughter of
a potter.[3] These writings testify to the general knowledge of reading, just as much as our epitaphs testify to
the same state of education. The Athenian potter's
daughter of the seventh century B.C. had her epitaph, but
the grave-stones of highlanders, chiefs or commoners,
were usually uninscribed till about the end of the
eighteenth century, in deference to custom, itself aris-
ing from the illiteracy of the highlanders in times past.[4]
I find no difficulty, therefore, in supposing that there

[1] Roberts, vol. i. pp. 52–55.
[2] For Abecedaria, cf. Roberts, vol. i. pp. 16–21.
[3] Roberts, vol. i. p. 76.
[4] Ramsay, *Scotland and Scotsmen*, ii. p. 426. 1888.

were some Greek readers and writers in the eighth century, and that primary education was common in the seventh. In these circumstances my sense of the probable is not revolted by the idea of a written epic, in *Greek* characters, even in the eighth century, but the notion that there was no such thing till the middle of the sixth century seems highly improbable. All the conditions were present which make for the composition and preservation of literary works in written texts. That there were many early written copies of Homer in the eighth century I am not inclined to believe. The Greeks were early a people who could read, but were not a reading people. Setting newspapers aside, there is no such thing as a reading *people.*

The Greeks preferred to listen to recitations, but my hypothesis is that the rhapsodists who recited had texts, like the *jongleurs'* books of their epics in France, and that they occasionally, for definite purposes, interpolated matter into their texts. There were also texts, known in later times as "city texts" (αἱ κατὰ πόλεις), which Aristarchus knew, but he did not adopt the various readings.[1]

Athens had a text in Solon's time, if he entered the decree that the whole Epic should be recited in due order, every five years, at the Panathenaic festival.[2] "This implies the possession of a complete text."[3]

Cauer remarks that the possibility of "interpolation" "began only after the fixing of the text by Pisistratus."[4] But surely if every poet and reciter could thrust any new lines which he chose to make

---

[1] Monro, *Odyssey*, vol. ii. p. 435. [2] *Ibid.*, vol. ii. p. 395.
[3] *Ibid.*, vol. ii. p. 403. [4] *Grundfragen*, p. 205.

into any old lays which he happened to know, that was interpolation, whether he had a book of the words or had none.   Such interpolations would fill the orally recited lays which the supposed Pisistratean editor must have written down from recitation before he began his colossal task of making the *Iliad* out of them. If, on the other hand, reciters had books of the words, they could interpolate at pleasure into *them*, and such books may have been among the materials used in the construction of a text for the Athenian book market. But if our theory be right, there must always have been a few copies of better texts than those of the late reciters' books, and the effort of the editors for the book market would be to keep the parts in which most manuscripts were agreed.

But how did Athens, or any other city, come to possess a text?   One can only conjecture ; but my conjecture is that there had always been texts—copied out in successive generations—in the hands of the curious ; for example, in the hands of the Cyclic poets, who knew our *Iliad* as the late French Cyclic poets knew the earlier *Chansons de Geste*.   They certainly knew it, for they avoided interference with it ; they worked at epics which led up to it, as in the *Cypria ;* they borrowed *motifs* from hints and references in the *Iliad*,[1] and they carried on the story from the death of Hector, in the *Æthiopis* of Arctinus of Miletus.   This epic ended with the death of Achilles, when *The Little Iliad* produced the tale to the bringing in of the wooden horse. Arctinus goes on with his *Sack of Ilios*, others wrote of *The Return of the Heroes*, and the *Telegonia* is a sequel to the *Odyssey*.   The authors of these poems knew the

---

[1] Monro, *Odyssey*, vol. ii. pp. 350, 351.

Iliad, then, as a whole, and how could they have known it thus if it only existed in the casual *répertoire* of strolling reciters? The Cyclic poets more probably had texts of Homer, and themselves wrote their own poems— how it paid, whether they recited them and collected rewards or not, is, of course, unknown.

The Cyclic poems, to quote Sir Richard Jebb, "help to fix the lowest limit for the age of the Homeric poems.[1] The earliest Cyclic poems, dating from about 776 B.C., *presuppose the Iliad,* being planned to introduce or continue it. . . . It would appear, then, that the *Iliad* must have existed in something like its present compass as early as 800 B.C. ; indeed a considerably earlier date will seem probable, if due time is allowed for the poem to have grown into such fame as would incite the effort to continue it and to prelude to it."

Sir Richard then takes the point on which we have already insisted, namely, that the Cyclic poets of the eighth century B.C. live in an age of ideas, religions, ritual, and so forth which are absent from the *Iliad.*[2]

Thus the *Iliad* existed with its characteristics that are prior to 800 B.C., and in its present compass, and was renowned before 800 B.C. As it could not possibly have thus existed in the *répertoire* of irresponsible strolling minstrels and reciters, and as there is no evidence for a college, school, or guild which preserved the Epic by a system of mnemonic teaching, while no one can deny at least the possibility of written texts, we are driven to the hypothesis that written texts there were, whence descended, for example, the text of Athens.

We can scarcely suppose, however, that such texts

---

[1] *Homer,* pp. 151, 154.   [2] *Homer,* pp. 154, 155.

were perfect in all respects, for we know how, several centuries later, in a reading age, papyrus fragments of the *Iliad* display unwarrantable interpolation.[1] But Plato's frequent quotations, of course made at an earlier date, show that "whatever interpolated texts of Homer were then current, the copy from which Plato quoted was not one of them."[2] Plato had something much better.

When a reading public for Homer arose — and, from the evidences of the widespread early knowledge of reading, such a small public may have come into existence sooner than is commonly supposed—Athens was the centre of the book trade. To Athens must be due the præ-Alexandrian Vulgate, or prevalent text, practically the same as our own. Some person or persons must have made that text—not by taking down from recitation all the lays which they could collect, as Herd, Scott, Mrs. Brown, and others collected much of the *Border Minstrelsy*, and not by then tacking the lays into a newly-composed whole. They must have done their best with such texts as were accessible to them, and among these were probably the copies used by reciters and rhapsodists, answering to the MS. books of the mediæval *jongleurs*.

Mr. Jevons has justly and acutely remarked that "we do not know, and there is no external evidence of any description which leads us to suppose, that the *Iliad* was ever expanded" (*J. H. S.*, vii. 291–308).

That it was expanded is a mere hypothesis based on the idea that "if there was an *Iliad* at all in the ninth century, its length must have been such as was compatible with the conditions of an oral delivery,"—

---

[1] Monro, *Odyssey*, vol. ii. pp. 422–426.   [2] *Ibid.*, p. 429.

" a poem or poems short enough to be recited at a single sitting."

But we have proved, with Mr. Jevons and Blass, and by the analogy of the *Chansons de Geste*, that, given a court audience (and a court audience is granted), there were no such narrow limits imposed on the length of a poem orally recited from night to night.

The length of the *Iliad* yields, therefore, no argument for expansions throughout several centuries. That theory, suggested by the notion that the original poem *must* have been short, is next supposed to be warranted by the inconsistencies and discrepancies. But we argue that these are only visible, as a rule, to " the analytical reader," for whom the poet certainly was not composing ; that they occur in all long works of fictitious narrative ; that the discrepancies often are not discrepancies ; and, finally, that they are not nearly so glaring as the inconsistencies in the theories of each separatist critic. A theory, in such matter as this, is itself an explanatory myth, or the plot of a story which the critic invents to account for the facts in the case. These critical plots, we have shown, do not account for the facts of the case, for the critics do not excel in constructing plots. They wander into unperceived self-contradictions which they would not pardon in the poet. These contradictions are visible to " the analytical reader," who concludes that a very early poet may have been, though Homer seldom is, as inconsistent as a modern critic.

Meanwhile, though we have no external evidence that the *Iliad* was ever expanded—that it was expanded is an explanatory myth of the critics—" we do know, on good evidence," says Mr. Jevons, " that the *Iliad* was rhapsodised." The rhapsodists were men, as a rule, of one day recitations, though at a prolonged festival at Athens there was time for the whole *Iliad* to be recited. "They chose for recitation such incidents as could be readily detached, were interesting in themselves, and did not take too long to recite." Mr. Jevons suggests that the many brief poems collected in the Homeric hymns are invocations which the rhapsodists preluded to their recitals. The practice seems to have been for the rhapsodist first to pay his reverence to the god, "to begin from the god," at whose festival the recitation was being given (the short proems collected in the Hymns pay this reverence), "and then proceed with his rhapsody"—with his selected passage from the *Iliad*. "Beginning with thee" (the god of the festival), "I will go on to another lay," that is, to his selection from the Epic. Another conclusion of the proem often is, "I will be mindful both of thee and of another lay," meaning, says Mr. Jevons, that "the local deity will figure in the recitation from Homer which the rhapsodist is about to deliver."

These explanations, at all events, yield good sense. The invocation of Athene (Hymns, XI., XXVIII.) would serve as the proem of invocation to the recital of *Iliad*, V., VI. 1–311, the day of valour of Diomede, spurred on by the wanton rebuke of Agamemnon, and aided by Athene. The invocation of Hephæstus (Hymn XX.), would prelude to a recital of the *Making of the Arms of Achilles*, and so on.

But the rhapsodist may be reciting at a festival of Dionysus, about whom there is practically nothing said in the *Iliad*; for it is a proof of the antiquity of the *Iliad* that, when it was composed, Dionysus had not been raised to the Olympian peerage, being still a folk-god only. The rhapsodist, at a feast of Dionysus in later times, has to introduce the god into his recitation. The god is not in his text, but he adds him.[1]

Why should any mortal have made this interpolation ? Mr. Jevons's theory supplies the answer. The rhapsodist added the passages to suit the Dionysus feast, at which he was reciting.

The same explanation is offered for the long story of the *Birth of Heracles*, which Agamemnon tells in his speech of apology and reconciliation.[2] There is an invocation to Heracles (Hymns, XV.), and the author may have added this speech to his rhapsody of the Reconciliation, recited at a feast of Heracles. Perhaps the remark of Mr. Leaf offers the real explanation of the presence of this long story in the speech of Agamemnon : " Many speakers with a bad case take refuge in telling stories." Agamemnon shows, says Mr. Leaf, "the peevish nervousness of a man who feels that he has been in the wrong," and who follows a frank speaker like Achilles, only eager for Agamemnon to give the word to form and charge. So Agamemnon takes refuge in a long story, throwing the blame of his conduct on Destiny.

We do not need, then, the theory of a rhapsodist's interpolation, but it is quite plausible in itself.

Local heroes, as well as gods, had their feasts in post-Homeric times, and a reciter at a feast of Æneas, or of his mother, Aphrodite, may have foisted in the very futile discourse of Achilles and Æneas,[3] with its reference to Erichthonius, an Athenian hero.

In other cases the rhapsodist rounded off his

---

[1] *Ibid.*, VI. 130-141.   [2] *Ibid.*, XIX. 136.
[3] *Ibid.*, XX. 213-250.

selected passage by a few lines, as in *Iliad*, XIII. 656–659, where a hero is brought to follow his son's dead body to the grave, though the father had been killed in V. 576. " It is really such a slip as is often made by authors who write," says Mr. Leaf ; and, in *Esmond*, Thackeray makes similar errors. The passage in XVI. 69–80, about which so much is said, as if it contradicted Book IX. (*The Embassy to Achilles*), is also, Mr. Jevons thinks, to be explained as " inserted by a rhapsodist wishing to make his extract complete in itself." Another example—the confusion in the beginning of Book II.— we have already discussed (see Chapter IV.), and do not think that any explanation is needed, when we understand that Agamemnon, once wide-awake, had no confidence in his dream. However, Mr. Jevons thinks that rhapsodists, anxious to recite straight on from the dream to the battle, added II. 35–41, " the only lines which represent Agamemnon as believing confidently in his dream." We have argued that he only believed *till he awoke*, and then, as always, wavered.

Thus, in our way of looking at these things, interpolations by rhapsodists are not often needed as explanations of difficulties. Still, granted that the rhapsodists, like the *jongleurs*, had texts, and that these were studied by the makers of the Vulgate, interpolations and errors might creep in by this way. As to changes in language, " a poetical dialect . . . is liable to be gradually modified by the influence of the ever-changing colloquial speech. And, in the early times, when writing was little used, this influence would be especially operative." [1]

To conclude, the hypothesis of a school of mnemonic

[1] Monro, *Odyssey*, vol. ii. p. 461.

teaching of the *Iliad* would account for the preservation
of so long a poem in an age destitute of writing, when
memory would be well cultivated. There may have
been such schools. We only lack evidence for their
existence. But against the hypothesis of the existence
of early texts, there is nothing except the feeling of
some critics that it is not likely. " They are dangerous
guides, the feelings."

In any case the opinion that the *Iliad* was a whole,
centuries before Pisistratus, is the hypothesis which is
by far the least fertile in difficulties, and, consequently,
in inconsistent solutions of the problems which the
theory of expansion first raises, and then, like an
unskilled magician, fails to lay.

INDEX

ABU SIMNEL, Greek inscriptions at, 319
Achilles, Character of, 29, 30
—— Quarrel with Agamemnon, 53
—— Indifference of, to feudal custom, 58
—— *Wrath of,* supposed early poem on, 80
Æolic Epic, Helbig on, 91, *et seqq.*
Agamemnon and Charlemagne, 303–309
Agamemnon, Position and character of, 51, *et seqq.*
Aias, has no chariot. His great shield, 117, 118
Alcæus, speaks of linen corslets, 151
Alcinous, his sleeping chamber, where? 216
Algonquins, their shields, why large? 135, *et seqq.*
—— their corslets, 140, *et seqq.*
Allen, T. W., on the Pisistratean legend, 49
—— on the *Doloneia,* 256
—— defends antiquity of Epics, 257
—— on the *Catalogue,* 287, 288
Anachronisms, alleged, in Homer, 27
Ancestors, Cult of, un-Homeric, 86, *et seqq.*
Angling. Heroes angle in Cyclic poems, 20
Archæology of Shields, 130, *et seqq.*
Archaism, not practised by poets in uncritical ages, 1, 2, 3
—— of painters and poets, 5

Archaism, Moellendorff on, 10
—— Helbig on, 10, 13, 14
—— unsuccessfully attempted by Quintus Smyrnæus, 106
—— False poets accused of, 120
—— by early poets, Leaf on, 126, 127
Archers, Achæan, 136, 140
—— Trojan, 136
Areithous, his iron mace, 179, 180
Aristarchus and legend of Pisistratus, 44, 45
—— on corslets, 151, 159
Aristonothos, Vase of, 121, 123
Aristotle on *Iliad,* II. 558, 44, 45
—— on Homer's art, 124
—— on Illyrian spears, 174
Armorial bearings, Greek and Mediæval, 36, 121
Armour, 108, *et seqq.*
—— defensive, Evolution of, 172
Arms, disposal of those of the dead, 89, 90
Arrow heads, bronze, at Mycenæ, 135
—— head, one of iron, 179, *et seqq.*
Arrows, poison for Arrow heads, 253
—— with stone tips. Not in Homer, 125, 126, 134, *et seqq.*
Assarlik, Graves at, 87
Art ("Mycenæan"), Changes in, 84, 85
—— Chronology, 84
—— at Enkomi, Vaphio, Knossos, 85
Assembly, in Book II., 56, *et seqq.*